Sparring with Charlie

Motorbiking Down
the Ho Chi Minh Trail

Sparring
with Charlie

Christopher Hunt

ANCHOR BOOKS
DOUBLEDAY
New York   London   Toronto   Sydney   Auckland

An Anchor Book

PUBLISHED BY DOUBLEDAY
a division of Bantam Doubleday Dell Publishing Group, Inc.
1540 Broadway, New York, New York 10036

ANCHOR BOOKS, DOUBLEDAY, and the portrayal of an anchor are trademarks of
Doubleday, a division of Bantam Doubleday Dell Publishing Group, Inc.

Book design by Maria Carella
Map designed by Martie Holmer

Library of Congress Cataloging-in-Publication Data
Hunt, Christopher
Sparring with Charlie : motorbiking down the Ho Chi Minh trail /
Christopher Hunt.
p.   cm.
1. Vietnam—Description and travel. 2. Ho Chi Minh Trail.
3. Hunt, Christopher, 1954–   —Journeys—Vietnam. I. Title.
DS556.39.H86   1996
915.9704′44—dc20   95-36322
CIP

ISBN 0-385-48128-4

First Anchor Books Edition: May 1996

1 3 5 7 9 10 8 6 4 2

To the memory of Richard P. Hunt,
my father and my friend.

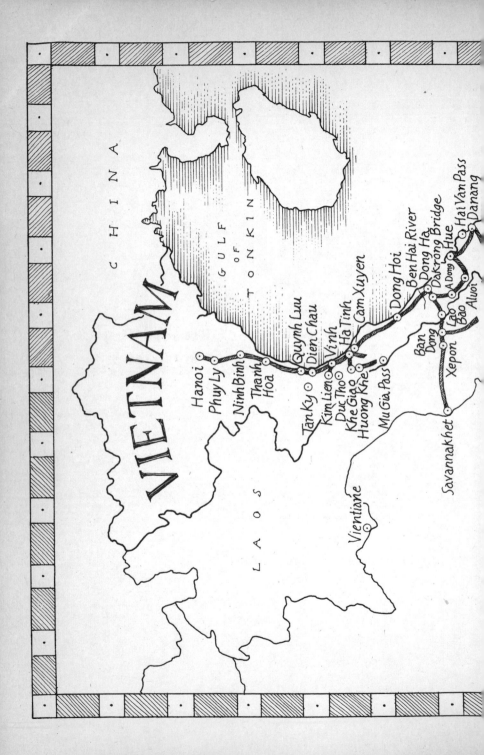

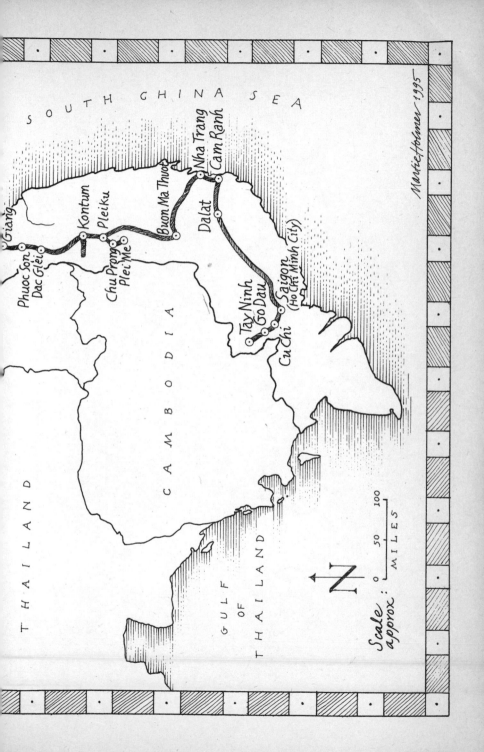

Sparring with Charlie

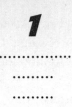

1

Vietnam is no place to drop in for lunch.
Traveling south from Hanoi, I started scanning for signs
painted with the words *COM* and *PHO*—rice and soup noodles
—at half past eleven. Picky, or maybe just skittish, I rarely ate
before one o'clock. Food shacks that didn't look unsanitary were
often too dark, too scary. Joints with no customers had to be
empty for a reason. Gatherings of more than six made me nervous.

Why? For starters, my compatriots had dumped bombs
equal to several Hiroshimas and a couple of Nagasakis on North
Vietnam. What's more, in South Vietnam hundreds of thousands of Hanoi's soldiers and sympathizers had been shot,
burned, or simply blown to bits. Not that a decade of destruction had anything to do with me. I was teething when the war
was gathering steam and flipping Frisbees as the fighting wound
down. But would the Vietnamese appreciate that mine was the
postwar, Nixon-hating generation?

Maybe it didn't matter. Locals said the war had been for-
given, if not forgotten. "That's all history," was the phrase that
jumped off tongues from Hanoi to Saigon. (Sorry, Ho Chi

Minh City.) Still, I found it hard to believe that twenty years would dull every taste for revenge. Odds were that somewhere there lurked a rice-paddy Rambo looking to take a potshot at a lone American.

These and other jitters were overruled by hunger as I passed through Quynh Luu, an unremarkable, unpronounceable town about 200 kilometers below the capital. I stopped at the last restaurant on the right. The design was pre-shanty. Crooked wood poles supported overlapping sheets of tin. Packed dirt masqueraded as a floor. From the rafters hung a fuzzy carcass which might once have been a goat.

Ten sets of eyes, among them two policemen's, tracked my entrance. The stiff stares showed more confusion than surprise. After checking that the tea hadn't been spiked, the diners broke the nervous silence with quiet speculation about my nationality.

"Russian," said one of the cops. His partner nodded without taking his eyes from me.

"French," said somebody else.

I cleared the air: "American."

Silence followed a collective double take. Unnerved, and wondering what latent patriotism had inspired the ill-considered admission, I fled the limelight. Moving toward a woman stationed by a mound of uncooked food, I asked for soup noodles and chicken, Vietnam's peanut butter and jelly sandwich.

The cook didn't react. Her face had gone rigid. Her eyes were blank with fear and surprise, as if Bigfoot had ordered a pizza. I repeated the request. The cook shook her clenched jaw. When I tried a third time, another woman stepped in.

"There is no chicken," she said.

"Beef?"

"No beef."

"What *is* there to eat?"

The woman poked a finger into a fleshy gap in the rafter

beast's black fur. We agreed that soup noodles, hold the meat, was an excellent choice.

My linguistic ineptitude relaxed the lunchtime crowd. Some of the diners returned to sucking at unfinished bowls of noodles. Others worked on third and fourth bottles of beer. The cops nodded and grinned, which I took as a sign that my arrest wasn't imminent. Unless someone convinced them otherwise. Whispering into the ear of one of the officers while sneaking sidelong peeks at me, a wiry man in spotless gray slacks and a white dress shirt raised the possibility.

The conference ended and Gray Slacks headed toward my spot on the bench. Noticeably cleaner than the rest of the dusty lot, he gave the impression of being a man of means, perhaps the owner. As he extended an open palm, I deduced that he had sought and received the official go-ahead to roll out the red carpet.

The assembled diners and drinkers fell silent as Gray Slacks paced the ten-yard gulf between themselves and the foreigner. Their nervous anticipation was understandable. Though Americans filled Vietnam's war stories and propaganda films, I was probably the first to appear in the flesh in Quynh Luu. For the onlookers, the imminent handshake of former foes would be a capsule of détente, a workingman's Paris peace talks. Cast in the role of Henry Kissinger, I cleared my throat and practiced my accent.

The incoming hand arrived before I reached my feet. The grips missed their meeting. The owner's palm bypassed my wrist and headed south. Confused, and embarrassed to have botched a simple handshake, I found myself in a half crouch, right arm extended. Would my social flub worsen America's reputation?

Then the Vietnamese hand took purchase. Overloaded, my sensory system required several split seconds to register what the cops, the cooks, and the customers could plainly see. There were four fingers and a thumb latched onto my crotch. Inches from my nose, the owner's mouth cracked into a crazed grin.

The grip was firm, like a barnacle's on a boat, but not painful. With slow precision, it shifted up, then down, left, then right. Unaccustomed to the sensation of a strange palm on my zipper, I had no response. When instinct finally took charge, I grabbed the intruder's wrist and guided it to a safe distance. Displeasure contorted my face. Fisticuffs didn't seem unlikely.

Fortunately for me, Gray Slacks retreated. Turning to his mates, he held his hands apart like a weekend fisherman describing a catch. In rapid-fire Vietnamese he announced the details of his research. When he finished ten sets of eyes looked into mine and drifted down toward my belt. I blushed, sat down, and crossed my legs.

By the time my noodles arrived, the handshake, Vietnam style, started to make sense. Clearly, a rumor had been going around town. Word had spread that Yankee proportions were unlike those of the average local. We were alleged to be . . . different. A man of intense curiosity, not to mention fast action, the owner was unwilling to let pass the opportunity to learn whether it was true what they said about American men.

2

What was I doing in Vietnam?

For months I asked the question nearly every day. As often
as not, the trip made no sense. Yes, Oliver Stone had gone to
the same New York City high school as I. *Good Morning, Vietnam* was one of my favorite movies. But nobody I knew had
fought in Vietnam. As a thirty-something, my interest in the
war was purely academic.

I traced the answer to Stanford University. One year at the
law school taught me that splitting legal hairs wasn't for me.
Words such as "interrogatory" and "dispositive" tired my
tongue. I lagged behind classmates who learned Latin with irk-
some ease. Two more years of the same? Followed by another
thirty of counting billable hours? I wanted something more
from life. At the time, dropping out to write pulp fiction made
sense.

My plan was to author a novel set in contemporary Vietnam, an exotic location sure to lure jet-lagged browsers. The
story's premise was simple: an embittered North Vietnamese
veteran learns that his old nemesis, an American diplomat, will

6

be returning to hoist the Stars and Stripes atop the old U.S. Embassy in Saigon.* Driven by some inner demon, the Northern vet would journey south to murder his rival. When a local cop discovers the plot, the assassin detours down his wartime route, the Ho Chi Minh Trail.

There was, however, a snag. I knew very little about the Trail. The road was named for Ho Chi Minh, formerly Hanoi's leader and Washington's public enemy number one. It was Hanoi's route for shipping weapons and men to South Vietnam. And it had been hard to find. My college history professor had said America might have won the Vietnam War had the supply line been cut.

Research deepened my knowledge. Library books said that the Ho Chi Minh Trail wasn't one road but a web of tracks and paths. Nor was it known by that name to Vietnamese. Northerners called the supply route Infantry Route One and the Old Man's Trail. Perhaps the most common name was the Truong Son Trail, a name derived from the mountains encompassing the network.

The Trail's first hikers were elephants foraging for food in the dense jungle blanketing the mountains along Vietnam's western edge. Other animals and local tribes followed these heavy footsteps, forming thin tracks. These came in handy when Ho Chi Minh and his comrades needed avenues for hit-and-run attacks during their war to expel the French. Paris waved the white flag and the network was reclaimed by Mother Nature.

But not for long. South Vietnam called off the promised

* The place was relabeled Ho Chi Minh City by the war's winners. I preferred the more natural ring of Saigon. So did most Vietnamese. Besides, decades of Communism didn't keep Russians from switching Leningrad back to St. Petersburg at the first opportunity.

nationwide vote shortly after the 1954 Geneva Accords temporarily split Vietnam in two. Hellbent on reunification, Hanoi began building up the infamous Viet Cong, Northern supporters living in the South. Saigon's forces controlled the lowlands along the coast. So an end run through the mountains was the best way to arm the rebels.

In early 1959 five soldiers were ordered to clear a supply path. Guided by an ancient mountain man, the crew scaled peaks, forded streams, and hacked jungles. Six months later, barely below the Ben Hai River, Vietnam's Mason-Dixon Line, they handed over the Vietnam War's first cache of guns and ammo.

The next year soldiers cleaved another path, this one farther west, where Saigon's increasingly alert patrols were less likely to spot infiltrators. Later, trails veered into territory belonging to Vietnam's neighbors, Laos and Cambodia. Broadened and smoothed, some tracks were soon accommodating bicycles. Later, pavement allowed trucks to make the trip. By the end of the war the Ho Chi Minh Trail was a 20,000-kilometer grid.

The first account I found of the Trail was written by Wilfrid Burchett. The Australian journalist went to Vietnam in the early 1960s, a time when growing Communist pressure on South Vietnam had Washington stepping up military aid to an indisputably corrupt regime. He wanted to see the budding battle through the eyes of "Charlie," the American moniker for the enemy's soldiers and supporters. So Burchett persuaded Hanoi to walk him to the South. When he got there, he wrote *Vietnam: Inside Story of the Guerrilla War*.

The book described hours of snaking down tunnellike trails cut into the damp foliage. According to Burchett, the tedium of walking was rivaled by the fatigue of scaling, rock by rock, near-vertical ridges. The payoff? "Occasionally we were rewarded by a magnificent panorama, serried folds of mist-covered forest stretching away into purple infinity."

But the perils far outweighed the pleasures of traveling the Ho Chi Minh Trail. Bridges of vines and bamboo threatened to tip trekkers into ravines. Leeches dropped from branches and sucked their fill. Once in the South, Burchett's group was menaced by reconnaissance planes and bombers. From the safety of a public library, the account read like an adventure.

I considered following Burchett's footsteps. A walk down the Ho Chi Minh Trail would help me fill my novel with the sights and sounds of the jungle. Locals met along the way would relate reams of war stories. By Saigon a bestseller would have written itself.

The trip appealed for other reasons. I wasn't tied down by the inconvenience of a job. More important, my girlfriend, an Ivory type with Einstein brains, had recently decided that we had nothing in common. She may have been right. I thought sports cars were a waste of money. She didn't. I fantasized about wallowing in a bathtub of chocolate pudding. She didn't. I wanted to stay together. She didn't. Skipping town seemed a reasonable response.

My friends and family disagreed. They had already suffered plenty. Few understood my sudden exit from the journalistic fast track. Fewer grasped the logic of my next career move, a stab at stand-up comedy. That flop bred a six-month walkabout in Latin America. Certain that my admission to Stanford signaled the return of sanity, my people cringed at the sight of yet another psychological free fall.

"Vietnam? Vee-et-nam? VEE-ET-FUCKING-NAM?" said a wordsmith who writes for the *New York Times*.

"Where *exactly* did you get this idea?" wondered my mother, as if it weren't too late to search-and-destroy the polluter of her son's once promising mind.

"The trip is likely to kill you," said Sherie, a journalist working in Southeast Asia.

"Kill?"

"You would definitely get malaria. But, having had it myself, I can tell you that malaria is the least of your worries. What you really have to look out for is dengue fever, which is ten times worse. They call it breakbone fever because you feel like every bone in your body is broken. It's the worst thing you can get and not die."

Sherie described more bogeymen. One was Japanese encephalitis, a mosquito-borne disease which swells its victim's cerebrum. The rare survivor is left with mush for brains. One also had to watch out for cobras, vipers, and the like. Then there were the hill tribes.

"It sounds romantic to go and visit hill tribes, but they're very unhealthy to be around. They live in filthy conditions in the middle of nowhere. A lot of them have malaria, and cholera breaks out from time to time. You wouldn't want to spend a night out there even if you could."

If? I had assumed my search would be unencumbered. True, totalitarian regimes often restricted foreigners' movements. But the newspapers were full of stories about Vietnam's renaissance. President Clinton had lifted the ban on commerce with the former foe and would soon restore diplomatic ties. Why would our new pals mind a wanderlusting American?

"The Vietnamese still don't like foreigners running around, particularly near the border areas," said Sherie.

I chose to discount talk of trouble. And though historians said jungle fever claimed at least one in ten of the Trail's wartime hikers, I didn't expect to get sick. Five inoculations and a healthy stock of malaria pills would see to that.

In fact, the well-meant warnings steeled my limp will. Navigating the Trail would give me more than decorative details. The jungle was sure to teach me about the type of man who could survive the bugs, bombs, and bullets.

One more thing. I was now hooked on Vietnam. I had to know what had happened, both during and after the war. Was America really in the wrong? And how did things look from the other side? Did Vietnamese think the result was worth the death and devastation to the place they called home? Mine was a privileged curiosity. As a noncombatant, I couldn't help but wonder how I would have fared under the miserable conditions that Americans and their enemies shared in Vietnam.

3

Billboards as big as moving vans loomed above my head. Three of them advertised swanky hotels. Two others pitched imported beers, Carlsberg and Tiger. One promoted a golf course. The print on the customs form in my hand read "Independence—Liberty—Happiness." I had, it seemed, deplaned at the wrong stop.

Vietnam was run by Communists, right? To me, that meant the country valued austerity and function over luxury and form. That consumer goods were not encouraged. That golf, the ultimate bourgeois sport, had been banned from the moment the tanks rolled into Saigon. Independence, liberty, and happiness? But for the sea of Asian faces at Hanoi's airport, I would have guessed that my Airbus had made a U-turn and gone back to California.

A uniformed immigration officer validated my visa with a swift chop. Another official barely glanced at my customs declaration. The first person to pay any attention to this incoming American was a small man in a brown suit. Breathing beer through teeth which matched his clothes, he said that I needed a taxi to Hanoi, which was 35 kilometers from the airport. The price would be thirty dollars, about the monthly wage of the average Vietnamese.

"I'm taking the bus."

"There is no bus. And it is not comfortable."

Another man sidled up when the first suitor moved on. He called himself a "special" driver, and proved it by flashing a laminated card. A third, pie-faced driver undercut him by bidding twenty dollars. When I accepted, he confirmed the kill by snatching my bags and marching out of the arrivals hall. I followed.

A mob converged on me. At least thirty men were acting like teens greeting the Beatles. Eyes widened, voices vibrated, hands grabbed for my clothing. They were drivers who, for lack of clout or cash, weren't allowed into the airport. One of the sharks trailed me all the way to his rival's car.

"Fifteen dollars for car to Hanoi," he said.

Should I stick to the bargain or save five bucks?

"You pay him twenty dollars. I take you for fifteen."

To renege would send the wrong message to the budding capitalist. Worse, a shift would mean more hassle when my main goal was finding a bed. The shark relented when the driver slammed the trunk's lid over my luggage. But there was something he had to know: "Why you so stupid?"

The airport scene uncovered just the tip of my ignorance about Vietnam. My preconception of Vietnam as a sleepy backwater took another battering when, after a fourteen-hour nap, I woke up under the gouged plaster and exposed wires of a windowless hotel room. Odd sounds were seeping through the concrete vent above the bed. I thought I heard the Mamas and the Papas—"All the leaves are brown. And the sky is gray . . ."—followed by a Bee Gees medley.

Downtown Hanoi was already vibrating at 7 A.M., when I rose to investigate. The retro rock was coming from a loudspeaker mounted on a movie house opposite my hotel on Trang Tien Street. The music was being drowned out by the engines and horns of puny motorbikes whizzing along the two-way street. The hurried riders relegated bicyclists to the street's edges. Those without wheels hitched rides with others in the growing river of traffic. All scrambled for cover when a car shouldered into the flow.

The sidewalk was no less cluttered. A pair of painters had spread a ladder in the center of the walkway. A wrinkled woman was pounding a pile of tin cans. Thirty schoolchildren dressed in cheery flower patterns propelled themselves down the pavement by pushing off of pedestrians.

A few tentative steps into the human tangle I found more signs that Vietnam was coming alive. Shopwindows brimmed with imported gadgets. One displayed dozens of Seiko watches. Another offered ten variations on the Walkman. A stationery store carried everything from Filofaxes to Post-its.

I wandered around Hoan Kiem Lake, the capital's placid breastbone. Near its top, in Hanoi's labyrinthine Old Quarter, a duty-free shop had run amok. Narrow streets once specializing in silk, rice, or broiled fish had been restocked with Marlboros, Tanqueray, and Johnnie Walker. Nearby lanes brimmed with shoes, paint, and sunglasses. Towers of washing machines blocked one sidewalk. Televisions barricaded another.

The service sector was also booming. Old women set out scales and charged a few pennies per weigh-in. A Xerox machine on the sidewalk did a brisk business. Twenty barbers had set up a row of chairs, mirrors, and girlie pictures on a downtown stretch.

Locals' ingenuity was underlined by the loads carried aboard cyclos—three-wheeled bicycle rickshaws. I watched a trishaw driver steam ahead despite the weight of eight kids in the front seat of his vehicle. A makeshift tow truck carried four motorcycles. Stacked with two coffins, a third cyclo served as a hearse. Who was tougher, the driver transporting four caged pigs or the one pedaling three unfettered Frenchmen?

Hanoi's fleet of motorbikes carried loads nearly as large. The sight of a Honda carrying a family of five made me smile. Another rider carried three televisions. The prize for ingenuity went to the man ferrying two refrigerators on his scooter.

I wandered into a bookstore. Among dozens of computer manuals and English instruction books were translations of Danielle Steel, Mario Puzo, and Jeffrey Archer. While leafing through the novels, I felt a grip on my elbow. The dead serious expression of the girl attached to the hand defied her age, which couldn't have topped eighteen. Stylish in black pumps and a pressed blazer, she demanded, "You like books?"

Without waiting for an answer, the girl grabbed my hand and yanked me from the store. Left down the pavement, left again into an alley, we arrived at a wall stacked high with books, pamphlets, and magazines. She shoved a bootleg copy of *The Quiet American* into my hands and said, "Good book." My purchase of no more than a cheap map of Vietnam left the bookseller grumpy.

Everybody was jostling for cash. Trishaws followed foreigners and whispered, "*Cyclo, cyclo.*" Tag teams of little boys carrying armloads of newspapers and tourist goodies pitched their wares. "Postcard. You like postcard. Very cheap."

When salesmanship failed, there was begging. "I am *sans famille*. No mother, no father," was the line mouthed by each miniature hawker. Skeptics were shown a laminated photo I.D. purporting to verify orphan status. A ragged mother carrying her infant took a less subtle approach. Latching onto my sleeve, she moaned "Money" until a second woman slapped her away.

Farther along the main street a skeletal man with crazed

white hair greeted me in French, which was spoken by old and educated Northerners. I shook the extended hand bones.

"May I ask you some questions?" he asked.

American, thirty-one, and don't know were my answers to queries about my nationality, age, and hotel address.

"Are you married?"

"No."

"Don't worry." After a quiet moment, he added, "I am poor and I am hungry. Give me a dollar."

The state-owned department store was the exception to the Hanoi hustle. I entered looking for toilet paper and a comb. Displayed in glass cases, goods were arranged randomly. Sunglasses were next to shampoo, shuttlecocks beside sun hats. Batteries, berets, and bike parts all shared a cabinet.

Two salesgirls glared when I interrupted their chat to pantomime my request. One nodded and walked away, presumably to fill my order. Her colleague showed me a plastic comb, which was bent like a boomerang. The vendor shrugged. The toilet paper never arrived.

The explanation for the incident was old. Most of the world had accepted long ago that private firms were the best providers of goods and services. Government employees had far less incentive to be productive or polite. Because the state "owned" everything in Vietnam and other countries which had marched to Karl Marx's drumbeat, lazy, rude workers became the norm.

A newer phenomenon was behind the enterprise evident in Hanoi. In a café half a block from my hotel, behind a stack of local newspapers and a dog-eared Vietnamese-English dictionary, I met Glenn, an American with a droopy brown mustache, who introduced me to *doi moi*, or economic renovation.

For most of the postwar period Vietnam was the New York

Mets of international economics. The Vietnamese grew progressively poorer in the early 1980s despite official assurances that the country was making great strides toward socialism. Once their sweat and tears were spent, locals could only laugh. "Day by day, poorer and poorer" went the black humor of the times. As one government technocrat later put it to me:

"Our salaries were enough for only two meals a day for a family. Everybody had to find supplementary work. Workers would finish at the factory, go to a second job, and go back to the factory to sleep. Bureaucrats worked three or four hours then left to spend the afternoon working at a private job. Even generals had second jobs. We had nothing. Life was terrible."

Reform, said Glenn, began at the end of the last decade. That's when the government began to allow free enterprise and private ownership to replace central planning and state control. Though slow and piecemeal, *doi moi* did stop the economic rot. Its ongoing momentum was responsible for the current explosion of commerce in Hanoi. Mostly pleased with the results, the cadres were now focused on controlling the pace of change.

Seeking an accommodation upgrade—a cloud of flies gathered whenever I used the ceramic hole in the bathroom floor—I meandered past a sooty, shuttered church, and down *Hang Ga*, or Chicken Street. A sign saying "Mini Hotel" attracted my attention. Inside, the owner greeted me with the grace of a five-star concierge.

Sixtyish, Mr. Truy sported a jacket and tie. His skin was the deep bronze sought in St. Tropez. Though gravity had sagged his skin, his high cheekbones and jaw revealed a face that was the envy of round-faced guys like myself. Punctuating his French with *vous* and *monsieur*, Truy asked my origin. The novelty of an American Francophone rated a coffee.

Truy described the tedium of his life as a bureaucrat. Now retired, he had a fresh outlook on life thanks to *doi moi*. The happy days began when the government let individuals own structures built on state land. Truy razed his home and erected a four-story inn. With eight rooms to rent, and hotel space tight in the capital, Truy had a steady income. He was, in local terms, rich and successful.

Too successful, in my book. Truy had no lodgings to spare. He suggested we check with another mini-hotelier in the neighborhood. We found his friend Mr. Luc glued to the television in his establishment's cramped sitting room.

Like Truy, the cherubic retiree had spent his life working for the state. Unlike his pal, whose weak eyes relegated him to desk work, Mr. Luc had been a military man. A snapshot showed him decked out in the uniform of a colonel, his olive-green breast spangled with medals dangling from red ribbons. The three medals on the right, Luc explained, were for service to country. The seven on the left were for "battles, courage, excellence, etc."

Yet the colonel was far more interested in discussing his current pursuit: money. More than forty years in the army hadn't lined Luc's pockets. So when the government eased restrictions, he tapped friends and family for funds to turn his home into a mini-hotel. With two floors and four rooms, Mr. Luc giggled when discussing full occupancy, at more than twenty-five dollars per room. He quaked with joy when boasting of his latest coup: the government had granted him permission to add two rooms.

Luc took no less pleasure in discussing the plans of other budding tycoons. A buddy had bought a large tract of land outside Hanoi. There he planned to build villas with gardens, which he reckoned would bring in several thousand dollars per month once more foreigners moved to town.

"What if they don't come?" I asked.

"Vietnam is growing," said the colonel. "They will come."

4

"**Nobody ever asked me that before**," said Colonel Luc.

"But is it possible?"

"Why do you want to go *there?*"

"It's a famous place."

"Close to Hanoi we have many famous places: Halong Bay, Perfume Pagoda."

"But can I see the Ho Chi Minh Trail?"

Luc engrossed himself in silent thought, as if his life depended on knowing whether there was, in fact, anything barring such a journey. Over sixty, the colonel was more like a playful squirrel than a stalking tiger. These days he wore a cardigan, not a uniform. Pudge covered his cheeks and stomach.

"I don't think so," said Luc. "But maybe."

I spread the map sold to me by the stylish bookseller on a glass-topped coffee table. A spider of red lines emanated from Hanoi. Most of the roads led north to China. One twisted west to the border with Laos. Two routes headed south. A dotted line in black and white represented a railway running mostly along the coast. A parallel, red line was Vietnam's main road,

Highway One, which I deduced despite the absence of numbers on the map.

That cartographic oversight didn't bother me. I recognized the names of several of the towns. History books told me that seaside spots such as Dong Hoi and Vinh had been staging grounds for the North Vietnamese Army, or NVA. Inland, A Shau and Khe Sanh rang bells. In Laos, I noted a place called Xepon. The problem wasn't the dots but the connections. The Ho Chi Minh Trail had been omitted.

Luc helped me fill in the blanks. He eyeballed the map with military intensity. Then, placing an index finger on Hanoi, the little colonel traced his southbound course to the seaside town of Thanh Hoa. Tracing the coast road, he said, "We took Highway One for a while. But when the American bombers made it too dangerous, we used inland routes."

The finger followed the thinnest of red lines southwest from a place called Ha Tinh. It stopped at the Lao border, where tiny, black print said *Deo Mu Gia*, or Mu Gia Pass. "We called this the Door of Death," said Luc.

The colonel explained. Northerners had to cross the Truong Son Mountains to reach sections of the Trail in Laos. These were accessible by just a few passes. Once the Pentagon saw the gaps for what they were, bottlenecks in the Viet Cong's lifeline, round-the-clock bombing commenced. Already exhausted from the climb, heavily laden soldiers broke into a run at Mu Gia. Truck drivers floored it. Anything to get through the "Door of Death."

Lucky enough to have ducked the bombs, Luc continued describing his trek. He ran his finger down a roadless section of eastern Laos and hooked it east to a blank spot just inside South Vietnam.

The colonel spent the next seven years in Quang Tri Province, the northernmost in South Vietnam. There he commanded an antiaircraft battery. Hanoi credited Luc's missiles and cannons with downing 86 American planes. But for politicking—NVA artillery units were constantly claiming credit for each other's hits—the official tally might have been higher.

Army regulars lived in foxholes. As the commanding officer, Luc had a narrow trench to himself. Learning to sleep in a hammock took time. He never got used to the knee-deep mud. His biggest fear? Cluster bombs, which upon impact fired steel pellets in all directions. The colonel saw medics remove sixty or more pellets from the flesh of comrades.

"It was misery," he sighed.

I wanted to show sympathy, but I couldn't. Luc-the-innkeeper was a jolly fellow, but Luc-the-soldier made me uncomfortable. His medal-winning "courage, excellence, etc." had taken a heavy toll on courageous, excellent, etc., American men no older than myself. Was I supposed to make some apology for his pains? Or was it his place to express regrets for gunning down my countrymen? Unable to decide, I returned to the original question.

"Is it still possible to walk the Trail?"

"I don't know."

Two other Northern colonels helped me to navigate the numberless map. I first met them in a café near Hoan Kiem Lake. No more than a tin roof covering bamboo chairs, the place was reputed to brew the capital's best coffee. Seated, I felt a hand touch my shoulder. I looked up to find a seventy-year-old elf peering down through thick black spectacles. The former officer suspected I was American. My confirmation elicited a dentured grin.

"I fought two wars," the tiny fighter boasted in French even rustier than mine. "One against French aggression, and one against American aggression."

During the latter, the officer headed a communications unit in Quang Tri, which he assured me was the war's deadliest zone. When I asked a yes or no question—had he traveled the Trail?—the officer answered with an essay. The gist of the lecture was old news: the Ho Chi Minh Trail wasn't one road but a network of roads.

The Trail, said the officer, was any means of getting supplies or men to South Vietnam. Footpaths and truck routes were most obvious. To these he added communications and petrol lines. Nor should one neglect guns and ammunition sent by sea. He demonstrated the point by grabbing my map and arcing a line from north to south across the South China Sea.

The approach of an active military man hijacked my attempt to steer the conversation toward this officer's trip to the South. The intruder looked like a thug. A uniform of heavy, olive cloth stretched across his barrel chest. An undersized cap emphasized the mass of his pumpkin-sized head. His face was fleshy and pocked. He looked like a cross between Norman Schwarzkopf and Manuel Noriega.

"May I present my comrade, Colonel Sang," the old man said with European formality.

"*Enchanté*," said the newcomer with a slight bow.

Sang lowered himself onto a plastic stool and listened as the old man explained that I was an American interested in learning about the Ho Chi Minh Trail. The ensuing pause made me nervous. Perhaps honesty wasn't the best policy with Vietnamese soldiers. Or was it? Snatching the map from my lap, Sang said, "I will tell you about the Trail."

With my pen the beefy colonel drew a black line south from Hanoi. Sang's route veered toward the mountains farther north than Luc's. Perhaps it was because he was nearsighted; despite thick eyeglasses, Sang brought his nose to within six inches of the map he was trying to read. More likely, he had taken another of the Trail's many branches. To my dismay, none of the twisting course he drew along the Vietnam-Laos border region touched any of the printed red lines.

Without notice, Colonel Sang switched from doodling to making broad strokes of the pen, driving two arrows of ink into the area just below the North-South divide. "First we liberated Quang Tri," he said. "The decisive battle was at Dong Ha." My finger indicated the spot his eyes couldn't pinpoint.

The colonel marked the spot with a black X and continued. "At first the army of the North had little trouble gaining ground along Highway One. Then three days of bombing blocked travel along the coast. Supplies were cut off. Food ran short before alternate routes were reopened. Our rice ration was reduced from seven hundred grams to two hundred grams of rice per day."

He placed another X on the area north of Saigon where Southern forces made their last stand. "They tried to stop the advance. But our side was too strong. We controlled the entire country except for Saigon. Then we took Saigon."

Looking back, Colonel Sang was unsurprised by the victory. He complimented America's officers and tactics. He admired their superior equipment. In particular, he envied GIs' access to showers. "The United States was a colossal force," he said in a tone of disbelief, "a colossal force."

"So how did you win?"

"The United States was trying to be a global gendarme. We were fighting for our country," said the bulky man. He glanced at his wristwatch. It was lunchtime. He slung a satchel onto his shoulder and, without looking at me, said, *"Au revoir, monsieur."*

Sang's departure left an aged officer and me to share the ponderous quiet. Neither of us had spoken by the time a sturdy, graying woman brought two demitasses of tea. She spoke no French. But the waitress had caught the gist of our chat. She wagged a finger and delivered a brief lecture. The officer translated.

"She says Vietnam is the only country to defeat America in war. She also wants you to know that when she was young she carried food and weapons on the Ho Chi Minh Trail."

The waitress nodded. She spread her arms to their full span to demonstrate the size of her loads. Thumbing a puffed chest, she looked skyward and drew a bead on a moving target with an imaginary rifle.

"I also shot American airplanes," she said.

"Hit any?"

"Two, four, maybe it was five."

"You alone?"

"My team," she said with a flex of a sixty-year-old biceps.

The colonels had been helpful beyond expectation. In addition to describing their own travels, they had lengthened my list of towns on the Trail. In Vietnam, I circled dots named Loc Ninh, Giang, and Aluoi. Ban Dong joined the list in Laos. Still hopeful of finding a map that would link the historic pit stops with modern roads, I went to the Army Museum on Dien Bien Phu, a street named after the site of France's Vietnam Waterloo.

The museum was marked by a decommissioned jet mounted across the street from a statue of Lenin. Littering the concrete beneath the defunct MiG were the remains of an American B-52. A plaque below said that the bomber was but one of the 14 enemy aircraft the fighter had downed during a seven-month stretch of "The Resistance War Against the United States of America for National Salvation." Nearby stood an artillery piece that had bagged 124 imperialists and "American puppets," the jargon for Saigon's troops.

Propaganda was the main concern of the woman who sat in a room filled with poster-size photographs of John Kennedy, Robert McNamara, and the havoc wreaked by their foreign policy. Alone until my entrance, the museum guide wore a military cap over a jungle of kinked black hair. Though the rest of her clothing—matching olive jacket and pants—was also army issue, her high heels, lipstick, and eyeliner didn't look regulation.

Moving from exhibit to exhibit, the guide spoke to an imaginary audience.

"She's a Communist," said a soft voice behind me.

The speaker was an Asian woman, her twenties still ahead of her, wearing bright cotton clothes and gold costume jewelry. Barely five feet tall, she had three feet of hair. She introduced herself as Daisy. Why Daisy was in the Army Museum I don't know. She didn't seem to like what she saw.

"Where did you learn English?" I asked.

"In Hong Kong."

Like thousands of others, Daisy fled Vietnam in the late 1980s. The idea was her father's. The state had confiscated the family's French-style villa, a house authorities had deemed too grand. That was the day Daisy's dad rejected the country he had fought to build. And plotted an escape.

Five years later the family had saved $2,400, half the sum demanded by smugglers of human cargo. So the family split up. Daisy and a brother fled with their father to Haiphong, where they and 69 others boarded a boat and shoved out to sea. Met at the other side by Hong Kong's police, the boat people were quarantined.

"I learned many things in the camp: English, Cantonese, Mandarin," said the upbeat teenager. "I wanted to be ready to leave for a new country. But we could not leave. Things were better in Vietnam. More open. So we came back."

Optimism for the "new" Vietnam didn't taint Daisy's disdain for the scoundrels who made the mess. Together we examined a glass case holding a braided ponytail. My self-appointed guide explained that a woman had snipped her locks and sent them to Ho Chi Minh as a sign of her devotion. Then she snickered and moved over to a photo of JFK.

"How long was he President?"

"Three years. Then he was shot and we got a new President."

"Who shot him?"

"A man named Oswald was blamed. But he was shot too." After a breath, I added, "It's not really clear."

"Then Nixon became President?"

"No, Johnson. Nixon was after him. But he had to quit. He got caught lying to the American people."

"The Communists lied to us also. When I was in school they told us to love Vietnam. That our mountains were made of silver and the ocean was made of gold. If we have so much silver and gold, why are we so poor?"

I said nothing. She continued.

"When I was young I hated the Americans. I thought they wanted to kill every Vietnamese person and live in our country by themselves. Then my father told me they only wanted to control the government." She ended with a question: "Something I don't understand is why the Americans wanted to come here?"

My rambling response touched on World War II, the rise of the Soviet Union, fear of Communism, the Constitution, King George III, and the Boston Tea Party. I may have mentioned America's tendency to export its principles. Daisy's perplexed gaze forced me to admit that I really didn't know.

She moved over to a cardboard cutout of an American prisoner. Hands bound, the man towered over his North Vietnamese captor. Daisy then asked the question Americans had been asking for twenty years: "America is so big. Vietnam is so small. How can America lose?"

Daisy and I walked through the museum's other rooms. The largest depicted the war's last years. By the door was a black and white picture of the archvillain, Richard Nixon. What looked like a collection of bowling balls turned out to be an array of captured flight helmets. Above them hung a poster of pilots in prison uniforms being led from a bus in two lines of ten.

Photographs of the victory showed Northern soldiers as blurs of forward motion. The winners waved flags over bunkers strewn with Southern corpses. Live "puppets" were marched away with their hands on their heads. An enormous photo, three feet by two, showed the infamous image of the line of refugees waiting to board a chopper on the roof of the U.S. Embassy in Saigon.

I lingered longest in front of a giant painted map. What had been a wartime secret was on display for all to see. Painted on a white background, the tangle of red lines looked like spaghetti marinara heaved against the wall. The largest of the roads had numbers: 9, 10, 13, 14, 15, 16, 20, and 71. It had taken a week. But I had found a guide to the Ho Chi Minh Trail.

5

"No way they will let you go there," said the listener.

"They?"

The stranger shrugged.

"Who are *they*, and why won't *they* let me see the Trail?"

"Believe me," he said. "I know these people."

"WHAT people?"

I dismissed the prediction. After a week in Hanoi I felt wise to Vietnam's ways. The country was unfurling fast, presenting new possibilities by the day. Maybe this joker hadn't heard that Americans were the flavor of the year. Besides, why should I care about the view of some local with nothing better to do than chat up foreigners on the sidewalk?

"I'm only trying to help you," he said in perfect English and with unsettling confidence. "Where are you from? California?"

Taking my bewildered look for what it was, a sign that I needed to hear more, he continued. He called himself Van. Over fifty, but not nearly sixty, he was forever slouched, his hands shoved deep into the pockets of a pair of khakis. From beneath a mop of straight black hair Van looked at the world through dark chocolate eyes.

Van was American, probably more so than I. He believed in things like high taxes—"taxes made America strong," he said —and Richard Nixon, whom he admired as a man with uniquely broad geopolitical vision.

"You live here?" I asked.

"I'm Vietnamese."

Seeing my failure to catch his nuance, Van backtracked. His father had been one of South Vietnam's elite. The family-owned sugar and rubber plantations had generated the money to pay for the tony schools he had attended. There Van formed his guiding principle: aim high. Seeing his chums plan on careers as doctors, lawyers, and bureaucrats, the rich kid set his sights on the job of Prime Minister. With no one else shooting for the job, he hoped to be a shoo-in.

"I was a minister when I was twenty-eight," said Van.

I called the bluff; a former minister of South Vietnam's government couldn't be on the loose in Hanoi.

He ignored my doubts and continued his story. An academic competition won him a university scholarship in Missouri. Next came a place in a Berkeley Ph.D. program. Impatient with the pace of academia—"Who wants to do that boring research?"—he found a shortcut. While classmates nosed the grindstone, Van sifted through the unfinished dissertations of former doctoral candidates. One had tripped just short of the end zone. When Van solved the problem, his professors crowned him a prodigy.

"That poor guy drove all the way from the airport and stopped too soon," he said, more in disbelief than disrespect. "I just picked up the bags and carried them across the street."

While unknotting the analogy, I felt the whiplash of another implausible plot twist: "Then I worked for NASA."

"NASA? As in astronauts and Tang?"

"Only for a few years. I didn't want to be a scientist. I wanted to be a big shot. So I went home to Vietnam. They made me Minister of Housing. Later I went to the Paris peace talks and met Henry Kissinger. Before that I was Minister of Propaganda. I knew Walter Cronkite, Dan Rather, all those guys. When they got out of line, we tried to show them the big picture."

I bristled at the suggestion that the American press had been blinkered; my father had been a television reporter during the Vietnam War.

Van cited the famous image of a Southern soldier sending a bullet through the temple of a captured Viet Cong. The deception of the lone photo, said Van, was that it excluded the run-up to the summary execution. The VC had just entered a house and shot an officer, his wife, and his children. Enraged, the officer who discovered the scene raced out and shot the killer.

The man reeled off war stories like an auctioneer selling steers. He told of watching a captured Northern general bite a cyanide tablet. Back in Saigon, an invitation to ice cream saved him from a terrorist bomb in a restaurant. Resettled after the war in Orange County, California, Van was shot by a schoolteacher who opposed his vocal support of normalizing U.S.-Vietnam relations. Whatever the content, each vignette ended with the sober intonation "I've seen a lot of things."

And now? What was he doing in Hanoi? Van had visited Vietnam over sixty times since 1975. His first tentative steps had been attempts to mend personal and political fences. Lately, business was bringing him back more often, and for longer stretches.

Like the mini-hotel owners, he saw Hanoi real estate as the road to riches. But the former minister's dreams were bigger: he was angling to develop ritzy apartments to rent to foreigners.

I wasn't sure what to make of Van. His story was incredible. But was it true? Would NASA have hired a scientist who frequented pagodas to pray that his wife produce boys? What government would include a minister who swore he saw a ghost during a visit to a cemetery in Quang Tri? Was this stranger who insisted that *they* wouldn't let me travel the Trail a nut or a whiz?

I turned to other questions. I had known from the start that an American wasn't going to find the Ho Chi Minh Trail on his own. That's why my half-baked plan hinged on hiring a local fixer, a combination friend, translator, and bushwhacker. Man Fridays, however, were in short supply.

Colonel Luc laughed at the suggestion that he retrace his wartime route. Colonel Sang was keener, but reflection reminded him of a pledge never to repeat the discomfort of the jungle. Two younger men enthused about an adventure in the mountains. Neither, however, could spare the time. With Vietnam taking off, anybody who spoke English was booked solid.

I kept looking. Colonel Luc sent me to the Vietnamese veterans' outfit, which he said might be willing to organize a trip. Dumb idea, I thought. Would Charlie barge into an American Legion hall looking for a lift to Arlington National Cemetery? Still, with options dwindling, I hoofed across Hanoi to a varnished door beneath white letters that said "VETS."

The office behind the door was hardly smoke-filled. There wasn't a grizzled vet in sight. A teenage boy preoccupied with sinking the battleships on his computer screen ignored my entrance. A rosy-cheeked girl prim enough for a sock hop rose to her feet but didn't speak. She left that to the manager, a man in his mid-twenties.

I had come to the right place. To supplement their pensions, the veterans had set up a company to guide the rising number of former American soldiers visiting Vietnam. Veterans of the U.S. 1st Division were taken to their former base camps and combat zones near Saigon. Those who had served in the 9th Infantry Division were slated for Mytho Province and the Mekong Delta.

My request fitted none of their molds. That I wasn't a vet didn't matter; the problem was finding somebody willing and able to navigate the remnants of the jungle roads. The office driver said he could cope; he had spent the war steering a truck up and down the Ho Chi Minh Trail. But now he would need a Toyota Land Cruiser and thirty-five dollars per day. Done, I said.

The driver, a weathered man in an equally worn blazer, ticked off a list of supplies I had to buy. We would need water, food, tents, and mosquito nets. One more thing. We had to carry spare petrol since filling stations were few and far between along his old route to Saigon's suburbs. Stepping up to a map on the wall, the driver showed me the winding mountain path we would follow. Estimated travel time? Ten days, just like at the end of the war.

The plan unraveled just as fast. "The Ho Chi Minh Trail is not open," said the office director, a former army sergeant with caterpillar eyebrows. "It is too dangerous. There are wild animals. Tigers. And deer."

"Deer?"

"There are men who will rob you. The road is no good. There is nothing to eat."

The director came clean after I queried each obstacle. There were indeed tigers, robbers, and potholes. The real problem, however, was bureaucracy. His was just a branch office of Vietnam Veteran Tour Service, or VVTS. Permission for an expedition such as mine had to come from the bosses on Quan Thanh Street.

The headquarters was no more receptive to me or my travel ambitions. Ten sets of wary eyes watched me enter their lair, an unpainted room obscured by smoke from a shrine's incense. The old men dispatched a messenger, a scrawny youngster named Hung, who relayed my request. "No," was the swift answer of the company's vice-director.

"Yes" came the revised response after the former colonel consulted with the comrades about taking a foreigner down the Trail. He could provide a car, a driver, and, if I liked, a Vietnamese veteran to provide color commentary. Colonels cost twenty-five dollars per day. Captains came cheaper.

One more thing. The cost of such a trip would be roughly thirty-two hundred dollars. That, said Hung, was the rock-bottom price. As proof he cited higher rates paid by other Americans and the hundred dollars per hour extorted from Swedes who filmed interviews with Vietnamese vets.

"Is there another way for me to go?"

"We are the only ones authorized to take you."

Van had been right. There was no way *they* were going to let me see the Trail. At least not for free.

6

Minh became my best buddy. It didn't matter that we shared no language. Ours was friendship built on something more powerful than words. We met at a café. It was 2 P.M. and neither of us had a thing to do for the rest of the afternoon. Or week. Or month.

Minh was unemployed. Vietnam's withering public sector had been shedding jobs. Budget cuts were also forcing the military, a traditional sop for extra bodies, to cut back. And though the country was hoping to conjure Asia's next economic miracle, employment couldn't take off without more foreign investment.

The jobless hordes gathered to commiserate and drink tea. No fewer than twenty youths were lounging in low rattan chairs around my spot in the sidewalk café. Some snoozed. The rest directed passionless gazes toward two nearby televisions, one showing a soap opera, the other a videotape of a breathtaking blonde marching to and fro in a sparse bikini.

I was also out of work. The Ho Chi Minh Trail was closed to anybody without a few thousand bucks to drop. The premature death of my fact-finding journey was just the latest dagger in my would-be novel. Glenn from the café said my fictional assassin was implausible: Vietnamese tended to look ahead rather than behind. Van had a more obvious criticism. Because the next American embassy would be in the capital, not Saigon, the killer wouldn't need to go south to bump off the new ambassador.

Minh couldn't understand all that. What he could tell from my languid body language was that the American propped in front of the television had some time on his hands. He raised an eyebrow and broke our pensive silence: "*Bia?*"

"Beer" was one of the Vietnamese words I *had* picked up. I nodded and bought our third round of a watery brew called *Bia Hoi*. We clinked glasses. Minh dreamed of a job. I thought about going home.

Instead, I went to the Emerald Bar. Snuggled in the Old Quarter, the place was all brass rails and varnished wood. Spotless glasses dangled above the long runway of the bar. Tall stools supported more than a dozen well-padded, Western fannies. Flirtatious singles completed the picture of a yuppie watering hole indistinguishable from thousands of others around the world.

I glanced out of the window. In the shadows stood four cyclos, their drivers lolling in the chairs of the chariots. They were no doubt wondering about their passengers, who were spending the equivalent of two days' wages on a can of imported beer. A ragged woman pressed her child's oozing nose onto a windowpane. When our eyes met she spread an empty palm and waited for money.

Inside, another newcomer to Hanoi was getting the big picture from an American working for a local English-language newspaper: "Vietnam is the frontier. The people who come here are adventurers, here to get rich or break convention. They're cowboys and carpetbaggers."

A less indulgent appraisal of the bar's clientele was provided by Sue, an acquaintance from the time I lived in Hong Kong. Most of the crowd worked in real estate. Vietnam had dozens of joint ventures with firms from Hong Kong, Singapore, and Thailand. The lack of indigenous know-how led developers to import engineers, foremen, etc. Come quitting time, Hanoi's migrant worker force flocked to a place with a familiar feel.

The clatter of the front door's frame turned every head. All watched the lumbering entrance of one not so gentle giant. From a balding head down to muddy combat boots, the mustached man defined "rough customer." He stormed over to the bar and hammerlocked the neck of a lanky guy with a blond ponytail.

Sue told me that the giant was American, the foreman on the biggest building project in town. Apparently devoid of skill, the man was said to speak fluent Vietnamese, which he had learned during the war. It was also said that he had interrogated captured Viet Cong, many of whom left their interviews minus fingers. One more thing: it was best not to ask about the past.

The giant's drinking buddy was more approachable. After the hulking figure had moved on to pound another cluster of boozers, I introduced myself to him. Garrett was raised in Maine; the sinewy twenty-something had come to Hanoi to oversee the renovation of villas. And my story?

Garrett stood silent while I traced the travails of trying to find and see the Ho Chi Minh Trail. He frowned when I ended the story by saying that my next stops were a travel agent and San Francisco.

"There's a guy called Joe who might be able to help you."

"Where can I find him?"

"He lives in some mini-hotel in the Old Quarter."

The tip was more complete than it sounded. Truy-the-hotelier had boasted that his best client, an American vet named Mr. Joe, spoke fluent Vietnamese. Hoping there weren't two Joes who knew their way around Vietnam, and emboldened by desperation, I returned to the inn on "Chicken" Street the following night.

"How did you find out about me?" growled the human bear who emerged at Truy's bidding. Dressed in fading black, the barrel-chested man wore a graying buzz cut. His deep brown eyes and budding jowls showed no signs of smiling.

"Sorry, big mistake" is what I wanted to say. Instead, I explained what had brought me to Hanoi, and how a trail of clues had led me to him. Joe's smile didn't crack until I outlined the obstacles to my plan.

"Those assholes haven't got a fucking clue," he scoffed.

The confident disdain for the men who had blocked my trip lifted my spirits. The shadow that appeared over his shoulder brought them back down. Emerging from a room in the rear was the hulking figure, complete with rugged face and sagging mustache, I had seen in the Emerald Bar.

"You know Keith?" asked Joe.

"Uh, no."

"I've seen you before. You following me?"

"I don't think so."

Kidding, though not clearly enough for comfort, Keith plopped a hand onto my shoulder and said, "We'll have to interrogate you in the back."

Was this wise? Should I be disappearing into a back room off a dark street in Hanoi with two veterans? I had no idea who these guys were or what they were doing in Hanoi. I did know that a lot of Vietnam vets had eggshell psyches which tended to crack in post offices and McDonald's. Was Joe or Keith the type to have a flashback and splatter my guts against a wall?

"Act cool and avoid sudden movements," I told myself.

Easier said than done. I got a jolt from the sight of a head-to-toe American flag hanging on the far wall of Joe's room. I chuckled aloud. Inside, I wondered whether this wasn't some sort of clandestine operation. Surely Hanoi had laws that banned owning, not to mention displaying, the Stars and Stripes.

"Beer?" asked my host.

I accepted. The alcohol might smooth my nerves. At least I would be relaxed when the local gestapo, who would certainly have bugged the room, piled out of a Humvee, kicked down the door, and dragged us away to tiger cages.

I tried small talk: "You guys serve together?"

"I was over here in the early seventies and Joe . . ."

"Sixty-eight to sixty-nine . . ."

"The psychedelic years . . ."

"There were a lot of guys doing a lot of drugs . . ."

"Saying 'America sucks but get me home . . .' "

"But only after a thirteen-month tour . . ."

"It was part of the macho Marine shit . . ."

"An extra month to get killed . . ."

"Entire towns were bombed off the map . . ."

"But it wasn't all bad . . ."

"It was like McHale's Navy only with drugs . . ."

Joe cut short the beery reminiscing. "We're probably the first Vietnam vets you've ever met," Joe said.

He was nearly right. Glenn had done a tour in Vietnam. I had also chatted briefly with a vet on my flight from California. He was with a group that was coming to salve mental scars by building a hospital. But the odd couple in the mini-hotel was my first extended contact.

"You'll meet a lot more while you're over here," said Keith.

Joe jumped in: "You gotta meet Danny. He left a leg, an eye, and a couple of fingers over here when an antitank grenade blew up in his face. And you know what he's doing? He's living in My Lai. He's living in fucking My Lai installing solar heating panels!

"There's another guy you gotta meet. He was left for dead after a grenade opened his chest. But somebody saw a movement and they sewed him together. He came back here and researched, down to the unit, the North Vietnamese who were opposite him that day. He wanted to show them the scars, the shrapnel in his chest, and say, 'It's okay.' "

With nothing to contribute, I just listened. The longer I did so, the better I understood the lure of Vietnam to American veterans, a bunch my generation viewed as addicts, psychos, and panhandlers. Keith spoke of his respect for the North Vietnamese. He admired their motivation. He envied their commitment to their society. And, like Joe, the man I had mistaken for a thug felt he had a lot in common with his former enemies:

"I met a soldier whose unit went south with four hundred men. They were just like any other bunch of guys. How many came back? Ten. And those ten guys live every day knowing they have to carry the memories and the stories of the other three hundred ninety. They all live near each other here in Hanoi; share something like that and you don't want to be apart."

Keith asked why I was in Vietnam. He snorted at my plan for collecting string on Charlie's perspective. "What do you think it was like? Those guys were like us: scared shitless. They dug foxholes and when the bombing started they jumped in and prayed."

"I figured seeing the Trail would show me how that felt."

"If that's what you want, just talk to Vietnamese vets in Hanoi. Look for guys with the tattoos on their forearms."

"Who are they?"

"Guys expecting to get blown up wanted somebody to be able to identify the pieces for the sake of their families."

Joe provided another snippet of the North's experience. He had met a peasant who rose to become a twice-decorated officer. At the end of the war the peasant expected a decent government job. Instead, the man was ordered back to the rice paddies. Why? The Party learned of his bad marks in seventh grade.

"How's that different from us, Joe?" asked Keith. "What'd they give us when we got back? They didn't give us shit."

Joe began a counterpoint, but Keith shouted him down: "Bullshit, man. I call bullshit."

"No, I'll tell you bullshit . . ."

A bead of sweat slid down my ribs. It dried to salt only after Keith called it a night and went home to bed.

Joe then revealed his own reasons for returning to Vietnam. He came first as a grunt in the U.S. Marines. He returned as a tourist in the mid-1980s, a decade before the age of "Viet chic." He started to arrange landing rights for private planes. "Air America" had been tainted, so he called his firm South East Asia Air. "No plane, no gain" was his motto. What kept the former sergeant coming back, however, was something else.

"You should see their eyes when a fat, balding American vet speaks their language and sings their songs. It blows them away. I went to my old area in Quang Tri. The kids couldn't believe that I knew the province better than they did. I love it here."

To a rookie like me, Joe was a godsend. I sat, spellbound, while he spun yarns about the past—the thrill of manning a machine gun in the open door of a helicopter—and the present. He was seeing a doctor who prescribed bloodletting to cure poor circulation in his feet. The vet joked about opening "The USO," a bar to be staffed with singers called the Seoul Sisters.

I envied Joe's swagger in the face of Vietnamese officials, whom I had christened "Hanoinkers." When questioned, he claimed to be normalizing U.S.–Vietnam relations. When I asked about going down the Trail, Joe said, "Just go. They won't stop you." In the meantime, would I like to join him, Keith, and some visiting vets who were due to arrive in Hanoi?

"I think they're carrying," he said.

"Carrying?"

"Dope. Marijuana. What's the matter with your generation?"

Three nights later we found Keith and his buddies surrounding a jumble of beer glasses on a sidewalk table. These ex-Marines fitted my image of Vietnam vets. Tall and fleshy, Don had a chipped tooth and an earring that gleamed beneath ginger-colored hair pulled back in a ponytail. Sam, his sidekick, wore black jeans, a black shirt, and a thin black necktie. Between a belly that spilled over his belt and frizzed, graying hair with a beard to match, the man was a dead ringer for Jerry Garcia.

Sam didn't sing. Nor did he talk much. When introduced he offered a grunt and a quick shake with his right paw. I'd have been scared to give the guy a quarter on a street corner. So when he suggested a joint in his hotel room, I looked for an exit.

No plausible excuse came to mind, so I followed the vets down an unlit block and into a decaying building. Chemical relaxants appeared. Don handed me a can of unchilled beer. Sam rolled a funky cigarette. I weighed my options: inhale and eliminate a political career; fake it à la Clinton and risk the wrath of the vets. I tried to fit in.

"Did you get the tattoos during the war?" I asked Sam.

"This one I got in San Quentin."

I recognized the home of California's death row. Sam was free, which meant he wasn't a murderer. On the other hand, the man had done time in Vietnam. So he probably had killed somebody.

"This peace sign I got during the war," said Sam, touching a different tattoo. "I left a little piece out of it. This teardrop is peace crying."

I found another stupid question. What were the dents in his fleshy upper arm—shrapnel scars?

"Holes from heroin needles." Sam rolled over his forearms to show me similar marks. Then he lifted the legs of his pants to reveal more scars on the backs of his knees. "I started the first day I got here and didn't stop for fifteen years."

There was nothing to say. "Get over it, guys," had long been my attitude toward vets' obsession with the past. The honesty and humility of a man who had had it far tougher than I squashed my disdain. I felt like apologizing to Sam, both for my ill will and for a government that had ruined his life.

Keith began explaining the appeal of Vietnam even to a skeptic such as Sam. "Even if I have an ordinary day, look where I am. I go to sleep in Hanoi. And that's cool."

"I can never sleep in this place," said Sam.

"Why not?"

"Because I'm here."

"Hanoi?"

"Vietnam." The man in black elaborated. "I've been back three times. I have nightmares every time. I wake up with welts on my forehead from clenching it so tight in my sleep. Last night I woke up Don three times because I was screaming in my sleep."

"Why do you keep coming?"

"It's hell to be here, but it's the only way I can work this thing out."

7

My feet accelerated before my mind registered the reason. Locals scattered at the sight of a red-faced male punishing the pavement with boots meant for hiking, not sprinting. The refugees left behind an obstacle course of stools, bicycles, and lighted grills. The hazards were secondary to the visceral importance of catching my quarry.

A minute later, breathless and walking, I did. She was no beauty. Perhaps she was a he. Whatever its gender, the name written in white on the black motorcycle was "Minsk."

The bike was like no other I had seen in Hanoi. Sure, the buzz of tiny engines had been waking me at sunrise for nearly three weeks. And the rivers of two-wheeled vehicles had made street crossings my least favorite part of the day. But what made this motorcycle different was the rider, a blond-haired man.

Where had he gotten the bike? I oozed motorbike envy. How could I get one? I had to know.

The Minsk was parked outside the Darling Café, Hanoi's hub for unshowered backpackers who, having come to Asia to be near "the people," spent most of their time comparing hotel prices lest too much money pass from West to East. Inside, I found Manfred, a friendly but grimy German.

"Where did you rent the bike?"

"I bought it."

"Bought? Where? How?"

Manfred's answers were too good to be true. The soiled Teuton had bought the Russian-made motorbike in Saigon for $515. He drove it up the coastal highway. Now, just two days from his departure, he was desperate to sell. The asking price was $400.

"Do you need a license?"

"*Nein.*"

"Registration?"

"*Nein.*"

"Insurance?"

Manfred laughed. He had asked the same questions. The vendors had assured him that such formalities had yet to arrive in Vietnam. "Nobody has papers. You don't need them," he assured me. Was the German telling it straight?

It didn't matter. My gospel was Joe's assurance that nobody would stop me from roaming Vietnam. Even if he was wrong, I was ready to break some rules. My failure to organize a sanctioned expedition still smarted. I wanted to show the Hanoinkers that they couldn't stop an American with a will. Stupid? I wouldn't know how stupid it was unless I tried to see the Trail on my own.

Manfred came clean once my cash was deep in his pocket. The Minsk, in fact, did have a few quirks. Shifting from second gear to third required a special touch. Nuts and bolts didn't always hold fast. The luggage rack and the tailpipe had both fallen off. The handlebars had only loosened. But the 125cc engine was reliable. And it was mine.

Good deal or major ripoff? For some time, the latter

looked more likely. The trouble started the first time I pumped the manual starter with my left foot. The Minsk sputtered. Subsequent kicks produced light coughs or no reaction. I pumped harder. A sweat broke on my forehead. A gray-haired man in grubby pajama bottoms watched in despair.

A half-dozen unemployed Vietnamese also rubbernecked. They beckoned for me to roll the motorbike to their sidewalk tea party. When I didn't, all but one ambled toward me. The holdout raced into a beauty salon. He emerged with a set of socket wrenches. Shoving me aside, he began dismantling my new purchase.

"He knows what he's doing," said the spectators' nods.

"*Bougie!*" cried the mechanic after five minutes of twisting and clanking. Like Lady Liberty, he held high my spark plug.

The mechanic disappeared past a woman in mid-shampoo. I could only wait. The men in green army jackets waited with me. So did three schoolboys in red kerchiefs and two old ladies with seven teeth between them. One of the men wanted to talk.

"*Rooshkie?*" he asked, pointing at me.

"American."

"*Rooshkie,*" he repeated, indicating the lifeless motorbike.

I was also wondering why an American would buy such a vehicle. Hadn't the end of the Cold War just proved the superiority of Caddys and Harleys over Volgas and Minsks? It had. But Harleys weren't on sale in Hanoi. Hondas were going for over a thousand dollars in Hanoi. Mine was the best vehicle that four times Ben Franklin could buy.

The mechanic reinstalled the cleaned-up *bougie*. But to no effect. While he spread the rest of the Minsk on the sidewalk, another onlooker approached. This one spoke some English.

"I like very much American movies."

"Me too."

"I like *Girl with Wind.*"

"Which?"

"*Girl with Wind*," he repeated. "Scarlet O and Red Butts."

"I like that one too."

The mechanic located the trouble. The verdict, after stripping and reassembling my motorbike, was that I had no gas. When I started to push the Minsk to Petrolimex, the state's chain of filling stations, he grabbed me. He beckoned for the English-speaker to translate.

"He says you will be a good mechanic when you get to Saigon," said the movie buff.

Traffic laws posed another problem. The few that existed were unwritten. Speedsters drove near the dividing line. Slower vehicles stuck close to the sidewalk. But not too close. Wrong-way cyclos and bicycles claimed the strip nearest the curb. The sound of a car's horn meant yield or die.

Right of way was even murkier. Most intersections were motocross meets mud wrestling. The exceptions were the meetings of Hanoi's main streets, where traffic signals had been installed. The municipality seemed to doubt the effectiveness of newfangled technology. Old-fangled policemen were deployed near every light.

Hanoi's traffic cops were a dedicated lot. I watched one sprint after a pair of teenagers who ran a red light. As the driver sped ahead his passenger caught a brutal whack on the head from the officer's zebra-striped truncheon.

The penalty for my first infraction was lighter. Returning from my maiden voyage, I turned right instead of left toward my place. The flow of traffic carried me to the end of Tran Hung Dao Street. There, at Hanoi's train station, I took another right.

Two sharp whistle blasts told me I should have gone left. Turning to confirm the source of the sound, I saw a man in a bright green doorman's outfit. The policeman was seated, legs folded, on a wooden chair. A teacup and a scone wouldn't have looked out of place.

The arresting officer played a cool hand. Without flinching, he watched me panic. Nervous about my lack of license and registration, I lost my grip on the clutch. The Minsk stalled. Unable to start under pressure, I pushed the bike in a U-turn toward the lawman.

He stood and raised his baton. But the officer didn't bring the wood down on my skull. He simply tapped the tin one-way street sign and pointed south, the direction I should have turned. I felt lucky to get away with just a warning.

8

Rice, water, a hammock, and a mosquito net.
Colonel Luc thought hard about whether he had left anything
off the list of essentials one needed to travel along the Ho Chi
Minh Trail. "One more thing. Take extra socks. Your feet will
be in mud."

Mr. Truy was next on my farewell tour. His last-minute
advice? "It can be very difficult for a man to know the age of a
Vietnamese girl. Don't worry. But be careful."

Van offered less cryptic counsel. The one-time minister
thumbed the bridge of his nose several times and recommended
I carry spare petrol. Petrolimex outlets could be hard to find
away from Highway One. As in the capital, mountain dwellers
would sell gas stored in beer bottles. These, however, were best
avoided.

"They will put water in the gas. You get water in your
engine and it stalls. What are you going to do if that happens?
You can't do anything."

Van made another "suggestion." He directed me to strap
my pack to the gas tank, not the luggage rack on the rear
fender. The latter, he assured me, would invite robbery. Ignore

him and the odds of reaching Saigon with my belongings intact were long, maybe four to one.

Joe's parting shots also leaned toward the practical. Seated in a hole-in-the-wall café across from Hanoi's version of the Pentagon, the American vet reminded me not to fear Vietnamese officialdom. He also wrote out a few handy phrases:

"Which way to the Ho Chi Minh Trail?"

"Where is the People's Committee?"

"My motorcycle is a Russian piece of shit. Can you fix it?"

"Do you have a husband?"

Saving his best idea for last, Joe invited me to join him at Apocalypse Now, a bar on the edge of the Old Quarter which was no more than a room off the sidewalk. A portrait of Ho Chi Minh hung from an internal balcony and a stereo bounced 1960s tunes off the walls. Only when I had stepped inside did I notice the four men huddled around a bottle of Chivas Regal and cans of Coke. Buzz-cut, white, and fit, they had to be military.

"Meet Joint Task Force-Full Accounting," said Joe.

He elaborated. In the interest of warmer relations, Hanoi allowed the United States to station servicemen in Vietnam. Their job was to determine what happened to Americans who never returned from Vietnam. Like Rambo, they were looking for MIAs.

In real life, finding an MIA was a delicate business. The men began with intensive training at the navy's language school in California. Before landing in Hanoi, where they lived in a shady compound dubbed The Ranch, the sailors were also given a list of dos and don'ts. Do avoid talking about politics. Don't wear a uniform in public.

The pressure made Hanoi a hardship post. John, a fresh-faced sailor in a Penn State sweatshirt, reminisced about his tour at Subic Bay in the Philippines. The young man shook his head while describing the lost paradise where bars were bars and full of girls, some as young as twelve. "Here, the fun police make sure we don't have a good time."

Another sailor, Greg, asked what had brought me to Hanoi. His jaw slackened as I described the now comatose plan to write pulp fiction set in Vietnam. The father of two rolled his eyes when I described my motorcycle purchase. And he smirked when I outlined my itinerary down the Ho Chi Minh Trail.

"This guy's going to Aluoi," screamed Greg.

"Aluoi?" said Jim, an athletic sailor from California.

Others joined in to laugh at, not with, me.

"What's wrong with Aluoi?"

"It's a bad, bad place. You don't want to go there."

"I won't," I lied. "But tell me why."

"For one thing, it's the home of the two-step snake," Greg said. "You get bit, you take two steps, you die."

"What kind of motorcycle you got?" asked John.

"A Minsk. It's Russian."

"I hope you've got first gear because you're going to be going uphill a lot."

"If you break down there you're in deep shit," said Greg. "There's no place to fix a flat tire and nobody will be passing by to help. Be prepared to spend the night out there."

Keith entered the bar just as the crew began speculating as to how long it would be before I came down with malaria. The hulking veteran's invitation to join him at the bar spared me more gang ridicule. Keith, however, had his own scheme for mocking the only customer who hadn't served his country.

He pointed to a glass jug high on a shelf behind the bar. Big enough to hold two gallons, the container was decorated with layers of black and brown stripes. Keith asked the bartender, a clumsy Vietnamese youth, to bring the bottle for inspection.

"Snake brandy," said the former interrogator.

Sure enough, each stripe was an inch-thick snake floating in alcohol. The longer I examined the jug the more hideous it became. One snake's head poked vertically, as if sniffing for an exit. Another was nestled between layers of bodies. Among the serpents were brown, wormlike twigs.

"What's the recipe?"

"Snakes, herbs, and brandy. They let it brew for a month and . . ." The effects on male virility were said to be qualitative rather than quantitative.

The snakes swayed in the liquid as the barman filled Keith's order for two shots. I checked that a floating eyeball hadn't found its way into my glass. Keith downed his quickly. I paused.

"If it killed you there would be bodies everywhere. Right?"

I took a tiny sip. More than the taste, the whiff of the brown liquid flared my nostrils, which threatened a walkout. Only after more prodding—"Don't you want to be a man?"— did I toss the shot over my terrified tongue.

The sailors followed suit. Several rounds of Tiger beer followed the snake brandy. The music drifted from the Doors to the Rolling Stones and back. Joe swayed and sang along: "Come on, baby, light my fire. Come on, baby, light my fire." One of the MIA team, maybe Greg, asked if I spoke Vietnamese.

"No."

Greg just shook his head.

9

Highway One made few early demands. Once clear of Hanoi, the direct route to Saigon was a southbound beeline, not the tortuous disaster area described by Vietnamese and American vets. A plane of asphalt covered both lanes. The dirt shoulders were nearly as smooth. I felt good about my decision to ignore the menacing gray clouds.

Vendors lined the route out of the capital. Many displayed bottles of petrol, cans of oil, and tire-repair equipment. Others sold cookies, Cokes, and snack food. The shortage of customers left the proprietors idle. All along the highway women squatted and men scratched. Dogs chewed their mange.

The road wasn't much livelier. Bicyclists quietly pedaled past water buffalo towing wooden carts without complaint. Few motorcycles were headed my way, though a steady drip of Hondas and Minsks buzzed toward Hanoi. Every few minutes all scattered to make way for trucks and buses which blasted horns and flashed headlights to clear the road's center.

Few Vietnamese missed the opportunity to stare at a motorbiking foreigner. In fact, life stopped as soon as a pinkish, unshaven face came into focus. A group of twenty schoolchildren in red kerchiefs went bonkers, dropping book bags in mud and puddles to free hands for waving and energy for cheering. An entranced four-year-old nearly fell off his buffalo.

Adults showed a little more restraint. A few simply gaped. Others raised a hand and smiled. Two women in a field dropped their hoes and held open their arms as if Jesus himself were passing. I waved back, pretending I was Neil Armstrong in a blizzard of ticker tape.

A stunning young woman seated on the rear of a passing scooter looked extra long. I figured her focus was my overloaded Minsk. My backpack straddled the gas tank. A jerrycan with twenty liters of petrol claimed the luggage rack. One handlebar carried a cloth satchel with bottles of mineral water. The other held a baggie with Van's goodbye gift, two rolls of toilet paper.

The longer she looked the more I doubted my conclusion. The woman was flawless. The whiteness of her *ao dai*—flowing trousers and a form-fitting top with splits on the sides—was punctuated by shoes which matched her scarlet lipstick. A black mane of waist-length hair flowed in the wind. I watched her signal the driver to slow to my speed. Just beyond arm's reach, the woman smiled. There was no mistaking her body language.

"Your turn signal has been on for the last five minutes," she said with a series of simple gestures.

The looker, who sped away laughing with her partner, wasn't the only local staring at me. A dozen men gaped when I stepped into a roadside noodle shack in Phuy Ly, a town which red-tipped milestones said was 40 kilometers from Hanoi. Those who missed my entrance whiplashed their necks while spinning around to catch a glimpse of something stranger than a Sasquatch.

I couldn't blame them. A relentless drizzle had soaked my

clothes. Spray from the road had turned my pants brown. Truck exhaust had tarred my face. But Phuy Ly's breakfast crowd had a solution.

"*Bia Hoi?*" asked a man behind a trio of empty beer glasses.

Alcohol might have improved the local fare. After three attempts to pronounce *com*, which meant rice when properly enunciated, I learned that the rice was sold out. Chicken was also out of stock. So my soup noodles arrived garnished with beef bits shaved off a catcher's mitt.

The travails of securing a simple meal stirred my old anxieties. My destination was Thanh Hoa, one of many assembly points for soldiers headed down the Ho Chi Minh Trail. Just 150 kilometers from the capital, the town might as well have been on Pluto. I would know nobody. I wasn't even sure whether there would be a bed for hire. To complicate matters, I spoke virtually no Vietnamese.

Glenn had been the first to suggest that English and French wouldn't go far outside of Hanoi. At the very least, a few words of Vietnamese would break the ice with locals who were wary of foreigners. For the price of a coffee he taught me some basics.

The vet started by penning "*ma*" six times. Five of the *ma*s were adorned with slashes and wigglies. The accents, he said, indicated the word's vocal inflection. I failed to hear any difference when the American veteran demonstrated the tones.

I had sought professional help. For five dollars per session, a Hanoi University teacher had agreed to take on a new student. Invariably dressed in leopard-pattern tights and a blazer, Mrs. Van came to my room six times per week for ninety minutes of torment.

The importance of accurate intonation meant that we spent half the lesson making sounds intelligible only to dol-

phins. *"Bi, mi, phi . . ."* The subtlety of the differences between tones escaped me. I got headaches after ten minutes of
repeating my own incomprehensible errors and suffering my
teacher's grating corrections. After a tea break, we worked on
basic dialogues. Class ended with Mrs. Van saying, "You exer-
cise."

I did, though not very hard. Still, I preferred to blame the
teacher for my inability to learn her language. Her pedagogical
technique went like this: read aloud a sentence, look the dumb-
founded student in the eye, say "Understand?" and move on. I
usually didn't understand, so we spent our time digging through
dictionaries.

Somehow, we parted on good terms. Not because I could
speak Vietnamese; I resigned myself to hunting through my
phrase book for any word more complex than "hello." And not
because Mrs. Van cottoned to me. The heart of our bond was
the twenty-dollar bonus I paid after glimpsing her dank home
in the Old Quarter. At the end of our last duet she said, "Good
lucky."

Lucky was what I would need to be with no lingo to
deploy. South of Phuy Ly, I felt increasingly remote. Rows of
shacks gave way to miles of green rice plants. The paddies were
dotted with the hats of peasants up to their knees in water and
mud. Scenic? Yes. Reassuring to a city kid worried about his
next meal? No.

Highway One crumbled even faster than my confidence.
The road narrowed to a lane and a half. The surface turned to a
patchwork of loose gravel and buckled pavement. In places,
Vietnam's main pike was no more than a slalom course of mud,
dirt, and jagged rocks. By weaving I saved tires but lost time.

Orientation was less of a problem. The provinces just below Hanoi were among the country's poorest. Towns had no
money to build roads. Asphalt was out of the question until

malnutrition was cracked. Highway One, then, was the only hardtop in sight.

That rule of thumb wasn't enough to guide me through Ninh Binh. At a roundabout I looked for a sign pointing to Thanh Hoa. Drawn by the sight of a battered spire rising behind the rest of the town's decrepit structures, I turned left onto a broad boulevard. At the end of the avenue three policemen were idling by an electric blue motorcycle with a sidecar.

They took no notice of an outsider turning right onto a muddy road. It was my U-turn away from a narrow path snaking into barren hills that caught the eye of the lawmen. One beckoned for me to pull up to their spot. Panicked, I stalled and used a phrase I *did* know: "My motorbike is a Russian piece of shit."

Two of the officers smiled. The third, who was wearing a white belt broad enough to be a corset, stayed serious. He slapped his palm and barked at me. I didn't need Vietnamese to know he wanted to see my travel papers. I pulled out a map.

"Which way is Thanh Hoa?"

White Belt slapped his palm and repeated his demand.

"Thanh Hoa. I'm going to Thanh Hoa."

The cop's face reddened as his demand went unmet.

My theory was that you couldn't bust somebody who couldn't understand the proceedings. "Thanh Hoa. Which way?"

"That way. Sixty kilometers," said White Belt, who failed to link my quick departure to some understanding of his language.

A crew of kids didn't let me off so easy. I found them playing near the elusive spire, which loomed over the rubble of the rest of a church. A woman of fifty stopped her bicycle and told me what must have been a history of the building. Again, I didn't need words to know that the church had been leveled twenty-plus years before by American B-52s. She quickly lost interest and left.

The boys stuck around. Armed with toy guns modeled on Russian AK-47s, each kid seized the occasion to scream "hello" at the top of his prepubescent voice. One proposed a trade, his fountain pen for my Minsk. When I turned him down, another tyke pointed his wooden rifle at my head and said, "*Lien xo.*" Literally "linked socialists," the words meant "Russian" as well as "cheapskate." I denied both charges.

My captor tried again: "*Phap.*"

Not being French, I shook my head.

The kids were stumped. None guessed that I might be American. That was beyond possibility in a small town in northern Vietnam. Nor was I going to volunteer this fact as adults began taking notice of the foreigner near the bombed-out church.

The children tried to force me to talk. They leveled their weapons and repeated their guesses. "*Lien xo.*" "*Phap.*" When I didn't answer, the rascals opened fire.

10

I was too tired for historic ruminations by the time the Ham Rong Bridge rolled under my wheels. To many a Northern soldier, the river crossing on the edge of Thanh Hoa represented the beginning of the Ho Chi Minh Trail. To American strategists seeking to stop the flow of supplies, the bridge was a point to be choked. Decades after the carpet bombing, the gaping craters remained.

I should have stopped to examine the holes big enough to hide a Cadillac and to ruminate on the horrors of another era. But I had been on the road for nine hours. But, having skipped lunch, I was hungry enough to eat tire rubber. Above all, however, my nerves had been rattled.

It happened in Len, a town too tiny to appear on the map. The first signs of trouble were the sharp crack and shard of metal zinging past my cheek. My left fingers lost their grip and the Minsk skidded to a stop in front of a slow-moving truck. Mercifully, the driver braked while I shoved my vehicle off the rocky road to assess the damage. My clutch cable was shot.

I thought I had it bad. Looking around Len reminded me just how lucky I was. The place was a shade above ghost town.

Big chunks were missing from all of the dozen concrete buildings by the road. The dusty wooden shacks looked unlikely to withstand a summer breeze. To me, the only sign of civilization was "Honda" scrawled on a plank of wood in front of a dark shanty. Praying for a mechanic, I peered into the windowless frame.

A muddy infant peered back. So did the ragged woman holding her. She gasped and dropped the baby when I reached for one of the wrenches strewn on the floor. The woman was out the back door before I could explain.

An underdressed man of thirty halted my exit. The grease layered onto his hands said it all. I had broken down ten yards from Len's body shop. The mechanic set to work without a word.

A crowd gathered. The entire population of forty, or maybe fifty, silently circled me. Gradually, they pressed in for a closer look at the unwashed intruder. A leathery man who was bent like a question mark addressed me with an elaborate pantomime. Why, he asked, was a rich foreigner riding a Minsk instead of taking a plane?

The penniless town reminded me of Duong Dan Dam, a retired Communist Party bigwig. I had met the hefty, white-haired octogenarian in a noodle shop near my guesthouse. Speaking in elegant French, Mr. Dam ran the highlight film of a life spent riding the right coattails.

Dam boarded Ho Chi Minh's bandwagon at the end of World War II. This foresight won him the job of governor of Nam Ha, the province where rubber beef and beer were breakfast favorites. There he spent seven years ducking French soldiers. Then Uncle Ho summoned him to plan the siege of Dien Bien Phu.

"I was very close to Ho Chi Minh," he whispered. "And I was in the cabinet of his successor."

Dam's clout was clear from the deference paid him. Other diners bowed their heads when passing our table. Some tried to catch his eye, which rarely strayed from the loose blouse of our fawning waitress.

Dam was reluctant to discuss the war. He would only say that he had survived B-52s, helicopter gunships, and, perhaps most painful of all, an eight-year separation from his wife and sons, who spent the war in Thanh Hoa. "We don't forget the past. We just don't talk about it," said the Party hack.

What he did talk about was soup noodles, or *pho*. Squatting on a low wooden stool beside mine, the one-time government minister boasted that this, his local joint, served Hanoi's finest *pho*. To ensure my agreement, he added a spoonful of fiery red paste and a half cup of chicken fat to my steaming broth. When I mentioned my plan to find the Trail, the old man closed his eyes. "Take the train," he said. Unaccustomed to impertinent Americans, Dam stiffened when I rejected the tip. He leaned close and said, "I was very close to Ho Chi Minh." The link to Vietnam's George Washington was meant to lend credibility to the preceding advice, as well as the warning that followed.

The mountain road, said Dam, was deadly. There were tigers, which he said were kittens compared to the panthers I was sure to encounter. Oddly, he believed bears to be more dangerous than either of the big cats.

Then there was the human threat. Robbers lurked along mountain roads. So did "Montagnards," the French word meaning mountain dwellers. Dam drew back on an imaginary crossbow and let fly an arrow. "If you go into a Montagnard village, you won't come out," he assured me.

How seriously should I take the warnings? I wasn't sure until Dam described more exotic threats. Once a thirty-foot python lay across a mountain road Dam was traveling by car. The driver wouldn't pass over it for fear the snake would wrap around and crush the vehicle. Elephants in the Central Highlands posed a similar threat. Those who got too close were trunk-wrapped and beaten like pestle on mortar.

At the end of our conversation, he handed me a business card, which he said was carte blanche should I encounter trouble with police or other officials. The big talk never panned out. Nobody ever recognized the name, not in Hanoi, not in Len, and not in Thanh Hoa.

That town's church bells were ringing when I arrived. But the rest of Thanh Hoa ignored me. Men in dusty clothes labored to turn bicycle pedals down the stretch of Highway One that bisected two rows of decomposing buildings. Pedestrians milled around, kicked stones, and listlessly tracked the progress of the only foreigner in town.

On the west side of Thanh Hoa's one and only street, I found Thanh Hoa's one and only guesthouse. Greeted in French by a pleasant, but hardly friendly, woman, I selected a cut-rate room in the dingiest of the three unpainted blocks of concrete. Five bucks bought me a wooden bed covered by a straw mat, a foam pad, and a mosquito net. There was no extra charge for peeing in the public bathroom's rusting, rancid trough.

I asked the receptionist where she had learned French.

"At university. In Hanoi."

"And you came back here after you finished?"

"This is my home."

Cutting to the chase, open to offers, I asked what people did for fun. Where was the action on a Friday night in Thanh Hoa?

"There is nothing."

I rephrased the question: "Young people, what will they be doing tonight?"

"Nothing."

"Nothing?"

"There's nothing to do here. I watch television in my home. Then I go to sleep."

My early evening stroll didn't contradict this information. Men and women, old and young, sat on stools and stared at the street or each other. It wasn't clear whether they would budge if the circus came to town. If Ringling Brothers did show up, admission had better be free. Thanh Hoa's residents looked broke as well as broken. The dinner menu was soup noodles or nothing.

The guard had changed by the time I returned to the guesthouse. The receptionist had been replaced by a smooth-skinned forty-year-old. As bored as I, he wanted to talk. "*Habla español?*"

The night clerk had learned Spanish in Cuba. What was he doing there? Poverty drove tens of thousands of Vietnamese to work in Communist countries where wages were higher. Sadly, for families that depended on remitted wages, most of the guest workers had to return home following the fall of the Soviet bloc.

A few found work elsewhere in the Third World. I met a pharmacist who spent three years in Algeria. I heard of a middle-aged government engineer who was sent to Iraq to build a road. The trip's timing couldn't have been worse.

The engineer arrived shortly before the start of the Gulf War. At a time when most countries were recalling citizens, Hanoi lacked the funds to repatriate its people. Stuck in a trailer in the desert, the engineer couldn't miss the cruel irony of facing American bombers for the second time in his life.

Poor though Thanh Hoa was, the night clerk felt lucky to

live there. Vietnam, he said, had many poorer places. One was Tan Ky. Colonel Luc said the town in Nghe An Province had been the assembly point for his Trail-bound unit. I said it would be my destination the following day. The clerk said stay away. Well off the coastal highway, Tan Ky had no food, gas, or lodging.

"If you go there, you will have trouble," he assured me.

More tired than worried, I called it a night. The next morning the receptionist was back. Friendlier than before, she asked, "What did you find last night in Thanh Hoa?"

"Nothing."

11

One day on the road made me leery of late
starts. Thanh Hoa was just 150 kilometers from Hanoi. Put
that distance on an interstate under construction, add a potty
stop, and the drive would still last no more than two hours in
any state of the Union. In Vietnam, the trip took nine hours.

The multiplier—one Western hour equals four Vietnam
hours—didn't dissuade me from heading for Tan Ky. Nor did
the night clerk's warning. Armed with a full jerrycan and a new
clutch, I was confident that I could make it to the source of the
Ho Chi Minh Trail and back to the coast by sundown.

About 100 kilometers down Highway One there was a dot
labeled "Dien Chau." From there a red line drifted northwest
toward Laos. That road would take me to a right turn which led
to Tan Ky. An eight o'clock departure from Thanh Hoa should
have had me there in time for a late lunch.

Again, I misjudged the travel time. Again, Hanoi's highway department was the culprit. At its best, the road surface was
uneven. At its worst, the bumps and potholes demanded a pace
too slow for third gear. A Minsk on the road felt more like a
boat on the high seas.

Bomb craters, distinguishable from natural divots by their roundness, continued to show the way south. Looking at the gray sky, I wondered about the day the holes were made. There was no natural shelter on the flat, only a brown expanse where mud and marshes had replaced rice and paddies. Collections of planks passed for luxury houses. Most locals lived in clumps of mud and sticks. Neither looked ready to stop a bomb or its blast.

A row of six roadside restaurants—shacks with signs to attract truck and bus drivers—was the first sign of life. A sagging man with a neck-to-navel tattoo of Buddha brought me a glass of coffee. A DeSoto bus stopped and disgorged three dozen shaken, but not stirred, passengers. The driver, who spoke fragments of English, told me to look him up when I got to Danang.

The southern city seemed impossibly distant. I completed the 80 kilometers to Quynh Luu, a town north of the turn to Tan Ky, at one o'clock. Where the hours went I couldn't say. What I could say was I was hungry and nowhere near my target.

It was hunger that convinced me not to flee the café after the owner confirmed (or denied?) the niggling rumor about American men. My bell had been rung. But I still wanted some soup noodles, hold the meat. Besides, after reporting his findings, the owner welcomed me with a more conventional handshake.

The rest of the group also warmed to me. A proud trucker showed me the cab of his vehicle. One of the policemen grinned and made a peace sign. His partner poured some of his beer into a spare glass for me. The rest of the customers looked equally delighted to have an American in town. I had, it seemed, misjudged Quynh Luu's lunchtime crowd.

A pudgy man in an untucked white shirt tapped my shoulder as I finished my bowl of noodles. He raised a finger that said, "Wait a minute," and scurried through a door at the rear of the shack. The overgrown man returned with something that was sure to impress a visitor.

The leather book in his grip held a collection of postage stamps. The heavy fellow claimed the place next to mine on the wooden bench and turned pages holding sleeves of stamps decorated with flowers, birds, etc. Four other men in various stages of insobriety looked on. I forced a smile and hoped my impatience was invisible. It wasn't. The collector spotted the drift of my attention and forced me to examine his prize stamps.

My lowered eyes found a picture with stars and stripes. I saw some familiar letters: USAF. Something didn't fit. Why did these Vietnamese stamps have American acronyms?

A closer examination revealed what the collector had been trying to show me: his stamps were vintage North Vietnam. Printed during the late 1960s, each one conveyed the inspirational image of American aircraft in distress. One featured a B-52 with flames pouring from its wings and tail fin. Another displayed an open parachute beside an exploding fighter.

Hanoi's postmaster general had contrasted the villains with the heroes. Four antiaircraft cannons pointed toward one flaming plane. The thousand-dong stamp deployed a bayonet blade in the place of a 1. Teams of women, perhaps not unlike the gunner-turned-tea-lady at the Hanoi café, operated several of the batteries. Other artillery was manned by square-jawed patriots.

The collector rested his finger beside the lower border of one of the stamps. The print said "*4181 May Bay My.*" The men around my seat used gestures to translate Hanoi's pride that it had shot down 4,181 American airplanes. The warmth of our male bond was evaporating fast. So was the novelty of being a lone American in Nowheresville, North Vietnam.

Charlie had me surrounded. A man in a green pith helmet was glaring at me from across the picnic table. To my left a beer-gutted fifty-year-old, his skin tanned and dried from outdoor labor, looked even less pleased. Seeing no quick exit, I kept my eyes cast down.

A stamp dated 1967 depicted a tiny Vietnamese woman pointing a fixed bayonet at the back of a hulking American pilot with his hands tied behind his back. Another stamp showed an airman in the green and white stripes of a prisoner of war.

I tried to acknowledge the patriotic victory over imperialism. When the tight spot didn't loosen, I wrote "1963," the year of my birth, on a piece of paper. That was my way of saying, "Look, guys, those bombs had nothing to do with me."

The rough customers didn't buy my story. The laborer grabbed me by the wrist. Then he lifted his right leg onto the bench and placed my hand on the flesh beside his shin. I searched his reddened eyes for hints of what would happen next.

The laborer used his free hand to poke the stamp with the B-52. His other hand guided my fingers to a spot on his calf. The flesh was hard, more like rock than muscle. Looking at the scarred skin, I understood what I was feeling. The hard spot beneath the surface was metal, or, more specifically, shrapnel.

But the sun-darkened man wasn't mouthing the familiar dismissal that followed most talk of the war between Vietnamese and Americans. He wasn't saying, "That's all history." For twenty or thirty years the laborer had been walking around with pieces of America in his hide. The guy was mad and he wanted me to know it. He looked angry enough to punch and drunk enough to think it was a good idea.

Across the table, the man in the pith helmet took less than playful swings at air. A half turn of my head revealed that the police had returned to their beats. If a fight broke out, would they have stepped in or piled on?

The laborer separated the flaps of his shirt and pulled my hand to another scar, this one near the top of his ribs. Fear surged and adrenaline rushed as I felt more metal lumps in his flesh. Maybe, just maybe, I had strayed too far off the beaten path. Maybe one Northerner was about to seek his own brand of war reparations. The bombing victim's relentless glare underscored that very impression.

The collector must have sensed the tension. Why else would he have distracted the antagonists by exposing and indicating the inside cover of the leather album? All heads turned. Instead of stamps we saw a five-by-seven-inch picture of two Rubenesque women stroking each other's naked white skin. Momentarily shelving plans to exact a pound of American flesh, the men of Quynh Luu pressed in for a closer look at the dog-eared pornography.

"Americans?" asked the laborer through a filthy grin.

I nodded.

"Wow," said a collective round of gasps. When the crew of five returned their attention to the nude models, I paid for my lunch and fled before I could make any more misjudgments.

12

....
....
....

The westbound road looked unlikely to lead
anywhere but trouble. The fat red line marked 7 on my map
wasn't a superhighway to Laos but an ordinary dirt trail. No
sign marked the road to Tan Ky. It was simply the only right
turn in Dien Chau. I paused before turning.

Quynh Luu had spooked me. "That's all history" had always sounded too pat to be heartfelt. The menacing Northerners left me even less convinced that the war was a distant memory for the Vietnamese. Did that negate the exuberant greetings
from others along the highway? No. But the cordial majority
didn't mean there weren't still plenty of sore toes. I resolved to
watch my step.

There was another argument for skipping Tan Ky. The
dogleg route was about 50 kilometers. At top speed, my motorbike could cover that in an hour. Crappy roads cut my average
pace to 20. That put Tan Ky at least two hours away, and it was
already two-thirty. What if I broke down? I continued south.

The road was mine. Lone cyclists or pedestrians appeared
every few minutes. As many as ten could pass between sightings

of motorbikes or trucks. Cars hadn't made it to this area rich in mud but poorer than dirt. I wove down the center of Highway One's two unmarked lanes and angled my face toward the sun, which appeared for the first time since I left Hanoi.

The rays led me into Vinh, where I expected another chilly reception. At one time the city had been all broad boulevards and colonial villas. That charm had been flattened by a series of brutal poundings.

The destruction started in the 1950s, when France bombed the city, which was resisting its rule. Local earth-scorchers followed. Reluctant to leave anything for the French to rule over, Ho Chi Minh's retreating supporters wrecked most of the city à la Sherman. A chance fire incinerated what the Viet Minh missed.

Vinh's curse was its port. Closer to the fighting than North Vietnam's other big harbor, Haiphong, the city was a hub for war supplies bound for the Ho Chi Minh Trail. The Pentagon caught on and ordered massive bombings of this source of the supply route. Nearly a decade of shelling had left the city with just two buildings intact.

Hanoi's postwar allies inflicted more durable damage. In the late 1970s, East Germany offered Vinh the financial and technical support to rebuild. What started as charity turned into an architectural nightmare. To drive into Vinh was to enter Moscow, Warsaw, or any other Eastern-bloc city reconstructed after World War II.

"*Khach San Nang Luong,*" said big letters on the first building along Vinh's six-lane main drag. *Khach san* meant hotel. *Nang Luong* may have meant "too ugly for words." It was a box without features, nuance, or paint. It was a stunning achievement for an architect who must have been trying to perfect the eyesore. It was rivaled only by the buildings farther along; a cluster of identical residential towers made New York's Co-op City look frilly. The tour ended when I recalled an unrun errand.

My one-month visa had neared expiration toward the end of my stay in Hanoi. One-month extensions were said to be a snap. Maybe so. But the two government offices I tried refused to even consider my request for more time in Vietnam. "Hanoinkers," I grumbled. At a third office, state-owned Vietnam Tourism, a muscular woman offered a two-week extension, as well as some advice. She told me to get out of town.

The problem was not me but Hanoi, said the bureaucrat. In Vietnam, adherence to rules was directly proportionate to proximity to the capital. Lawmakers said foreigners could only add two weeks at a time. Closest to the enforcement mechanism, bureaucrats in Hanoi tended to follow the letter of the law.

"Go to Hue, Danang, or Ho Chi Minh City," counseled the woman. "Because they are far from the center there are fewer rules." She endorsed Vinh as a source of paperwork, cheap and speedy.

But there were reasons aplenty for not visiting the port city's immigration office. For a start, any encounter with Vietnamese officialdom led to more questions than I could answer. The lunchtime run-in had made me wary of Northerners. Finally, it was four-thirty on a Saturday. What self-respecting official would still be at work?

Something simpler finally overruled the combined weight of those arguments. My visa would soon expire. With no extension, I became a prime candidate for the gulag should a policeman or even a hotel clerk take a close look at my travel documents.

Blue, English letters identified a low yellow building on

Le Hong Phong Street as the immigration office. Hearing the commotion of an idling Minsk, a relaxed gent in a loose-fitting shirt stepped from one of four doors and onto the dirt road.

"Hello; do you need a visa?" he said in flawless English.

The official led me through the door on the far left. If you ignored two broad desks in the back, the office could have been a living room. Four armchairs were split evenly on opposite sides of a long wooden coffee table. On the table's surface, five dirty glasses mingled with empty bottles formerly filled with six liters of beer.

"Everybody went home already," said the official. "Maybe I can help you."

Had I come to the wrong address? Was this attentive, articulate fellow really a government employee? Was I still in Vietnam? Maybe the official was just moonlighting from a job at a five-star hotel.

"How long do you want to stay in Vietnam?" he asked.

Hoping to curry favor, I sat back and sucked up. I detailed my deepening affection for Vietnam. There was just so much to see: Vinh's world-famous port, the home of Ho Chi Minh, blah blah blah. I outlined my plan to drive to Saigon. Sorry, sir, Ho Chi Minh City. If only I had more time.

The official agreed. There *were* many important places to see in Vietnam. He asked for my passport and the separate piece of paper with my visa. Concentration brought a frown to his smooth-skinned face.

"This is no good," he concluded.

It was a mistake. There had to be a mistake. I was too sensible to break the rules and too savvy to turn myself in to the sheriff. Right? Right. The official had seen the expired front of my visa instead of the valid renewal on the back. We shared a laugh, mine nervous, his relieved not to be reading a foreigner his rights. Still, I would have to wait until Monday for an extension.

The business finished, we relaxed. The official excused his English, the best I had heard in a week. Did I speak Russian, which he had picked up during six years in Moscow? No. How about French?

"You are an American who speaks French?"

"Sure."

"You are in America's security forces."

"What? . . . No."

"I think you are in the security division," he insisted.

Saved from one hole, I felt myself falling into another. Because only an elite group of Vietnamese received language training, the official inferred that I was CIA or some other breed of agent. For all I knew, he had already sounded a silent alarm and scrambled the local storm troopers.

"I'm just a student."

The official laughed at the quiver in my voice. He flipped the back of his hand and said, "Don't worry. You are security. I am also security. No problem."

That bond led to an exchange of personal details. The official volunteered that he was thirty-five, had a wife, three kids, and a home in Vinh's suburbs. Me? Thirty-one, no kids, and still looking. The last answer elicited a laugh and another question.

"What kind of woman do you like? Young?"

"About my age."

"How many?"

"Three."

"You want three. No problem."

But there was a problem. I was kidding. The official wasn't. The Vietnamese man confessed to a lifelong lust for American women. In particular, he admired their "big breasts."

"Do you like big breasts?" he asked.

"Well . . . uh . . . sure."

"How about vaginas?"

My comfort level plunging, I wished the official weren't still holding my passport and visa. I had suspected an American might get the third degree in Vietnam. I just hadn't expected it to be on his preferences in partners. Impatient with an uncooperative witness, the interrogator raised the stakes of the interview.

"I can help you get a Vietnamese girl," he said in a tone saturated with conspiracy. Confusing my silence with assent, he described the logistics. In Vinh, the hotels near the beach were the place to party. As elsewhere, the price of a prostitute was directly linked to physical merits. Beautiful girls cost a hundred dollars. At the opposite end of the scale, a quickie could be had for ten. "I can help you," the official repeated.

Trying to refuse without offending, I observed that a family man such as himself probably didn't want to spend Saturday night pimping for an American. He denied the charge and continued his plotting. Did I have a choice? Perhaps procuring hookers was the way local cops greased their palms. Twice caught off guard at lunchtime, I felt unable to judge natives' intentions in Nghe An Province.

"I am in the security forces. You will have no problem."

"You have a wife. I'm sure you want to go home."

"My wife knows very little about my work. She only knows that I work with security for foreigners. I can call her and say I must work with a foreigner tonight. Later, I can meet you at your hotel."

There was no dissuading the official. I pointed out that I would need my travel documents to check into a hotel: all over Vietnam, desk clerks were responsible for reporting the movements of foreigners. That observation brought my passport and visa back into my hands for the first time in a half hour.

"Which will be your hotel?"

"Uh . . . Khach San Nang Luong."

"I will talk to my wife," said the libidinous official. "You have a shower and I will meet you in a few hours."

13

Maybe the immigration official decided that Saturday night with a CIA agent was a bad career move. Maybe his wife insisted he baby-sit. Or maybe the security forces hadn't trained him to know that a foreigner wouldn't patronize an eyesore like Khach San Nang Luong. Whatever the reason, the official never came to my guesthouse, a rotting block favored by itinerant truckers.

I regretted his absence the following morning, when I needed directions. Several roads ran west off of Le Loi, the city's central street. One led to Kim Lien, Ho Chi Minh's birthplace. Which one, however, was a mystery. Road signs were among the oversights of Vinh's planners.

My clueless demeanor drew the notice of a group of five young men. They waved me over to their table on the dirt shoulder of a westbound street. A muscular twenty-two-year-old in a stained shirt spoke enough English to see my problem. He grabbed my map of Vietnam and put the question to the rest of the group.

The sound of metal tearing at pavement interrupted their deliberations. Heads spun in time to see a Honda sliding under the grate of a truck. Free of his vehicle, the rider rolled into the front tire, which stopped just before impact. A crowd gathered to assess the damage. When there proved to be little—though limping badly, the rider appeared unhurt—the jury of five resumed its deliberations about my map. Their conclusion?

"You are on the road to Kim Lien," said the map reader, who poured me a cup of pale tea as I rose to leave. "Can you introduce yourself?"

I plodded through the basics of my life. In his turn, the map reader called himself a student even though he hadn't lifted a book in years. Why the outdated label? He *was* taking night classes in English. But the real reason was that the youth had been unemployed since finishing high school. His profession had not been determined.

He wasn't alone. My Saturday night spin-around Vinh revealed more motion than action. The owners of open-air cafés along Le Loi played videotaped movies on televisions that attracted fifty or more youths. Other kids had pressed their clothes and gelled their hair for an evening of loitering outside the Workers' Cultural Complex. Hundreds more spent the night cruising the dark streets on motor scooters or bicycles. All dressed up, Vinh's Generation X had no place to go.

"I am very unhappy," said the map reader. "No work for two years."

"What job would you like to have?"

"You can help me?"

"I'm just a tourist."

"Maybe you can help me?"

"I really can't."

The glum bunch returned to their tea. I drove west, over a short bridge, past five bathing water buffalo, and toward the hometown of the fellow known to all as *Bac Ho*, or Uncle Ho.

Young or old, Communist or capitalist, Vietnamese had a

soft spot for a leader best identified by the long wisps of gray hair hanging from his chin. Locals explaining their feelings for Ho Chi Minh cited the leader's unaffected love for Vietnam and the Vietnamese. Harder to pinpoint was the source of the man's magnetism.

"It was nice to be near to him, like your father," said a toothless woman who had met Ho in her youth.

"When *Bac Ho* arrived at a meal he checked the toilet and kitchen," said a former infantryman. "If they were dirty, or if the other food was not as good as his, he refused to eat. Those were signs that the hosts were not treating everybody the same."

"We think of him as a member of our family," said a young woman who was born in 1969, the year Ho died.

A quarter century later Ho Chi Minh's personality cult was still alive and well. His picture hung in all government offices. His likeness could also be found in homes, restaurants, and places of business. His face plastered billboards on the streets of any city. His words could be read on equally pervasive banners. Every time I reached for a banknote, there was Uncle Ho.

To blaspheme the dead leader was to invite a Niagara of trouble. During a meal in the capital, a British friend had referred to Ho as "The Expanding Plastic Man," a reference to the effect that years of taxidermy had had on his corpse, which had been pickled and displayed in a mausoleum in Hanoi. The response of his Vietnamese wife was swift and sharp: "You cannot say these things about Uncle Ho."

The wife's shrill tone may have been motivated by fear. The Vietnamese police had a history of filling cells with people who had criticized Ho. Objective, or correct, critiques were often used as pretexts to punish enemies. An American businessman told me how a neutral comment akin to "Clinton could use a haircut" earned him a month of surveillance by security officers seeking an excuse to expel him.

Uncle Ho was even beyond reproach for the millions of deaths during the wars to drive foreigners from Vietnam. Here, fingers pointed at Vo Nguyen Giap, the head of Hanoi's military during and since the Vietnam War. A retired Northern officer summarized General Giap's strategy for me: "He put 10,000 of ours against 1,000 of theirs and let them blow each other up."

The only open discussion I ever heard about Ho Chi Minh related to his ideology. Most everybody agreed that post-1975 Vietnam had Communism and corruption to thank for its economic woes. A dead leader couldn't be accused of taking bribes. But what about his choice of economic theory? Had Uncle Ho steered his people down the road to ruin?

Ho was twenty-one years old when he left Vietnam as a cook on a French steamship. He traveled to Africa, Europe, and both of the Americas. He built a résumé that included waiter, gardener, and snow sweeper. But distance didn't damp Ho's affection for his homeland. Settled in Paris, he was consumed by the question of how to liberate his colonized countrymen.

Communist doctrine provided the first satisfactory answer. A young man's despair turned to confidence that Marx and Lenin held the keys to Vietnam's leg irons. Visits to Moscow confirmed that he had found a way to free his people. Though descended from aristocrats, Ho and his disciples stuck to Communist knitting while adapting its ideology to fit Vietnam's long history of foreign invasion and occupation. At least that's how local propagandists told the story.

A bookish British journalist offered an alternative view. Seated beside me in a Hanoi restaurant, the diner pointed out that, as a young man in Paris after World War I, Ho had seen the Americans as the natural allies of subjugated people. He courted President Wilson with a series of letters. During World War II, American operatives trained Ho's men to fight the Japanese.

They also helped launch Vietnam's fight for freedom. On September 2, 1945, Ho Chi Minh proclaimed to an outdoor rally that the Democratic Republic of Vietnam had been born. Stuck for rhetoric the previous night, Ho had turned to a group of Americans near his table in a Hanoi tea house. They were agents of the OSS, the CIA's predecessor, which had trained Ho's men to resist Japanese occupation. The Americans suggested something along the lines of "all men are created equal."

Cribbing from the Declaration of Independence didn't win Washington's support. France was bent on reassuming control of its former colonies. While it may have been sympathetic to Ho's cause, America chose to support its wartime ally. So North Vietnam's future leader turned elsewhere for help.

Dogma, said the journalist, was far less important to Ho than evicting foreigners. To do so, he needed guns and bullets, which Moscow was willing to supply to those willing to talk their talk. "They were really more nationalists than Communists" was the bookworm's conclusion.

Nobody debated whether Ho Chi Minh was still a deity in Vietnam. His successors ignored Ho's clear request for cremation. They justified the betrayal, and the public display of Ho's embalmed corpse, by saying that "the people" wanted to keep him around. "When Uncle Ho is near, we feel safe" remained a popular expression.

On the other hand, unofficial skepticism about the founding father's achievement was rife. Daisy, the returned refugee, was baffled by my interest in visiting the mausoleum. Her main memory of Vietnam's favorite uncle dated to her schooldays. Every Monday she had to face the flag and sing songs about

Ho's wisdom, immortality, etc. Twice a week "special teachers" lectured on Ho Chi Minh and the victory over rich imperialists. "We wondered what was so bad about being rich," said the trendy teen.

Daisy viewed the widely sold Ho Chi Minh busts as relics for old people, many of whom had stowed theirs during the five years of *doi moi*. Her generation respected Ho's kindness, but they couldn't help but associate him with their lousy lot in life. When I expressed interest in visiting Ho's mausoleum, Daisy agreed to take me. She added, "I would never go there by my-self."

Many of those who had lost faith in Ho's vision continued to exploit his name. Dam, the Party hack, thrice reminded me how "close" he was to Uncle Ho. A friend in Hanoi told me about a woman who, having devoted her life to painting pictures of Ho, had earned a place among Vietnam's elite.

Another Northerner described how towns or provinces seeking government funds shamelessly leveraged Ho's popularity: "Anybody who wants a school or a bridge makes up a story about Uncle Ho. Ho went fishing here. He caught frogs there. This is where Uncle Ho helped a wounded buffalo. That was forty or fifty years ago, so we can't tell what's true. And because it's Uncle Ho, nobody can say no."

His face on every banknote, Ho's name became a synonym for cash. Meeting for business or pleasure, Vietnamese greeted each other by saying, "Did you bring Uncle Ho?"

A local entrepreneur described a more colorful exploitation of the name. The businessman needed an import license. A bureaucrat at the relevant ministry set twelve thousand dollars as the price of his approval. Accustomed to the practice, the importer duly returned with a packet of hundred-dollar bills. The bureaucrat stuffed the money into his breast pocket and said, "When Uncle Ho is near, I feel safe."

The house where Ho Chi Minh grew up stood at the end of a tidy path through a vegetable garden. The sparse dwelling emphasized the phase of the family's fortunes most in line with the Party's ideals, i.e., the period after Ho's father, a mandarin who had supported anti-French activities, had been stripped of his property.

Like Lincoln's log cabin, Ho's home was simple. Two compact, perpendicular buildings of wood were covered by the high V of a thatched roof. There were no doors; straw flaps on hinges covered the sides. Inside, a family sleeping platform was the main furnishing on a floor of hard-packed dirt. The walls were bare.

My visit coincided with that of a school group. Torn between a functionary's lecture and ogling a dust-covered American, thirty teenagers chose the latter. "I came to see my Uncle," said the eagerest of the beavers, who were surprised that I knew their hometown, Quynh Luu.

The mob followed me down a path to a Ho Chi Minh museum filled with examples of colonialism's horrors. One photo showed Vietnamese men wearing wooden neck frames. Another featured grim-faced rows of Viet Minh prisoners. I concentrated longest on the French-issued identification papers carried by Ho's father.

Beneath front and profile photos worthy of any police mug shot was a description of the bearer. There were basics—race, height, and age—as well as details. Head: big. General appearance: skinny. Color: yellow. Forehead: big and of average incline. A separate note remarked on lumps and marks on the father's face and head. Subjected to such scrutiny by a Frenchman, I too would have rebelled.

14

....
....
....

"Voo. Pair-doo."

I looked up at the sun-darkened man who had joined me at a crossroads. I could fault his French but not his conclusion. I was indeed *perdu*, or lost.

One blue arrow pointed left, toward a mud-brown river where children played and women washed. It said "Do Luong." A second arrow pointed right and said "Dung." Neither place showed up on my map, which was splayed across my gas tank. When I appealed to the man beside me, he tugged on a yellow T-shirt that said "Marina Del Ray, California."

His home, Nam Dan, was indistinguishable from other Northern towns. The one concrete building bore the government's red and gold seal. The main street was a strip of bumpy dirt on which scrawny chickens pecked lazily. The other residents, panting dogs and drooping humans, stared lifelessly from the shade of shacks constructed from flaps of wood, tin, and plastic.

I passed through the town and meandered for a few more kilometers before admitting that I had been given a bum steer. Somebody in Hanoi had called Nam Dan a staging area for the

Ho Chi Minh Trail. The source said I would even find a working army base on the outskirts of town, which lay just 7 kilometers from Kim Lien.

A half-naked man of seventy rescued me at the crossroads.
Bald but for a few gray spikes, built of little more than ribs and
skin, he doddered toward me. Once close enough to box my ear,
the old man shouted into it: *"JE PARLE FRANÇAIS."*

"Can you direct me to the army base?"

"YOU'LL HAVE TO SPEAK LOUD BECAUSE I'M A
LITTLE DEAF. COME HAVE TEA AT MY PLACE."

Ribs walked away. I rolled the Minsk toward a narrow
table in front of the shack he called home. Marina Del Ray
followed. Teapot in hand, the old man lowered himself beside
me on one of the benches flanking the table.

"I AM THE FRENCH TEACHER IN NAM DAN.
HOW OLD ARE YOU?"

My answer evoked an increasingly common response.

"DO YOU LIKE VIETNAMESE WOMEN?"

I expressed mild interest.

"VIETNAMESE WOMEN ARE VERY . . . *COM-
MODE.*"

My French faltered. Did *commode* mean comfortable or
accommodating? I couldn't remember. Nor could I discern why
the nugget was being proffered. Mindful of the immigration
official's hands-on approach to normalizing U.S.-Vietnam relations, I feared what, or whom, Ribs might have in mind.

The intentions of a pair of reddened eyes looking hard into
mine were even more worrying. The glare belonged to a flabby,
tanned man who had silently seated himself across from me.
With four of us seated, there should have been eight limbs on
the table. I counted just six.

Red eyes had no hands or forearms. Below the elbow, each
of his branches dissolved into a fleshy stump, which he used to

scratch his chest and nose. I didn't doubt his mutilation was war-related. But I couldn't guess the cause of the symmetric damage. Had he tried to lift a land mine?

The amputee looked curious rather than angry. A man who lived on the outskirts of a suburb of a minor city in one of Vietnam's poorest regions was far removed from the renewed inflow of foreigners. Moreover, I was probably the first live American he had seen. The rest would have been anonymous demons loosing explosives on his head and, of course, arms.

"HE WAS INJURED DURING THE VICTORY OVER THE AMERICANS," shouted my host. The old man's hearing was such that he hadn't picked up the heavy accent in my French. Under the circumstances, that was just as well. "WHEN ARE YOU RETURNING TO FRANCE?"

"Soon."

I rose, but Ribs wasn't ready to let me go. "MONSIEUR, THE SUN IN VIETNAM IS VERY STRONG."

He had a point. On this, my first cloudless day on the road, the breeze of a moving Minsk hadn't been enough to cool me. Sweat had stained my T-shirt by the time I reached Kim Lien in late morning. In Nam Dan, nobody moved out from the shade after noon.

"DO YOU HAVE A HAT?"

"No."

"GET ONE."

That was the best tip I would get in the greater Vinh area. Back in the city, I wandered the concrete warren that was the indoor market. One row of vendors sold cloth. The next offered T-shirts. I stopped when I found the aisle of hat dealers.

A brown golf hat emblazoned with "USA, California" seemed out of sync with the low profile I aimed to maintain. A baby-blue model saying "Buick Exclusive" was just too tacky. So I went native. A green pith helmet of the type worn by cyclo drivers, paddy farmers, and other paupers looked least likely to attract attention or bad reviews.

I asked the vendor to direct me to the source of much of Vinh's history of destruction, its port. "Take a right at the top end of Le Loi" sounded like good directions until a jeep jammed with soldiers pulled alongside. Shouting, gesticulating, they wanted a word on the shoulder of an empty stretch of road. The word was that my license plate was dangling loose. The soldiers drove off.

I got lost. At the road's end I found a single pier rather than a port worth shelling. Backtracking, I turned left down a dirt track along a beach. Bomb craters, wider than they were deep, suggested that former targets weren't far off. Unable to spot the mark, I retreated.

Seeing my pink face for the second time, a barefoot, middle-aged woman waved one frantic arm and blocked my way. Rags covered her hips, head, and shoulders. By her side were two half-naked children, a girl and a boy. I leaned forward to hear her story and to get directions. Instead I got an infant wrapped in rags.

"*Di*," she said. "Go."

The mother of three motioned for me to drive away, to take her baby and raise it in Russia or France or wherever I came from. Any place foreign had to offer a better life for her child than her squalid corner of the world. With no hesitation she turned and walked away with her remaining pair of kids.

Speechless, holding the baby away from my body like a tub of toxic waste, I waited for her to turn back and say "April Fool." When she did neither, I shouted. I wasn't ready for motherhood, or even fatherhood. Unable to drive after her with an armload of infant, I dropped the motorbike and gave chase on foot. The mother didn't smile when I thrust the load back into her arms. She just shrugged and kept going.

The following morning I finally located Vinh's port. By then I had lost my license plate and bought it back from the pack of tattooed toughs who demanded a hundred dollars for their find. They settled for ten thousand dong, or a dollar. That was one fifth what I paid a local mechanic to spend two hours fixing the front fork of my motorbike.

The much-embattled port had become a secondary interest. I wanted to follow the route taken by tons of Viet Cong war supplies. The map showed a westbound road out of Vinh. Labeled "8," it wasn't on my list of Ho Chi Minh Trail survivors. But what else could a road that drove straight into Laos be?

I filled my tank at Petrolimex and asked the attendant to direct me to Duc Tho, a town midway to the Lao border. She finished freshening her makeup and sent me across a toll bridge, where a road sign said, in English, "Good Luck to You." On the far side, I confirmed the directions.

"Duc Tho?" I asked a man leading a water buffalo.

"Duc Tho," he said with a nod and a wave.

The Trail beneath my tires brought a smile to my face. Knowing that I had made it, that I had done what *they* said I couldn't, made the road feel smoother. The scenery, rice and mud, mud and rice, now looked exotic. So did the town of Can Loc, which I reached after a half hour.

The day's fourth map consultation delivered the bad news. I was on Highway One, not the Ho Chi Minh Trail. Twice told that I was en route to Duc Tho, I couldn't imagine the reason. Was there a conspiracy afoot? Was I being steered clear of secret military installations? Or live prisoners of war? Or were locals simply steering me clear of rough terrain?

15

Pham Tu Quang stared hard at the wall map of Vietnam and the bordering countries. He was a former NVA officer, a retired general, and a national hero. The diminutive gentleman had earned the latter distinction for his role as the designer of the Ho Chi Minh Trail's petrol pipeline. In refined French, General Quang told me about his crowning achievement.

The port of Haiphong, he said, was too dangerous, too often hit by American bombs. Arcing a finger over Vietnam's northern border, the general outlined what he had judged to be the more prudent course. His digit meticulously twisted down the country's western frontier and crossed into Laos.

I asked how Laos felt about a pipeline on its territory.

"We dug a trench and buried the pipes underground so nobody could see them," he said. Not quite a *mea culpa* for a strategy that invited a deluge of bombs on a neighbor, the general's story continued with his indicator back in Vietnamese territory. "But we also had a pipeline over here. The jungle formed a canopy. So we didn't need to bury that one."

Times had changed for General Quang, whose smooth

skin defied his seventy-something years. A powder-blue suit had taken the place of an olive uniform. His customary audience, military brass, had been replaced by an unshaven American. He didn't seem to mind. Moments after we met in a café near Hanoi's Pentagon, the general had jumped at the chance to brief me on the fuel line which had made possible the North's victory.

"Impossible" was the general's snap answer to my riff about following his Trail to Saigon. That hard line softened after I bought a round of coffee. "There is too much jungle to travel the entire Trail. But you can see many sections," he said.

Route 9 west from Dong Ha was my best bet. I was also instructed to stop in Hoi An: "The seafood is excellent." The general rummaged through his pockets and produced a business card. Then he lowered his voice.

"You ought to leave Hanoi."

I leaned in to hear more.

"Hanoi is boring. Go to Saigon. It's livelier."

I asked for one final tip. I pointed to a solid red line parallel to the Lao border. Labeled "15," it mirrored the route of the Ho Chi Minh Trail. Was it open now?

"There was a road there," said General Quang. "Now, maybe."

In Ha Tinh before noon, I had time to learn more about the condition of road number 15. It lay about 20 kilometers to the west of the latest dusty, concrete town. The road was linked to Highway One by two thin red lines. Find either on-ramp and I was on my way down the Trail. A filling station on the town's four-lane main artery looked to be a source of reliable know-how.

The pump jockey let me down. Or maybe I didn't focus on his explanation. My attention was focused on the lighted cigarette dangling from the attendant's lips as he topped my tank.

Anyway, a nosy trucker seemed better informed. After examining my map, he pointed down the heat-stricken street, hooked his hand right, and gestured ahead like a football referee signaling a first down.

The exit from Highway One dissolved my dour mood. Petrol peddlers and repair stalls disappeared. Their place was taken by the grassy bank of a winding river. Bathing buffalo paid no mind to the putt-putt of elongated canoes or the clamor of my Minsk. In a five-shack village, kids whacked each other with sticks while a woman threw rocks at chickens.

Other signs of violence were unavoidable. Brown bomb craters scarred the green palate. After the asphalt gave way to dirt, I slowed to consider the silhouette of the pedestrian ahead. Wearing only a pair of dirt-stained shorts, the man alternately swung forward his crutches and his one remaining leg. I sped by.

Then I slowed again. Farther west was a complex of buildings which looked like a high-tech military installation. That assessment was revised to telephone station after a closer look at the plantation of steel towers and wires. In either case, it wasn't the sort of place where xenophobes would welcome a foreigner.

It was, however, the end of the line. On the far side of the plant, through the midday haze, I saw layers of mountains. Undulating foothills gave way to a row of low semicircular rises. Behind these stood broad-shouldered masses of rock topped with rounded towers. Driving over the peaks wasn't an option.

Nor could I find a pass through the hills. Past the plant, the road deteriorated. Flat earth was replaced by deep ruts left by trucks churning through mud. Baked dry by the sun, the hardened ground gave way to jagged rocks. My thoughts turned to flat tires. After fifteen minutes and one kilometer, I stopped.

The rocky road showed no sign of improving as it wound into lifeless shrubs and hills. Tens of thousands of foot soldiers had negotiated the route. Why couldn't one American? First, my Minsk was likely to break at any moment. Next, my gas wouldn't last. Finally, I was scared of rotting to death in Vietnam's wilderness. Greg-the-sailor had warned me: "Be prepared to spend the night out there." I wasn't.

"Bad road," said the café keeper I consulted once back in Ha Tinh. The road I needed, the road that linked Highway One to Route 15, could be found one kilometer north of town. Accurate directions now in hand, I had only myself to blame for the next wrong turn.

Ha Tinh's hotel charged twenty-five dollars per night. Cheaper digs, said my guidebook, could be found in Cam Xuyen. Ten kilometers south of Ha Tinh, the town had but one structure sturdy enough to withstand the slam of a door. That was the concrete police station. What crime, I wondered, carried a sentence of one night complete with steak-and-eggs breakfast? A roadside mechanic showed me the alternative, an inn at the base of a dirt incline.

The local Hilton exhausted my thesaurus. Decrepit, crumbling, ugly. Health hazard, disaster area, a shithole. The one available room, at three dollars per night, featured a wooden board for a bed, a straw mat for a mattress. Holes in every wall insured the free flow of dusty air. Parking was the lone bright spot. The manager rolled my mud-caked motorbike right into my room.

Cam Xuyen grew on me. A restaurant on the east side of Highway One specialized in rice and mystery meat. I made a friend, a nine-year-old boy named Phuc. He followed me back to the guesthouse, where I taught him to count to ten in English. He reciprocated by showing me how to lure a woman: the boy mimed grabbing a girl, tossing her to the ground, and jumping on top.

One of my fellow residents took a more subtle approach to

courtship. She looked like a ghost flowing toward me through the evening haze. Most of her face was as white as her robes. The exceptions were her angry-red lips and shocking-pink eyelids. Some sort of crown capped the head of this waking nightmare. The feel of a strong grip reaching inside my shirt awakened me to the fact that I was once again in the hands of a Vietnamese man.

He was an actor. The getup was not drag but a costume for a Chinese-style opera. A traveling troupe was camped out two doors from my room. Less clear by the time the star had mussed my hair, pecked my cheek, and left for work was whether the performer was getting into character or making a pass.

I padlocked my door from the inside. Exhausted, I couldn't sleep. Invisible bugs nibbled at my skin. A bus parked and vomited dozens of relief-seeking passengers into the field behind my room. When they departed, the opera's atonal tunes and soprano shrieks pierced the humid air for hours. When silence fell, I wondered whether the tactile actor would return. Just before midnight, I heard a knock.

I played dead. The tapping persisted, a little harder and a little faster. It stopped after a third unanswered round. Relieved, I nodded off until a more violent pounding rattled my chamber. The familiar voice of the manager persuaded me to part my mosquito net and tiptoe to the door.

Peering down through the angled slats of the door, I saw two pairs of trousers. A dusty gray pair belonged to the manager. And two bright green legs to his right were unmistakably those of a police officer. My last legal brush, the encounter with the sex-crazed immigration official, made me doubly reluctant to open up.

The constable continued his pounding. Relenting, I found a stern young man with his mitt on my visa, which I had left with the manager. Already briefed on my shortage of language skills, he jammed a fingernail on the past expiration date on the front of my visa. The officer prepared to collar his first American, the catapult to many a Northerner's career.

Disappointment, then anger, crossed the cop's face when I pointed out the valid extension on the back of my visa. His eyes blazed at a wise guy in need of a pistol whipping.

"One person?" he demanded in Vietnamese.

"One."

Incredulous, the officer pushed past me and goosestepped around my room. Nobody under the bed. Nobody in the cabinet. Satisfied that I had no cohorts, he paused at the door. I probably read too much into the policeman's hard glare. In case I hadn't, I fled his beat at first light.

16

A bus blasting through the morning mist confirmed that I was on track. "Huong Khe–Ha Tinh" read a sign in the vehicle's window. Having just turned west from Highway One, I recognized the former as a town smack in the middle of Route 15. Adjacent holes, both wider than backyard pools, supported the view that I was on a course formerly traveled by Charlie and bombed by Sam.

The road narrowed and roughened as I twisted up a hill. The brush grew thicker, the trees taller. Away from Highway One there were no villages. No children cheered my every move. The only sound was the buzz of the Minsk kicking up dirt and pebbles. The only sight was an empty road burrowing into the wilderness.

In the middle of nowhere, Khe Giao felt urban. Located where my dirt road formed a T with another, the village consisted of ten huts. The population of forty dropped everything to redirect a pale-faced traveler who claimed to be en route to Saigon. A four-toothed man pulled me into his shed for a cup of tea and some homespun wisdom.

"Saigon?" I asked, pointing left.

"Highway One," he replied, pointing backward.

After tea, gentle hills rolled for miles. The climb up a steeper incline rewarded me with a view of tropical serenity. In the silent valley below me, water buffalo soaked in a lake where bleach-white birds posed on one leg. Behind the water, peasants in cone-shaped rice hats worked glimmering fields of green. At the rear of the bowl rose low mountains, bare but for lollipop-shaped trees along their crest.

Two hours after exiting Highway One, the sight of railroad tracks tipped my imminent arrival in Huong Khe. Its grubby collection of plywood sheds looked more Wild West than Far East. Indeed, the whistle stop was the last outpost before the long ride to Dong Hoi, a coastal city about 100 kilometers away. I bought gas and ate noodles.

Then I headed for the Mu Gia Pass, one of the gaps in the Truong Son Mountains, which formed Vietnam's border with Laos. Like Colonel Luc and countless other Northerners, I aimed to climb the Mu Gia Pass. Unlike Charlie, I planned to turn around once I reached the "Door of Death."

Hanoi's soldiers would have been better prepared than I. At similar points in their own journeys south, NVA soldiers had spent several weeks in training. Riflery and camouflage were two of the basics. So was carrying heavy loads. Soldiers weren't permitted to go south unless they could manage a load of at least 30 kilograms, or about 65 pounds. Few failed the test, even though the average North Vietnamese weighed just 50 kilos.

The typical load included a spare uniform and a pair of black pajamas, as well as a tent, hammock, and mosquito net. Each soldier had a small supply of medicine, and vitamin pills to last one month, the average walking time to the first big camp. Cubes of antidote for snake venom were also standard issue.

The weight was most odious near the start of the Trail.

The Mu Gia Pass was more than 400 meters high. Other passes were nearly twice that. Soldiers took days to reach the crossings, which were mercilessly bombed and strafed.

Once in the mountains, the balance of dangers changed. The heat and the damp took a slow toll of trekkers' bodies. As few of the teenage fighters had ever traveled far from their villages, homesickness sapped their souls. Soldiers filled their diaries with yearnings for families they would probably never see again. Food, much of which was supplied by stations spaced eight hours' walk from each other, often ran out.

Hungry soldiers were more susceptible to illness. Most infiltrators caught colds during their first days in the jungle. Untreated, the sniffles often turned to pneumonia during the monsoon season. That was also when mosquitoes were at their worst. Malaria killed as many as ten percent of the people on the Trail. Other fevers and parasite-related diseases were common.

All that before anybody dropped a bomb or fired a shot? How, I wondered, had any Northerner survived?

Riding toward the Mu Gia Pass, I saw mountains that lived up to their reputation. A row of low peaks blocked an escape to the east of the uneven road of dirt and pebbles. The western side of the long valley was a wall of rock. The severe incline was seamless. For a soldier marching with others behind, forward down the natural corridor was the only way to go.

I looked harder at the Truong Son Mountains. Higher peaks I had seen. But more solid? I couldn't recall. How the Trail's blazers had chiseled a route over these Alps was beyond me. Only a superhuman would even contemplate such a barrier.

My southbound progress stuttered an hour below Huong Khe. Narrow planks were the only way over the railroad ties suspended forty feet above a shallow river. Later, I skidded around a bend and braked on the lip of an outsized puddle.

Where Route 15 should have been I found a child up to his ribs in water. A stocky hag with betel-reddened teeth guided me to a shallower crossing.

Nobody could help me clear the next obstacle, a three-foot drop to a pond whose murky brown water defied judgments of its depth. A fifteen-foot jump would get me across the hazard. Another motorbike, a red Minsk which appeared on the opposite side of the chasm, demonstrated the other option.

The rider looked rough. Beneath a brown baseball cap with "USA, California" stenciled on the front was a tanned face pocked like a minefield. His clothes were soiled and torn. After a brief pause to consider the effects of slipping into the trap, he maneuvered the bike along a six-inch lip of mud. Could I repeat that miracle of balance?

"Mu Gia? How far?" I asked.

"Ten, fifteen kilometers," said the man named Tho.

"And Dong Hoi?"

Tho shook his head.

"This isn't the road to Dong Hoi?"

"Go to Ha Tinh. Highway One."

"What about *this* road?"

Tho shook his head. Down the road I would find more water. He showed me the depth of future obstacles by putting a hand to his chest. He made a swimming motion, front crawl. I didn't need a mock swan dive to understand that bigger and meaner obstacles waited to the south. Misdirected a dozen times in half as many days, I hesitated to believe him.

But Tho had credibility. His peasant's appearance told me that he was no café cadre; Tho traveled the road he described. His odometer had logged more than 30,000 kilometers. And because Tho drove a Minsk, I assumed he knew the limits of a Russian motorbike on Vietnamese terrain.

Going backward was not much easier than moving ahead.

Combining gestures and the occasional search through my phrase book, Tho suggested I load my motorbike onto a train to Dong Hoi. The idea appealed to me. It was the coach potato's way to see a section of the Ho Chi Minh Trail. The only problem was timing: Tho said the next train was in four hours, at 5 P.M., and departed from a town called Phuc Thach, which wasn't on my maps.

Tho promised to show me the station. He led me north before turning down a dirt lane cut into a wall of trees. I wondered if I had been too trusting. This rugged man had all the makings of a highwayman. With nothing but trees in sight, I could have been driving myself into a robber's lair. Indeed, Tho did demand some cash. But only as compensation for his guidance. And only after we arrived on the train platform in Phuc Thach.

I found the ticket agent beyond a row of vendors dozing in the shade of the eaves. She giggled at my attempts to balance an overloaded vehicle against the wall of her sauna-sized office. Well past forty, her beauty had lasted thanks to high cheekbones and black hair long enough to tie into a noose. Which is what I soon wanted to do with it.

"I want to go to Dong Hoi."

The ticket agent nodded.

"When is the train?"

Her head shook, wiggling her rope of hair.

"Dong Hoi. Train. What time?"

The rope wiggled again. Did VietTrak hire mutes?

"Is there a train at five o'clock?"

"No train."

Tho had promised me there was a train at five. Lest there be any mistake, I indicated the words, one by one, in my phrase book. Today. Train. What time? The ticket agent slid the booklet from my fingers and browsed for more than a minute. Then she turned the book for me to read her response: "Are you married?"

"Today. Train. What time?"

"Ten o'clock."

The answer wrinkled my plans. Eight hours was a long time to wait for a train. And if none arrived, a night on the outdoor platform would expose me to all species of insect-borne nastiness. Turning to leave, I slipped in a puddle of my own sweat and pushed through twenty rubberneckers. A station worker with a red band on his sleeve grabbed me by the arm.

"Train. Six o'clock," he said.

I whirled and glared at the ticket agent. She shouted at the worker. He shouted back. Five minutes later they agreed that yes, there would be a train at six.

"How much is the ticket?"

The ticket master mumbled a phrase I couldn't understand. So I asked again. She repeated the mystery phrase. I pointed to a phrase in my book: "*Bao nhieu?*"

"How much?" She repeated her phrase, which included no numbers. I wrote some possible fares on a scrap of paper. The mystery phrase, again. Dripping sweat, I begged to be told the fare to Dong Hoi. The ticket agent stonewalled. As a roundhouse punch to the head began to make sense, I left.

A man of sixty beckoned for me to join him in the shade of a tree. A devotee of the school of thought that said foreign-language comprehension increased in line with volume, he shouted in my ear. Within five minutes I learned that the fare was roughly twelve thousand dong, a buck and a bit. The money was payable to the conductor, which was what the ticket agent had tried to explain. When she joined us outside, I apologized.

"How much to put my Minsk on the train?"

"No motorbikes."

"What?"

"Six o'clock train. People only."

"No motorbikes! After one hour I learn no #@ motorbikes on a #@* train you told me didn't even #@*& exist. You saw my %#$, @*^% Minsk leaning against your *^#* wall. Did you think I wanted to $!@ leave it behind?"

I bolted for Ha Tinh. Watching Tho weave his native roads had taught me to slalom potholes the Vietnamese way. I already burned gas like an American. Between the two, I kicked up more dust than a stampede of buffalo. The clatter of my 125cc engine revving at top speed drowned out rational thoughts.

A cow brought me to my senses. A cat would have scatted, a chicken scattered. But the one-ton beast standing broadside in the road stoically held its ground, fully prepared to hip-check a speedster rounding a bend. I skidded to a stop a yard from a meeting with its hide and my Maker.

Five kilometers from Ha Tinh a bus bound for Huong Khe forced me to the side of the road. My engine sputtered to a stop. Adding gas produced no motion. I took out my tools and cleaned the spark plug. Nothing doing. Looking around for help, I found none. The nearest tow truck was probably in Hanoi. The only option was to start pushing the loaded bike.

17

The Trail took a heavy toll. Back in Ha Tinh, a mechanic stroked his thin, Rhett Butler mustache while examining my grimy, lifeless Minsk. Then he examined me. Deciding that I was in the sorrier state, he led me through his home to the backyard. A bucket of well water darkened as I rinsed away the sweat, dirt, and oil.

The motorbike's dead engine was only the start of the damage report. In just one day I had lost a handful of screws, broken the fork supporting the front wheel, and loosened the spokes to the tension of linguini. My rearview mirror was missing in action. That I had returned alive made me a hero in the eyes of Rhett, who, after two hours of work, refused payment.

More humiliating was my weakness to the lure of Ha Tinh's high-price, low-class hotel. After a sleepless night and a waking nightmare, I wanted nothing more than air conditioning and running water. Both conked out when the power failed, leaving me with nothing for my money but the flattery of the hotel staff, who never failed to greet me with an unctuous "Hello, handsome."

The biggest concession in the fiasco's wake was made the

following morning. Spooked by the proximity of disaster—
where would I have been stranded had Tho not turned me
around?—I changed my plans. No more solo rides along the Ho
Chi Minh Trail. Until further notice I was sticking to Highway
One.

New dangers cropped up along the coastal route to Dong
Hoi. Driving in a drizzle, I twisted up a peak near the southern
edge of Ha Tinh Province. It was there that I learned of Vietnamese truckers' habit of killing the engine and coasting down
the middle of mountain roads. Fair enough; gas was dear and
the curves had no rails. My sense of propriety downshifted
when a runaway bus forced me into a wall of rock.

"Welcome to Quang Binh Province" said a McDonald's-
size billboard at the top. Though the rest of the text was in
Vietnamese, the cornucopia of fruit depicted on the billboard
suggested that a land of plenty lay ahead. Why, then, were three
girls kneeling, their rice hats upturned, beside the road? And
why, about a mile later, did I see a begging midget with only his
hands to cup?

A different kind of greeting met me in Dong Hoi. "You
look like an American soldier," said Kwok, a Hanoi University
grad who had found no better use for his fluent English than
minding the register at a guesthouse. Before I could correct
him, a young maid jabbered something else. I picked up just
two words: "Clinton" and "Bill."

"She likes Bill Clinton very much," Kwok explained.

"Why's that?"

"He lifted the embargo."

The maid jabbered again. Kwok translated: "Also, he
didn't fight in Vietnam."

Kwok couldn't do enough for me. The eager graduate
parked my Minsk, aired out my room, and unpacked my bag.
He suggested we take in a movie, maybe hit a dance club.

When I said I wanted a quiet dinner on my own, Kwok steered me toward the best seafood in town.

At least thirty heads turned to watch me sit. All but two returned to their meals following the spectacle of an American trying to order shrimp, vegetables, and rice. One of them, an athletic man in a Nike tennis shirt, asked, in English, where I came from. It took less than a minute to establish that our California homes were only an hour apart.

He called himself Phap. Raised in San Jose, where his refugee parents had settled after the war, he logged ten years as an engineer in Silicon Valley before starting his own business. But material success felt empty without a wife, who had to be Vietnamese. When we met, Phap's future Mrs. was by his side.

The woman was stunning, easily the most beautiful woman I'd seen in Vietnam. Deep brown eyes hovered over full lips painted burgundy. Her shimmering mane of black hair poured down the back of a green *ao dai*, whose split sides revealed most of her soft rib cage. The smile that spread across her mouth and eyes as she shook my hand was unpracticed.

But Phap's courtship sounded odd. The couple had met in Saigon eight months before, when the American was on a business trip. The match was made in the disco of a hotel. Phap wondered whether the nineteen-year-old nymphet was "the right kind of girl." The trans-Pacific correspondence that followed convinced him that she was. Now he was in Dong Hoi to meet her family, take the vows, and take his bride to America.

Phap's future in-laws, seven of them, migrated from their table to mine to hear about their sister's new home. Anxious about her imminent relocation, the nymphet listened hardest. Egged on by her fiancé, the shy girl asked questions.

"Is it cold in California?"

"Will they let me drive a car?"

"Do Americans eat rice?"

Couldn't Phap answer these? He explained: "To them, I look Vietnamese. But you have white skin and blue eyes. You look like an American. So they believe you."

The Californian translated an even odder question on behalf of his male companions: "Do you have any interest in pilots?"

I was stumped.

"Men in airplanes. American soldiers."

"You mean MIAs?"

"Yes."

Phap looked down the table at three of his in-laws. He said the trio had bought some bones from villagers in the Truong Son Mountains. The Montagnards claimed to have found the remains near the wreckage of a jet. Now Phap's friends wanted to recoup their investment.

My thoughts flashed back to Hanoi. At the Apocalypse Now I had met the men responsible for finding Americans missing in action. They explained to me how one sailor was responsible for sifting through Hanoi's documents for tips on where to search. Another specialized in oral history: gleaning information from live interviews. A third was in charge of "special cases," the euphemism for tracking down soldiers who might still be alive.

The magic number for the Joint Task Force-Full Accounting was around sixteen hundred. That was the total number of soldiers, sailors, and airmen who hadn't returned, dead or alive, from Vietnam. Another six hundred or so men disappeared in Laos and Cambodia. But that broad definition of MIA exaggerated the hangover from the war.

"The idea that there are hundreds of hidden prisoners is bullshit," one of the sailors had said. "Most of the guys missing were pilots who crashed in jungle or over the water. Everybody knows they're dead. But they stay on the list until we find their remains. There are less than eighty people whose fate we don't know."

"Who are they?"

"Some of them just walked off. I've heard of guys who have been living in Thailand since the war. How am I supposed to find them? For all I know, *you* could be one of the guys I'm looking for."

Dead servicemen were no easier to locate. The MIA team didn't expect to find entire skeletons neatly seated in their cockpits. The reason for their low expectations was clear from Greg's description of how the impact of an airplane hitting the ground sheared teeth off the jaw. Realistically, all they could hope for when excavating a crash site were bits of uniforms, or fragments of hair or bone. When found, these artifacts were flown in flag-covered coffins to a laboratory in Hawaii.

Treating a dental filling to full military honors sounded silly to an American who had never served. Expensive too. In the three years prior to 1995 the Pentagon ran up a $160 million tab searching for MIAs in Southeast Asia. During that period just sixty names were scratched off the list of the missing. Why did they bother?

One reason was the clout of the groups representing those who lost sons or brothers during the war. An American vet eavesdropping on this barroom powwow made a related point:

"Soldiers have to know that, whenever and wherever you serve your country, you will get a decent burial. The widow in Vermont can't rest until she knows for sure what happened to her husband. So when these guys go out on the tarmac and salute a coffin leaving Vietnam, they know there's one less guy whose family is in doubt."

The young sailors nodded their agreement. They also agreed on the toughest part of their mission. It wasn't the Vietnamese government, which appeared to be bending over backward to be helpful. Nor were locals obstructing the search. Quite the opposite: more and more Vietnamese were offering information about dead Americans. With the word out that Uncle Sam was paying for bones, the new challenge was to separate fact from fiction.

What made the MIA team apoplectic were suggestions that they weren't trying, that they were part of a government conspiracy to whitewash lingering Vietnam issues. One muscular serviceman glared, as if I were such an accuser, and shouted, "Why would I lie? WHY WOULD I LIE?"

Joe-the-vet intervened, perhaps to keep me from catching a punch. "These guys aren't allowed to comment on U.S. policy. But they know it's bullshit. They've been ordered to do the impossible. There are no live prisoners in Vietnam. This isn't *Rambo*. So they're over here looking for people they know don't exist."

My certainty that there were no straighter arrows than the crew from the Apocalypse Now guided my response to Phap and his friends in Dong Hoi.

"Why don't they call the MIA office in Hanoi?"

"They are afraid. Not of the Americans. But of the Vietnamese. They think the police will find out and put them in jail."

The entire table looked to me. My instinct was to help— not a pack of greedy gravediggers, but the family of a dead American. But buying bones was beyond patriotism's bugle call. More likely than not, I would be sold a phony. Besides, how would I explain a skull in my carry-on?

I gave Phap the phone number of the MIA team.

"Maybe you can arrange a secret meeting?" he said.

"You're an American. Call them yourself."

18

Nguyen Ngoc Hung felt lucky when the North
Vietnamese Army drafted him in 1969. Until then, university
students such as himself had been exempted from military service. Expecting a short war, Hanoi tried to preserve an educated
class to run the country come peacetime. Fortunately for Mr.
Hung, the war's goriest years had passed by the time Ho & Co.
spotted the looming shortage of cannon fodder and forced the
intelligentsia to enlist.

Hung spoke in the velvety accent of England's upper class
as we chatted in the Hanoi language school he headed. Putting
off the task at hand, a blow-by-blow of days on the Ho Chi
Minh Trail, the teacher explained why he, unlike many of his
opponents, never considered resisting the draft.

"In the North, society was run by the old men of the
village. Ho Chi Minh had a gift for speaking with the elders.
He called on them to instill a sense of responsibility in younger
people. The old men told us that our forefathers had fought
against the Chinese and the French for more than one thousand
years. They told us it was now our turn. By the time you were
eighteen you were ready to fight."

Besides, not fighting didn't guarantee safety. There was nowhere to hide in a country carpeted with bombs; Hung said he never stopped worrying about whether his parents' home-made shelter would withstand the explosions.

Much of boot camp was review for the teacher-to-be. Schoolchildren in the North began handling AK-47s at age thirteen. For roughly six months Hung was taught to fight in groups of three and ten, in a platoon of riflemen and with tank support. In late 1969, after the Tet offensive, his unit headed toward Laos.

The previous year had been the Trail's busiest. By 1968 the road network had a full-time maintenance crew of 50,000 women and teenagers. Roughly 150,000 soldiers went down the route that year. To stop them, the Americans dropped about 175,000 tons of bombs. Survivors described the Trail as a round-the-clock purgatory of explosions and avalanches, burning vehicles and forest fires, screams of the wounded and silence of the dead.

"By the time I went south, to Quang Tri Province, there had already been so much bombing that what had once been jungle looked like the moon. You saw so many dead people and bodies torn apart that you stopped worrying about death."

"What kept you going?"

"Should we imitate the aborigines in Australia? Should we let white people take our country and turn us into second-class citizens?"

I mumbled meekly about saving Southerners from such second-class citizenship.

"What Americans don't realize is that most Vietnamese saw no difference between you and the French colonialists."

Hung returned to motivation in the jungle. "Life was simple. We would go to where the Americans weren't bombing and look for food. We had a little bit of rice. Local people showed us what we could eat from the ground. For meat we would fish in rivers or try to catch snakes and squirrels."

"What about tigers?"

"Tiger meat is tough," he said, his deadpan devoid of irony.

Hung came back up the Trail in 1970, when fear that the enemy might attempt a sea landing led Hanoi to beef up the defenses around Dong Hoi. Drawing a winding line west from that city to the Mu Gia Pass, the one-time grunt showed me the route he took to Laos the following year, when the North's goal was to block the South's attempt to cut off the western portions of the Ho Chi Minh Trail. Later, his and other units massed for the final drive to take Saigon, which Hung entered the day after the first tanks.

Dong Hoi reminded me of my plan to follow Hung's westward footsteps out of the coastal town. I needed no reminding of what had happened on the previous section of the Ho Chi Minh Trail. I dumped my decision to stick to Highway One but added a safety feature: a local pilot.

Sy worked as a driver for Dong Hoi's top hotel, a barren place lighted by naked fluorescent tubes. Puddles filled the floor's undulations. His boss, a Francophone named Lu, didn't flinch when I asked for a guide to the Ho Chi Minh Trail. Instead, he apologized. The one man who knew the jungle roads only spoke Vietnamese.

That wasn't entirely true. Barely older than I, and far better dressed in loafers, slacks, and a white tennis shirt, Sy spoke one word of English, "Okay," which is what he said to showing me the Trail. My Man Friday mounted the back of my bike and signaled for me to hang a right out of the parking lot.

Sy directed us west from the town's main roundabout and

across a concrete bridge over the rail tracks. The pavement gave way to orange dirt. A series of seemingly random lefts, rights, and "okays" took us past ramshackle houses and huts. Before long the broad road narrowed to a single lane cut into trees and reeds too dense to see through and too high to see over.

The promiscuous foliage parted at the top of a rise, leaving us face to face with a row of shadowed behemoths. Partly obscured by clouds in the valley below, the monsters ahead were the Truong Son Mountains. I looked back at Sy for assurance that there was in fact a way through the parabolas.

"Okay, okay," he said.

Sy didn't complain when a drizzle soaked our faces and turned the dirt road to mud. He took in stride the trail of hockey-puck-size stones that jarred us without mercy. The rear tire struggled to find a grip on the uphills and fishtailed on the downhills. Sy passively endured the punishment until a stream came into view.

I hesitated. He pounded my shoulder, egging me to plow across twenty feet of rushing water. Supported by Sy's mantra —"Okay, okay"—I plunged into the drink and across the bed of slick stones. The next water hazard was shorter but deeper. Encouraged to floor it, I soaked us both while spraying two-foot waves to either side of the Minsk. The maneuver earned me a "thumbs up" from my coach.

We were a team. My jobs were steering a course along a stony trail cut into the mountains and butting low-flying branches with my pith helmet. Sy jumped off to clear away obstructions and animals, such as ten cows who were reluctant to break from slurping spring water. A stick swung by the navigator persuaded the untended bovines to make way.

The tangles of foliage layered onto the mountains left me speechless. The shades of green challenged my color thesaurus. My list ran out after light green, dark green, forest green, pea green, kelly green, olive green, lime green, and Dartmouth green. As impressive as the shades was the flora's density. Trees were covered by moss which grew vines that vied for sunlight with ferns. Nowhere amid the chaos could I see any unclaimed earth.

Supplementing the fractions of his language I could grasp with drawings in the dirt, Sy pinpointed the position where we stopped to rest. More than 50 kilometers west of Dong Hoi, we were just 20 from Laos. The road, he said, was a branch of the Trail that originated at Thanh Hoa. It terminated near the mountain town of Khe Sanh, once the site of an American base near South Vietnam's northern border.

Downhill from our spot the Trail disappeared into a river more than a hundred feet across. As for its depth, a pair of men served as human yardsticks. Up to their waists in water, they were washing a truck whose wheels were hidden from view. The Minsk would never make it. The time had come to backpedal.

There were other reasons behind our decision to turn back. Sy had pointed into the hills several times during the drive. My hands full, I waited to ask why he kept saying *"Van Kieu."* Once my hands were free, I didn't like the looks of the answer: Sy pantomimed a man drawing back and firing a crossbow. It was, he said, the preferred weapon of the local hill tribe, the Van Kieu.

Nor did I like the looks of the truckload of soldiers that passed us. The border was known to be riddled with drug traders exporting their contraband from landlocked Laos. Vietnamese patrols nabbed a fraction of the smugglers crossing the jungled frontier. Some soldiers looked the other way. Others, it was said, were themselves smugglers, who I doubted would welcome a foreign face.

Sy clinched the argument with the tale of his last visit to the area. *"Cop,"* he said, pointing to the edge of the trees on the river's far bank. A flick through my dictionary brought me to the word "tiger."

"Tigers? Down there?"

The navigator nodded. I had been taking warnings about wild animals with a shaker of salt. Most came from men who hadn't left the capital for decades. Now Sy was saying that two weeks ago he had seen two tigers lapping water at this very spot. Though I envied his glimpse of the wild kingdom, I was glad not to have shared it.

My rear tire spun wildly over the stones covering the first uphill of the return journey. The road would have offered no less grip had it been coated with axle grease. Sy didn't notice the unnatural swinging of the back of the Minsk. I kept mum and hoped the problem would go away. When an attempt to dodge a small boulder caused a stall, I dismounted. Sy joined me.

Neither of us liked what we saw: a half-flat tube of Russian rubber. Neither of us spoke. Our silence left only the sound of buzzing insects and the beating sun. Though he spoke a different language, Sy must have been sharing my speculation about what was to become of us. We looked at each other. About 50 kilometers from Dong Hoi, 30 from the nearest village, the glance we exchanged communicated our common thought: "We're dead."

As we drove on, the tires took less and less hold on a trail made of jagged bowling balls. Traction neared nil as the loss of air left only rubber and rim to tear at the road. Spinning crazily, the rear wheel swung as much as a foot to either side. I used my legs like pontoons to keep us upright. After a near fall I shut off the engine and faced the fact that the tire was flat.

Minsks come with an air pump stored under the seat. Indeed, I found an eighteen-inch tube of the type that clips onto the frame of a bicycle. Unattached to each other, the pieces fell to the ground. Alone, I would have cried.

Sy didn't despair. He gathered the pieces and, in a snap, restored the pump to working order. He was jamming air into the flat tire before I could unscrew the cap on the drinking water. After fifteen minutes of taking turns we had pumped in enough air to move again. At worst we could shorten our walk to Dong Hoi.

The Ho Chi Minh Trail no longer looked like a Disney joyride. The pastiche of greens which had dazzled now daunted. A tiger attack seemed unlikely. But while the effects would be less immediate, a night exposed to mountain mosquitoes could be just as deadly. What if the spear-chucking Van Kieu tribesmen were still sore about the napalm dropped on their mountains? And if we got out of this mess, wouldn't Sy seek retribution from the bonehead responsible for the risk?

A downshift of the gears at the base of a hill probably helped Sy make up his mind. I pulled in the clutch with a squeeze of my left fingers. The loss of resistance to my grip, and the sound of metal splintering, were undeniable signs that the clutch cable had chosen this inopportune moment to call it quits.

Standing, once again, by the immobile motorbike, Sy combed his fingers back through his thick black hair. He tried on for size my look of fear. The loss of a clutch, he realized, was more serious than the flat. But it was my turn to be confident.

"I have a clutch."

The navigator recracked his laughing smile when I pulled a spare cable and set of tools from the storage space beneath the seat. He grabbed the tools and set to work. Having watched truckers and bus drivers working on vehicles stranded miles from the nearest garage, I understood my luck. As the driver of a hotel van, Sy had to be an expert mechanic. A quarter hour later the clutch was ready. And my second venture into the Truong Son Mountains was over.

19

A soldier clutching a rifle to his chest blocked the exit from northern Vietnam. Decked out in gray, chiseled by a cubist, the statue of the fighter stood at the base of an upright billboard of stone. Near the top, a yellow star stood out from the faded red background. So did two sets of numbers, 20-7-54 and 30-4-75.

The first was the date the Geneva Accord split Vietnam in two. The second was the day Saigon fell. Near the statue a plaque in Vietnamese said: "The river may run dry. The mountains may wear out. But one truth never changes. Vietnam is one country."

Before the war a flagpole had stood on each bank of the Ben Hai River, the line dividing North and South. A storm toppled the southern pole in 1985. As there was no longer a Southern flag to fly, nobody saw the need to right the damage. Hanoi's yellow star on a red background flapped proudly on the north bank while the defunct flagpole rotted on a bed of weeds on the south side.

Other scars abounded. Below Dong Hoi, Highway One was a showcase of sand traps and other scars left by American bombers. The decaying stumps of the original bridge, one of the first targets of strategic bombing, peeked out from the Ben Hai River. On the far side, a charred blockhouse built by the French had somehow withstood years of bombing.

How long, I wondered, would an American have lasted here in, say, 1969? The area had been saturated by Hanoi's troops. If Charlie didn't get you, U.S. bombers probably would. If they missed, a hike to safety required penetrating the so-called McNamara Line, a band of land mines, fire bases, and electronic detectors designed to deter trespassing.

My crossing from north to south went virtually unnoticed. A gaunt farmer whose brown chest was scarred in four places flopped back into his hammock after giving me a once-over. Another bony farmer didn't stop hacking his dirt. Fishermen continued to dry their nets. Water buffalo kept grazing.

I marked the crossover by losing my pith helmet. Cruising down a straightaway between two mammoth fields of green paddies, I felt the wind lift the lip of my lid up and over my head. A truck approached as I moved to recover my headgear. When a DeSoto's wheel flattened the canvas-covered plastic, my helmet days were done.

The loss spared me a fashion gaffe; golf hats were all the rage in Dong Ha, the first town below the Ben Hai River. The caps came in browns and blues and reds and greens with lettering such as "BOY," "JVC," and "USA." Everyone from cyclo drivers to noodle chefs preferred a soft hat to the hard helmets favored just a little way north.

I stopped at the corner of Le Duan and Tran Hung Dao. The intersection was the home of a clumsy ballet of jeeps, trucks, scooters, and bicycles trying to stay in motion. Poor choreography was the fault of two policemen parked near the meeting of the streets. The pair acted more interested in levying fines than directing traffic in the absence of signals.

Locals ducked in and out of the alleys between the market's rows of tin-roofed shacks. Across the street, low concrete buildings housed vendors selling gold and portable stereos. Food vendors cluttered the space in between. A girl in red pajamas squatted and stirred a pot of vegetables in broth. Beside her a woman monitored a mountain of oranges, melons, and grapes.

A westward turn revealed more signs of the South. Every street in Dong Ha enjoyed a layer of asphalt, a reminder of the Americans who once occupied the town. Nearby, a pile of military vehicles, twisted and rusting, rested beneath a giant billboard. One had been a tank before somebody, or something, twisted the turret. The tread of another armored vehicle had been torn from its wheels. While shocking to me, the debris of a war fought twenty years ago couldn't have been less interesting to natives pedaling past on old bicycles.

A tiny Honda motorbike pulled alongside mine as I looped back to the main drag. The driver, a stocky, deeply tanned man in a mock flight jacket and army cap, didn't look to be my kind of people.

"You need a hotel," he said in rasping English.

"I've got one," I lied.

"I show you mini-hotel five dollars one night you don't like you don't stay no problem."

The tout called himself Eddie. A former interpreter for the U.S. Marines, he boasted of his dozens of American friends. His rugged, second baseman's build and gruff demeanor added to the credibility of his story. "Now you in Quang Tri Province. I know every place. Anything you want I can do. I am your friendly."

I followed my new friendly one disconcerting kilometer down Highway One to a three-story building. He waited while I inspected a tidy room with a double bed and a fan. The middle-aged landlady secured my custom by guiding me to a vinyl armchair and pouring a cup of tea. Eddie plopped onto the adjacent couch and began firing off bursts of English.

Born in Dong Ha. Lived here his whole life. Learned English in high school. Graduated and got drafted. Translated for the Marines in Dong Ha and territory to the west. Jailed when the North took the city. Released to unemployment. Married. Two kids.

"Before I drink Seagram's and smoke pot. P-O-T. You can speak American to me. I was with Third Marine Corps. I understand son of a bitch, bullshit, fuck you, anything. I know what you mean."

I nodded, but felt no urge to ply my native tongue.

"You looking for MIA?"

My answer, "No," caught him off guard.

Eddie told me about a pair of Americans, a fat man and a woman, who had recently come to Dong Ha and left with some remains. But he couldn't understand my story, that of a lone American who (a) wasn't a veteran, (b) wasn't looking for bones and bodies, and (c) was in Dong Ha. Like the immigration official in Vinh, he gave me a wink that said, "Your secret is safe with me."

Fatigue and hunger kept me from clarifying my mission. As the sun set, I sat myself on a plastic chair in the mini-hotel's empty dining room. No service materialized. Downstairs, at the end of a narrow corridor, I found the kitchen, where a squatting woman was milking blood from a newly headless chicken.

Selecting a meal wasn't easy. The scarlet ooze and spastic flapping of wings had killed my appetite for chicken. Unable to grasp my order for vegetables, the owner opened the door of the freezer to let me select from her stock of beef, shrimp, and squid.

A human toothpick pushed his way into the crowded

kitchen. Dressed in a green bomber jacket, he looked no younger than fifty despite a young man's long thick hair. He demanded to know what I was doing.

"Trying to get some dinner."

"I was an interpreter for the Americans. I can help you," he said. Together we worked out a meal of fried squid and rice. He even managed to get some vegetables thrown in. The price? I had to consent to a drink with his friends.

Led through the fly strips of a private dining room off the corridor to the kitchen, I met three men seated on plastic chairs. A bony fifty-year-old named Chu jumped up to pump my hand with passion. I missed the name of another equally amicable fellow.

A dark-skinned man who had combed back his silvered hair offered neither a hand nor a name. He showed no expression and didn't unfold his arms from his green army jacket. A case of canned beer, a local brand called Halida, sat on a chair. Was he grumpy at the prospect of sharing? Or something else?

Dien was the host's name. He poured a beer and clinked his glass into mine. "Vietnam custom. We have one glass together. Then you are free to go. Friends." With that he tossed the beer down his throat with frat-boy ferocity. Sensitive to the importance of respecting local customs, worried about giving Americans a bad name, I followed suit.

Three women with no more than seventy-five years among them swept into the room with trays of food. After spreading the meal on the Formica table, they settled onto extra chairs around the table. A bucktoothed girl stroked my forearm en route to resting her hand on my thigh. I looked to Dien, who was making goo-goo eyes at another lady.

The scene resembled nothing I recognized as Vietnamese. Men in U.S. Army hand-me-downs, in a private dining room, drinking one-dollar beers like they were water, and consorting with tarts attracted by cash. Three sets of car keys on the table confirmed their wealth. Who had this kind of money?

Traders. That was how Mr. Dien described himself and his mates. "You want to buy anything, tell me," said the ringleader. "Uniforms, flak jacket, boots, helmets, anything."

"What about guns?" I joked.

"Sure, guns. Also grenades. Mr. Chu can get you anything in Dong Ha. I can get you anything in Quang Tri City. Whatever you like."

I liked the idea of locking myself in my room. Dien, on the other hand, liked to see Americans chug beer. So I stayed for more toasts to friendship, peace, prosperity, and whatever else the local mafiosos proposed. Eddie passed by the open door. A roll of his brown eyes told me that I had fallen in with a bad bunch. My exit blocked, I sweated while Dien described the rejection of his application to emigrate to America.

Nonetheless, the skinny veteran couldn't do enough for me. He proposed a family meal at his home while his personal waitress rolled tender beef bits into rice paper and held the morsel up to his mouth. Dien steered her chopsticks toward me and insisted that she feed me instead. More uncomfortable about refusing than accepting the gesture, I opened wide.

"I think Miss Hu loves you" was Dien's assessment of the electric moment.

"Maybe she's just doing her job."

"I think Miss Hu would like to come to your room later."

I protested that our relationship was still young. Dien laughed but ignored my diversion.

"Because you are far from home, it is my responsibility to help you. I think you will hear a knock on your door at midnight. Why don't you go take a shower?"

A young woman burst through the red, white, and blue fly strips before I could protest the unfolding chain of events. Her left arm cradled an infant. Her right grabbed for the shoulder of the nameless man. Before reaching her target, she began to shout.

His sheepish expression told the story. The man had clearly lied to his wife, perhaps hiding his intent to go carousing with a story about visiting his sick mother. The icy glare the newcomer cast over the three other women in the room spoke volumes about their line of work. Before leaving, the wayward husband plunked some cash on the table.

I followed suit. Upstairs, behind a locked door, I hoped Dien's plans for me had been lost in the shuffle.

20

Most of Dong Ha was wide awake at dawn.
Slackers were reprieved until 6 A.M., when a loudspeaker attached to the telephone pole by my window gargled static before spewing a patriotic ditty. The tune was drowned out by a trucker testing his horn. The buzz of motorbikes confirmed that day had begun.

I walked onto the terrace of the brothel. In the distance I saw a green sea of stumpy palms and other vegetation. Nearer, the uniformity was broken by ramshackle homes and patches of dirt. Below me a procession of women in pajamas and rice hats limped under the shouldered weight of bamboo poles bearing baskets of fruit or noodles at either end.

Joe had lined up a man named Pham, a local who pledged to take me to the Lao sections of the Trail. To my mind, 6:30 A.M. was too early to go calling. A bowl of noodles killed just twenty minutes. The search for Dong Ha's lone tourist attraction, a French blockhouse, took twice as long. Bulky, concrete, likely to withstand attack, the fort proved unfindable.

At eight o'clock I went to Pham's reputed hangout, a building on the edge of town. I did find an English-speaker.

Only his name wasn't Pham. It was Tuan. Dressed in an olive shirt and dusty black boots, he raised his face to examine mine. I saw a man whose dark skin sagged over once handsome facial bones.

"You're American," he said.

"Yes."

"Are you interested in dog tags?"

"What do you mean?"

"I can introduce you to a friend who has U.S. Army dog tags."

"From dead soldiers?"

"Some are dead."

With a gesture toward a pair of armchairs, Tuan invited me to sit. I followed as he limped toward the nearer of the chairs. He wasted no time divulging his life story, which he broke into three unequal parts: war, "reeducation," the rest. I asked Tuan what went through his mind when Hanoi's tanks rolled into Dong Ha.

"I thought my life was over."

Time had borne out his instinct. Nabbed along with other "collaborators," the gentle fellow was shipped to a so-called re-education camp. Unable to spare any books or professors, the jailers thought wood chopping and field tilling were the key to winning hearts and minds. The curriculum also included lectures on the joys of Communism and the misery of imperialism.

Released early, Tuan and others were given "jobs." Their mission was to clear the mines that littered the DMZ. One catch. The equipment provided didn't include a metal detector. The mine sweepers were handed bamboo poles with metal tips and told to go to work. They prodded the ground and trod lightly.

Tuan taught himself to detect metal with a pole. He also learned how to feel for the edge of explosives, which he had to unearth by hand. Few of his cohorts lived to collect their pensions. Still, Tuan didn't consider himself lucky to have lost just half a limb.

"One day I stepped on a mine and lost my foot," he said, pointing to his left shoe. "But the doctors botched the operation and my leg became infected. They put me back on the table and cut my leg off below the knee." His pain jogged by talking, Tuan removed the wooden shin which had been hidden by his trousers. He massaged his stump.

And since the war? What had he been doing?

"Until recently nobody who worked with the Americans was allowed to work."

"But in the North everybody says, 'That's all history,' when I mention the war."

Tuan snorted. Jobless for nearly two decades, he had supported a family of four by selling handmade raincoats.

The Southerner's story bugged me. Not the parts about maltreatment by the Communists; I had read about "reeducation." Nor the suggestion that Northerners hadn't forgotten the past; I had long suspected that Hanoinkers weren't coming clean. What bothered me was that Tuan was still paying for his past associations.

Washington had a way to help men such as Tuan. For years after the war, former soldiers, policemen, and administrators from the South poured out of Vietnam in anything that could float. The exodus, as well as the high death rate during flight, grated on the conscience of the West. So in the late 1980s the United Nations set up the Orderly Departure Program, or ODP, as a safe, legal escape route. The exit had been used by tens of thousands of refugees who proved their wartime links to the United States. Why hadn't Tuan done the same?

The man was trapped in a previous lie. Nearing the age of conscription, Tuan had dodged South Vietnam's draft by changing his birth date and name on a fake ID card, which he used to apply for safer work as a translator. His American bosses never learned his real name. Hanoi did. Because his current documents matched no name on America's lists of former employees, the man couldn't convince the ODP of his eligibility.

Admittedly miserable, Tuan wanted my help. He also wanted me to meet his daughter. We agreed to have dinner at his home the following night.

Tam, a French teacher at a local high school, was born too late to help the Americans, but early enough to resent the North taking over his hometown. Wearing flip-flops, a fishing hat, and wraparound sunglasses, he would have been as comfortable in a trailer park as in the roadside café where he answered my question about how the war was taught in schools.

"They change the facts, and talk only about victories and heroes. The biggest is Ho Chi Minh. Vietnam has thousands of years of history and many heroes. But you never hear about them. Only Ho Chi Minh."

This unexpected candor prompted me to ask another question that had been nagging me. Did a young man who grew up below the Ben Hai River, but after Hanoi's victory, see himself as a South Vietnamese or a Vietnamese, a loser or a winner?

It took Tam a few tries to sort out thoughts.

"Northerners are our brothers," was his knee-jerk answer. "We are one country so we have to get along," he added.

"A lot of people in the South were killed by the VC. Many people in the North were shot by Southerners. Nobody can forget this in one day." The teacher rested after saying, "Really, we don't like the Northerners. But don't tell anyone I told you that. Please."

I resisted joining the local consensus on Northerners. Time and again those who lived above the 17th parallel had bailed me out. Increasingly skeptical, I stayed loyal.

The following morning Eddie took me back to the North. Decked out in aviator shades and a U.S. Marines cap, the stocky sergeant led me to Vinh Moc, a town located in what the Pentagon had called a "free fire zone," an area where anything that moved was fair game for U. S. bombers. The deluge led the entire village to move underground in the mid-1960s.

Above the Ben Hai River, we turned right from Highway One onto a path that wound through the paddies. A left put us on a stretch that looked like a showroom for sandboxes. Few spots had eluded the bombs. Every ten feet the grass gave way to reddish-brown indentations in the earth. The depth of the holes could be judged by their residents: cows whose legs were hidden from view. The bovines appeared unconcerned about their ancestors, many of whom had died after kicking an undetonated bomb.

The dirt trail ended at a concrete building by the sea. Inside, black and white photos of bamboo homes reduced to charred matchsticks gave the official version of events: Vinh Moc's peace-loving population was minding its own business when the Americans started dropping bombs, napalm, the works. Their houses burned, the townsfolk dug two kilometers of tunnels to live in. "I will not move a centimeter," said the inscription below an oil painting of a square-jawed youth holding a pickax.

Eddie offered a different version. A run-of-the-mill village wouldn't have been subjected to intense bombing. Vinh Moc, however, doubled as a supply center for Hanoi's military operations near the DMZ. The village also served nearby Con Co Island, the site of antiaircraft batteries. That explained not only the regular attacks but also the sophistication of the tunnels.

A local led me underground. My urge to exit was immediate. Too narrow to accommodate my squared shoulders, the cool dirt tunnels weren't high enough to allow me out of a half crouch. I pressed ahead, but only because the guide had the sole flashlight. Sixty feet belowground, I didn't want to be left in the dark. The thought of huddling here while B-52s pounded at the surface weakened my knees. The residents had felt cozier: the local said that several children had been conceived and delivered in these tunnels.

"Are any of the survivors still around?" I asked Eddie after emerging and gulping several gallons of fresh air. He shook his head.

"They left, like everybody, in boats. Now they live in Australia, Canada, U.S.A., every place."

So much for not moving a centimeter.

Back in Dong Ha, Eddie asked me to meet with a friend who wanted my help. He overruled my protests that I was just a powerless tourist. In a shack burrowed in a grouping of trees, he introduced me to Minh, a graying and unusually flabby man in a country that knew more famine than feast.

"I knew you were American when I saw you come to Dong Ha, but I was afraid to speak to you," said Minh. He explained that former interpreters such as himself were discouraged from speaking to Americans. Then he cut to the chase.

Like Eddie, Minh had worked with the Americans during the war. He too had been jailed and banned from earning a wage. Both men wanted to leave Vietnam via the ODP. Unlike Tuan, Eddie had the proof of his wartime employment record. Were he to apply, he would probably get an American passport. What he couldn't get was permission to leave Vietnam. Eddie reckoned local officials would demand as much as fifteen thousand dollars for the exit papers.

Minh had a different problem. His son had fled by boat,

landed in Chicago, and saved money to bring Dad to America. He had submitted Minh's papers to the ODP's Bangkok headquarters and arranged for his father to be interviewed in Saigon. The time and place of the meeting were in a letter that never arrived.

"They open all of our mail," moaned Minh.

"*They?*"

"The police. They have people in the post office who take the letters of the interpreters. They read them. Sometimes they keep them. I never knew about the appointment. Now the ODP is forgetting about me. I want them to know what happened. But I cannot send a letter from Dong Ha."

The legality or illegality of my agreeing to smuggle and post Minh's letter was still on my mind when I got back to the brothel late in the afternoon. The owner reached behind her reception counter and handed me a sealed envelope. Inside, I found a note, handwritten and in English:

> *Dear Mr. Hunt:*
>
> *It was in good faith that I invited you to my place. I was unaware of the possible unpleasant consequences that might present themselves. In our locality, receiving a foreigner in one's home is a rare phenomenon and I have no intention of giving our "mutual friends" a peg to hang their accusations on. On second thought, I guess we'd better forget about our get together. We'd be less vulnerable if we were seen together in broad daylight. Sunday afternoon, for instance. I hope you are sympathetic with me and for give me.*
>
> *Thank you all the same.*
> *Tuan*

21

In Hanoi a young woman had described to me the crushing effect that the disintegration of the Soviet Union had on her grandmother. Like thousands of others, the old lady moved from South Vietnam to North in the mid-1950s. She saw Communism as a historic force. She wanted to be part of "the revolution."

Granny fainted when the TV news showed Lenin statues toppling all over the Soviet Union. Relegated to a sickbed, the woman's heart weakened. She recovered, but only after her family resorted to white lies. "It's not true," they swore. "This is all American propaganda." They were a dying breed, said the raconteur. But the true believers, people with unquestioning faith in Ho Chi Minh and his vision for Vietnam, weren't extinct.

I didn't believe her until I met Dang Sung. Hair mussed, shirt rumpled, rummaging in his shirt pockets for an elusive paper, Mr. Sung had looked too untidy to be a hard-core Commie. We met thanks to Alia, a Dutch woman who invited me to ride in her private van, with her private guide.

Sung showed his colors almost as soon as the van started to move. Following my gaze toward the collection of battered tanks and artillery pieces at the post office roundabout, he said, "Those are monuments of American spoils."

"Why do they keep that junk around? Doesn't the government want to put the war behind it?"

"We must educate the young generation about our victory over the Americans."

I hadn't met a Southerner, young or old, who showed much enthusiasm for Hanoi's victory. But Sung showed no sign of doubting his pronouncement. He continued plugging his side as we headed north and then west down an unmarked dirt road.

The guide's take on his country was simple. Hanoi and the surrounding provinces were the center of good. Its women were stylish, its men sophisticated. Everybody appreciated art, music, and poetry. He even found virtue in the poverty of the rural areas: the hard life drove Northerners to dizzying achievements.

Saigon and its vicinity, on the other hand, produced little of use. "Because they can grow all their food for the year in six months, Southerners are lazy," said Sung. His disgust mounted as he described that region's reliance on the United States. First, war money flooded the region. Later, relatives who fled to America supplemented the incomes of those left behind. "They spend money like water because they never had to earn for themselves."

Sung launched lectures faster than you could scream *Good Morning, Vietnam*. When I opened my map to get his take on the Ho Chi Minh Trail, the Northern veteran pulled from his pocket a black notebook as wide as a palm and as thick as a Tolstoy. He began to read: "There were seven Ho Chi Minh Trails. The Ho Chi Minh Trail for soldiers, the Ho Chi Minh Trail for trucks, the Ho Chi Minh Trail for boats, the Ho Chi Minh Trail for petrol . . ."

The booklet was his personal collection of facts and figures; he admitted to a fear and loathing of mistakes. Once opened, the booklet wouldn't be shut until the end of the passage. Interruptions were not unwelcome. They were simply ignored, as I learned while trying to redirect his attention to my map. Only after he finished—"Sometimes we carried only one pistol, sometimes only one kilo of rice. But we had patience"— did he lift his head from the tome.

Sung's favorite lectures focused on his hero. Did I know that Ho Chi Minh had tried to befriend the United States? That Uncle Ho was an excellent poet? Had I heard that Ho always finished every rice grain in his bowl? I wanted to despise this Duke of Dogma. But I couldn't.

The van stopped at the end of a deserted back road. We piled out to inspect the Truong Son Cemetery, a smaller, scruffier version of Arlington National Cemetery.

Built in 1976, this military graveyard held over ten thousand shin-high, gray headstones of the 559th Brigade, the army unit responsible for building and maintaining the Trail. Grouped by province, each stone carried a yellow star and in red lettering a name, dates of birth and death, and the words *Liet Si*, Vietnamese for martyr. Spent sticks of incense in blue and white jars indicated that relatives had paid their respects to the dead.

Located in the heart of the former McNamara Line, the area around the graveyard had never recovered from the destruction. Where there had once been thick jungle there were now rolling hills on which the low shrubs didn't hide the red earth. If there were no signs of warm-blooded beings, it was because the area was still riddled with mines and other live explosives.

Sung walked gingerly up the steps to examine the monument at the center of the cemetery. The tower bore giant red letters saying *TOI QUOC GHI CONG*, or "Grateful Fatherland." Behind it were groupings of graves, one for every region of North Vietnam. Sung stopped at each one, as if to remember fallen comrades from that province. I dared not intrude on the veteran's silence, though my list of questions was growing by the second.

We reloaded the van in silence and headed south, toward Route 9, a road built when the French needed a better access to their colony in Laos. The Americans hardened and widened the central artery of this, the province closest to the enemy. But American control of the road extended only to the frontier.

There, Charlie took over. The Lao section of Route 9 became the fifty-yard line of the Ho Chi Minh Trail's end run around U.S. troops. When the GIs pulled out, Hanoi incorporated the rest of the road into their supply network. The number "9" was dead center of the Trail map in Hanoi's Army Museum.

After a stop in Cam Lo, a place renowned for the sweet water that dripped from local trees and a wartime visit from Fidel Castro, I asked Sung about his war record. A lieutenant, he had gone south in 1969. A truck drove his unit to the outskirts of Thanh Hoa. At the Ham Rong Bridge they started a serpentine, 700-kilometer trek to their post.

For the next six years Sung served as an intelligence and agitation officer. Five times he met American prisoners and escorted them up the Trail to the Hanoi Hilton and other prisons. During tranquil stretches Sung and two guards transported POWs by jeep. During heavy bombing they walked, ducking in and out of caves and man-made shelters. Remembering my harrowing half hour in the tunnels at Vinh Moc, I wondered aloud how they managed far longer periods underground.

"I wonder people can live in New York City, where you can be killed if you have five dollars in your pocket."

I missed the connection.

"If you must, you learn to cope."

The places on the red-tipped milestones along Route 9 meant nothing to me. But to veterans on both sides, names such as Dakrong, Khe Sanh, and Lao Bao were legendary. Joe had given me instructions to visit Camp Carroll and the Rockpile, two other highlights of any tour of his old area. Neither was evident as the flat road began rolling over low hills. The only sights were increasingly high peaks covered by patches of greenery.

The van screeched around a sharp bend and began the twisting climb toward the Truong Son Mountains. Crested by lollipop trees, the severe mountains were packed tight like terracotta warriors. In the valleys below, the clusters of wood and thatch homes looked exotically simple, rather than desperately poor.

"It looks beautiful now, but during the war this was a terrible place," said Sung.

"You were here?"

"There," he said, pointing to the impossibly steep hills on the far side of the river valley, an area that was supposed to have been U.S.-controlled. "We hid in the jungle. Until they dropped defoliant and the leaves fell off. Then we spent more time in caves."

When not taking POWs north, Sung "agitated." His job was to demoralize, not shoot, the enemy. To do so, his unit moved as close as one kilometer from American bases and lobbed mortars carrying leaflets instead of explosives. The text informed GIs that they were fighting an unjust war against innocent people. It recommended they drop their guns and go home. The "or else" needed no elaboration.

The lieutenant also taught mountain villages to resist the Americans. Women and old men were taught to mess their hair, sob violently, and beg to be left in peace when enemy soldiers came to town. Little boys were told to distract soldiers and steal their weapons. Pretty girls were to flirt; Hanoi reckoned that aroused GIs would long for wives and lovers at home. And if a village didn't cooperate?

"We had to teach them," said Sung, showing no remorse for the practice of killing a countryman in the name of the cause.

Other operations were aimed at gathering ammunition. Sung's unit tried to contact Americans and offer a deal. GIs could deposit weapons and bullets at a designated spot in the jungle. In exchange, the Vietnamese would leave a few Soviet-made guns for use as "proof" of victories in the field. Fire bases that cooperated wouldn't be fired upon.

"That worked?"

"Of course," said Sung, grabbing my shoulder to make sure I heard his next exploit. By the time we reached the battlefield at Khe Sanh, Sung had built himself into a cross between Mata Hari and Sergeant York.

The site of the U.S. base at Khe Sanh defined "moonscape." The dirt was orange and barren. Holes not formed by bombs had been bunkers. The peaks surrounding the plain loomed like ghosts over the spot where roughly twenty thousand Americans and South Vietnamese withstood 170 days of rifle and mortar fire before withdrawing.

Sung's superiors had placed control of Khe Sanh high on their wish list. The owner of the patch on the corner of the Ho Chi Minh Trail and Route 9 could control infiltration to the South. As in other battles, Hanoi had accepted vast losses and in the end managed to expel their adversary from Khe Sanh.

Sung and I walked between craters to the remains of the airstrip which had linked the base to safer spots to the east. He lifted and then dropped a scrap of green military canvas before pointing out some barbed wire. The perimeter of a sunken sandbag station, said the Viet Cong vet. He looked into the hills and fell silent.

"Do you think it's strange to come here with an American?"

"Ho Chi Minh said, 'One year I may be your friend. The next generation my son will be the enemy of your son.'"

Though the sun was getting ready for bed, Sung insisted we visit a mountain village. The van headed east and then south, stopping about five kilometers below a steel bridge supervised by a detachment of cops. A narrow footpath took us down a ravine to a stream. From there, the jungle path began to climb.

"*This* is what the Ho Chi Minh Trail was like. To go from village to village we took small trails used by the hill tribes."

"The Americans couldn't find them?"

"It was dangerous to look for them."

We came to a clearing where eight sturdy wooden houses rested on fat, five-foot stilts. A woman stopped pounding grain in a stone basin with a four-foot baton to examine us. Mahogany brown, she had wrapped an emerald-colored cloth around her head and a tight cotton skirt around her waist and athletic calves. She puffed on a thin pipe and, unimpressed by whatever she saw, returned to her pounding.

Old men peered out from dark rooms. Pigs and firewood competed for space below the houses. Children, half naked and filthy, stared silently at the intruders. A tiny boy with no pants ventured nervously within five feet of me. Around his neck was a native necklace.

Moving closer to get a look at the tyke's jewelry, I found I was mistaken. The steel chain held the dog tags of an American soldier. Was Robert Mitchell still alive? Did he realize that a miniature Vietnamese was wearing his name, rank, and serial number?

I also misidentified a log protruding eight inches from the

ground. Looking closer, I found myself standing above an unexploded artillery shell. I showed it to Sung, who interrupted the woman's pounding to inquire.

"She says it won't explode," he reported. "They have tried to dig it up and hammered it one thousand times. Don't worry."

I didn't, once I was fifty feet away.

Though we disagreed on how to fix Vietnam, Sung clearly considered himself a friend. He warned against my habit of drawing circles and arrows on the map. The police, he said, would suspect I was a spy marking sites to bomb at a later date.

"What will happen if they arrest me?"

"The police will fine you, maybe one hundred dollars, and force you to leave Vietnam," said Sung. With a sigh of resignation he added, "The money will never get to the government. It will stay in the pocket of the police."

The candor continued. He volunteered that Vietnam was fighting a new war, this one against corruption. The problem permeated every facet of life. Sung told of his distress to see officials taking bribes for licenses, creating false receipts for goods, and selling political favors. A man who had helped send the Americans packing was less than optimistic of the prospects for victory.

Most Vietnamese accepted corruption as part of life. A businessman in Hanoi told me that understanding the nuances of bribery was the secret to his success. "You give a few cookies here and a few cookies there and you get what you want," he told me over coffee in Hanoi. "But you don't give cookies to everyone in the room. And not too many to one person."

It hadn't always been that way. Sung traced the change to 1972, three years after Ho Chi Minh died. That was when the lieutenant saw the North's discipline begin to slip. He used the ban on relationships as a case study: "Men and women were told not to fall in love, so we did not. I once shared a bamboo bed with ten women, very beautiful. But I never thought to sleep with one."

"Why not?"

"Our life was not like the Americans'. They had hot food. And showers. Also prostitutes. We lived like monks. That was our strength. The political officers said that we could not win without our discipline. They said you could lie to your wife but not to the Party."

"What if you met a nice girl on the Ho Chi Minh Trail?"

"I would be sent home and lose the honor of fighting for Vietnam. The Party would criticize me and I would live in shame," said Sung. He showed no signs of joking.

After Ho's death Sung noticed more pregnant women being sent home quietly. Bad reports and heavy-handed pressure to conform became a thing of the past. Worse, high officials kept in check by Uncle Ho's ascetic example began philandering. High officers who once ate and slept with their men began accepting luxuries, a sin Sung couldn't forgive.

"They began to form a separate class," said the veteran. "A privileged class. After the war they got Japanese cars and we got nothing."

"And if Ho had lived longer?"

"Things would be different. We would have realized his master plan. And we would all be equal."

No fan of his politics, I felt sorry for the disillusionment of a true believer.

22

Nobody neglected to warn me; everybody said, "Steer clear of Laos." I ignored them all. Why? Laos was the location of the Ho Chi Minh Trail's fast lane. My obstinacy cost me multiple migraines, gallons of sweat, and a detour that took me hundreds of miles off target.

The road to Laos began with a phone call to Washington. The man running the Lao Embassy's visa section was too brusque for any job but bureaucrat.

"What is the purpose of your visit?"

"Tourism."

"What is your agency?"

"I don't have an agency."

"You must have an agency. Or permission to go to Laos."

"I'm calling to get permission to go to Laos."

"You must get permission from someone inside Laos."

"How can I know anybody in Laos before I get there?"

"You have business contacts."

"I don't."

"Or maybe you have a relative there."

Last I checked, none of my Swedish, German, or English

ancestors had crossed the Pacific, schlepped over Vietnam, and settled in a promised land called Laos. Rejection of my oral visa application looked imminent. To clarify why, I paraphrased: "Those are the conditions? I need an agency or a business or a relative?"

"Laos does not have conditions. Just rules."

That assessment had been borne out when I visited the embassy in Hanoi. Situated in a barren courtyard of faded colonial buildings, the immigration office was marked by a sheet of paper thumbtacked to a post. Beside the words "Visas $25" was a hand-drawn arrow pointing up an outdoor stairway. At the top I found a room displaying a six-foot-long painting of gold-spired temples.

The lone employee, a brown man in a white shirt, gestured for me to approach his glass barrier. Bending to speak through a hole, I described my plan to take Route 9 overland to Laos.

"No," said the official, a man who enjoyed his work.

I repeated my question. He repeated his answer.

Then the official elaborated. True, the rules had changed and the land border *was* open. But only to Vietnamese. The rules said that foreigners could visit Laos only by flying to the capital, Vientiane. The city was hundreds of kilometers from Savannakhet, the Lao terminus of Route 9. But the government was stingy with internal travel permits, so I probably wouldn't be allowed outside the capital.

Experts on both sides of the war agreed that the sections in Laos were the key to the Trail's success. There, the NVA could outflank American ground forces until they found a soft spot in South Vietnam's defenses. The area was bombed silly once the Pentagon caught on. But the B-52s were opposed by as many as eighty thousand antiaircraft gunners, infantrymen, and engineers whom Hanoi stationed in Laos to keep the Trail open.

Xepon was one of the network's nerve points in the mountainous jungle. Located just a wind sprint from the Vietnam end of Route 9, the town was a hub from which supplies fanned out along one of dozens of hidden paths. Xepon, then, was where I intended to see the Trail's central business district. If I could get a visa.

The paperwork eluded me. I struck out at the Lao Embassy and ignored the Vietnamese bureaucrat who suggested I take the matter up with Vientiane's ambassador. Another local, a recent college graduate named Huynh, gave me hope.

Huynh had a contact in Dong Ha. He phoned Pham, who promised to arrange for me to drive into Laos. Skeptical of the coup, I asked Huynh to double-check. Pham reconfirmed. His words, "No problem," were clear despite a crackly line. But what sounded like idiomatic English was in fact technical Vietnamese for "You're doomed."

Once located, Pham said he had never heard of me. And he had no idea how to get me into Laos. He suggested trying a place called Tourist Guide Office.

I grimaced at the thought of returning to the shysters who had tried to sell me everything from a DMZ tour to a U.S. Army ring. I caved in upon recalling the urgency of going to Laos: extended twice, my visa would expire for good before I reached Saigon. Fresh visas were available only outside Vietnam. I had to leave.

The boss of the tourism firm's hogs, a porker named Duy, laughed at my plan to drive into Laos. Stumped for a money-making scheme, he consulted his cohorts in slime. Ten minutes of bickering generated a proposal. For a hundred dollars, the month's wage of three Vietnamese, the brain trust would wangle a permit for me to take a bus to Laos.

"The embassy in Hanoi charges only twenty-five dollars."

"We have expenses."

Not that I had much choice. I had to leave Vietnam. And

a hundred bucks looked cheap compared to the hassle and cost of flying to Bangkok, the Mecca for Vietnamese visas. Shocked by my quick assent, Duy's eyes bugged as I lifted a hundred-dollar bill from my wallet.

He looked set to slobber as I withheld the cash and posed more questions. Was there a Vietnamese consul in Savannakhet? Would he give me a visa? How long would it take? Duy's answer was the same on all counts: "No problem."

Indeed, two days later I had a Lao visa. The package included the services of a young man named Tho. The smooth-faced son of a diplomat taxied me to the bus stop on his Honda scooter. It was 8 A.M. and the mercury had already cleared ninety degrees. We settled in a café's canvas beach chairs and sipped sugary lemonade until the arrival of the Savannakhet Express, which stopped only when flagged.

Tho used fragments of English to tell me that the cost of food in Laos would be double the Vietnam price, beer three times as dear. He had two other predictions: "Road to Savannakhet very bad" and "Laos very hot." Worse roads and higher temperatures than in Vietnam? Uninformed hyperbole, I thought.

The yellow DeSoto showed no sign of stopping as it rumbled by our shady spot. Tho gave pursuit on his red scooter and, waving like a desert islander to a ship, attracted the attention of the driver. The bus slowed to a halt, leaving me with a quarter mile to sprint.

At the finish line a teenage boy snatched my pack and heaved it atop a pile of baggage in the rear of the bus. Then he whistled and the driver punched the accelerator. I jumped into the rear stairwell as the bus began chugging west. "Five dollars," screamed Tho. "Pay five dollars."

What did five bucks buy on a Vietnamese Greyhound? Not a seat. The DeSoto was already stuffed. Passengers sat three to a seat in fifteen rows. Spare baggage filled the aisles. Four men were stretched atop the freight in the rear. That left two empty stairs, the bottom one for the bus boy, the top for me.

The seatless were, in fact, blessed. Only the driver and the plastic Buddha on his dashboard looked comfy. My spot by the open door offered air and a view of Route 9. But even the historic highway could grow old.

How old? The Dong Ha brain trust had forecast a trip of seventeen hours. That had to be wrong. The ride was only 325 kilometers, a shade over 200 miles. Say we averaged 20 miles per hour, the speed at which most people look for parking. The pace would land us in Savannakhet in ten hours. What were the other seven for?

Pit stops. The driver eased the DeSoto to a halt outside a string of food shacks near Khe Sanh. Out poured the passengers for a group urination off a precipice. A four-course, eighty-cent meal followed. How we would fill seventeen hours was still a mystery when we reached the frontier at one o'clock.

A soldier offered some insight. I focused my camera on mountaintops that few, if any, Americans had had the leisure to admire. Cicadas screamed in the midday heat. Bad enough by bus, the heart of the Ho Chi Minh Trail looked like a nasty place to have had to hoof it. My ruminative spell was broken by a grip tightening on my elbow.

The soldier grabbed my camera and marched me toward the concrete customs building. The detention room was airy, furnished with a table and four chairs, really more like an office than a torture chamber. A baby-faced customs official with curly black hair arrived to begin the interrogation.

"How old are you?"

"What's your job?"

"Have you got a wife?"

I relaxed. My captor was just another local seeking to practice his English. A thin, mustachioed man in uniform took his duty far more seriously. The immigration officer thumbed slowly through my passport. I pointed to the Lao visa. He focused on stamps from China, Vietnam's archenemy. Without a word, he disappeared with my papers. When he returned, he asked whether he should take away my Vietnamese visa.

"What do you usually do with Americans?"

"We don't know."

The young official decided to keep my Vietnamese visa as a souvenir of the first American to pass his checkpoint.

Laos cast an equally wary eye on a red-faced foreigner coming down the pike, a gravel lane that wound a mile or so through the brush separating its checkpoint from Vietnam's. A guard in army pants and a white T-shirt rubbed his eyes and slapped the soldier dozing next to him. Both stared before resuming their catnaps.

The bus driver parked behind three trucks waiting to clear customs. Most of the passengers sought shady spots under trees. The bus boy and I climbed the steps to the porch of the immigration office, a broad, wooden building resembling a tree house on six-foot stilts. There I filled in an arrival card which asked me to state, among other personal details, "number of followers."

Two stocky men behind the duty desk passed my document back and forth like a live grenade. They punted the job to a woman, who spoke to the bus boy in Lao, who spoke to me in Vietnamese, which I understood well enough to know that she wanted money. When my answer, "No," reached her, she stamped my passport and waved me into her country.

Laos felt different than Vietnam. For a start, the west side of the border made the east look like Beverly Hills. The shacks were more dilapidated, the streets dustier. Unlike the Vietnamese poor, who always managed a bath, Lao adults were filthy. Many were not entirely clothed. I passed a wrinkled, topless woman who might have modeled for *National Geographic*.

I felt lost. Vietnam's Roman lettering was decipherable. Laos's strings of squiggles and loops looked like the product of a swami on LSD. Equally unfriendly were the faces of the brown men lugging loads of cigarettes and fans toward Vietnam. Nobody showed any interest in a stranger.

The yellow DeSoto didn't reload until four-thirty. That left nine of the estimated seventeen hours to cover just 250 kilometers. I looked forward to an early arrival in Savannakhet and a meal of whatever Lao cooks were famous for. I watched in pain as that fantasy evaporated.

Road conditions were the main cause of delay. Nobody had paved the Lao portion of Route 9 since . . . maybe ever. Bumps like ski moguls bounced me off my feet. The bus slowed to walking speed. I passed some of the time by thinking about history.

The famed jungle canopy was gone. In its place was a tangle of dry bushes, tall reeds, and dead stumps. Tiny footpaths led into their midst. Where there were gaps, there were also broad, round craters. Bare black football fields of slashed-and-burned land added to the sensation of moving through a war zone.

Frequent stops delayed our progress. First there was a group of five dark women dancing beside the road. Dressed in tight, ankle-length skirts and baseball caps, one of which said "U.S. Marines," they were Laos's welcome wagon. One woman tied "good luck" white strings on the wrists of visitors. Another pinned them with plastic flowers. An old woman followed the pair with a bowl, into which passengers dropped bits of money.

Several rattling hours later, we stopped for dinner. The bus driver led me through a dirt-floored kitchen where a ragged lady used a horror-movie prop to chop at a cooked chicken. The sous-chef tended pots on an open fire and scooped rice onto plates. After rinsing ourselves with hand-pumped water, we settled on benches in the open-air dining area.

The bus boy handed me a plate of rice and mangled chicken. Too late, I noticed that the table was crawling with flying ants. I was too tired to shoo the brave dozen which ventured onto my dinner. Leaving the food, I ordered two beers and watched a forty-something woman in a turquoise blouse shriek at a man in a white tank top. They must have been married; the guy didn't fight back when she walloped his cheek-bone.

I must have passed out. The hours that followed were too horrific to be real. There were two men lying on either side of my niche atop the baggage. One, a frail man of sixty, insisted on holding my wrist so I wouldn't fall out the door. Another snored and rolled onto me whenever he dozed off. A giant bump in the road bounced us all off the ceiling and into a pile. I kicked at the bodies on top of me. But I didn't scream.

That I saved for the moment it began to rain and the bus boy locked the back door. The air grew heavy with the breath and foul mood of sixty-plus passengers. Suffocation started when the old man lit a cigarette. I begged him to put it out. Then I begged to get off the bus. Laos's dark, rainy roadside appealed more than a Black Hole on wheels.

23

I had two goals when dawn slid under my door.
Half a night in a room infested with rat-size cockroaches—or
were they cockroach-size rats?—was one half too many. All I
wanted was a new visa and a ticket back to Vietnam. Neither
was available at 6 A.M., when I stepped into the Savannakhet
sunlight.

The Mekong River town felt like an outpost: Dodge City
meets French colonialism. Once elegant buildings were crumbling along the hard-packed dirt of the main streets. The few
people who had emerged from their homes showed little interest in me, as if staring invited trouble. Even roving packs of
dogs minded their own business.

Four blocks from the river, nature started getting the better
of civilization. Lao-style homes, products of the tree-house-on-
stilts school, filled the spaces between coconut trees, broad-
leafed plants, and farm animals. Jungle took over where the
residential section ended, a half mile from the Mekong.

Some might describe the town as "exotic." "Unsanitary"
was my adjective of choice. Gullies flanked Savannakhet's

roads. Three feet deep and about that wide, the ditches were half full. With what I don't know. Slicks, lumps, and chunks shimmied in shades of green, brown, and black.

The roadside troughs were textbook breeding grounds for *Plasmodium falciparum*, the deadly, drug-resistant mosquito. I thought back to my *Lonely Planet* guidebook's malaria warning: "The highest risk area in Laos seems to be the lower Mekong River Valley south of Vientiane."* That, plus speculation about what else might be growing, had me outside the Vietnamese Consulate's door before it opened.

Ho Chi Minh's smile never looked so friendly. Dominating the rear of Vietnam's gym-size reception hall on a street called Sisavangvong, the mammoth bust of Uncle Ho made me feel safe. I began looking forward to reuniting with my Minsk. Rat-bugs and sewer slime would soon be distant memories.

A graying man with thick glasses scrambled to his feet and bowed slightly when I entered. He showed me to an armchair by a coffee table, mumbled something in French, and scurried out of the building. He returned with a more senior diplomat, who poured two cups of yellow tea before saying a word. Leaning back in an armchair, he folded his legs and asked how he could help.

"I would like a tourist visa for Vietnam."

"You must wait one week."

"I understand that these things take time. I'll come back, say, this afternoon."

"You must wait."

"My friends in Dong Ha, employees of *your* government, said you could issue a visa in 'one day, no problem.'"

"You must wait."

---

* *Laos—A Travel Survival Kit* (Lonely Planet Publications, 1994), p. 85.

The procedure, said the diplomat, was standard. Visa applicants completed a form, which the consulate faxed to Hanoi. There a team of experts checked names against a list of enemies of the state. Henry Kissinger and Sylvester Stallone need not apply. As a rule, replies came within a week. "More tea?"

I demonstrated that a delay made no sense. I had just left Vietnam. In other words, Vietnam had already deemed me fit for consumption. At that very moment I could have been in Danang, Dim Sum, or any other place between Hanoi and Saigon.

"You must wait."

I sipped tea and plotted a new course. According to Joe, Sung, and anybody else who had ever set foot in Vietnam, Hanoi's underpaid officials accepted, and often demanded, bribes. The diplomat was probably looking to supplement his children's college fund. To me, fifty dollars would be an acceptable price to avoid another night in Savannakhet.

"Is there an application fee?"

"Twenty dollars."

"In America, you can pay a little more for faster service."

"Vietnam is not like America."

I ought to have admired the diplomat's integrity, not to mention his patience with a whiny traveler. His homeland would be a better place with a brighter future were there a thousand more like him. Instead, I hated the honest Hanoinker for ignoring my offer and condemning me to a week in a sweltering limbo.

I found a sympathetic ear at my hotel's shady dining area. Mr. Leng was dark, stocky, and, I think, blind in one eye. He volunteered that he had been a police officer in Vientiane before finding work as an interpreter for Americans stationed in Laos in the early 1970s. Like Laos's economy, he became depressed after "liberation," the unopposed coup by indigenous Communists in mid-1975. Jobless in the capital, Leng came home to Savannakhet.

My woes agitated Leng's dander. He sprinted over to a bald man sporting mirrored sunglasses. The pair returned in agreement: I need not worry, they had strings to pull at the Vietnamese consulate. Stroked by luck, I pooh-poohed midday heat reaching for the century mark and headed toward the town's central market in search of my first local meal.

The food sections inspired vegetarianism. Beef, pork, and fish smoldered in two rows of stalls separated by a stream of black ooze. Women fanned the meat in a futile attempt to shoo flies. Venturing down the rows of stalls to an open, concrete floor, I found a kaleidoscope of fruits and vegetables spread on straw mats. One squatting woman sold me a skinned pineapple. Another sold me a green coconut, which she readied for drinking with five swift hacks of a two-foot machete.

Walking north in search of sights, I found a convoy of trucks waiting for a barge to Thailand, an empty soccer stadium, and a billboard that said, in both English letters and Lao squiggles, "Pepsi, The Choice of a New Generation." I killed the rest of the afternoon watching my hotel's housekeepers channel-surf among music videos, Thai soap operas, and a dubbed version of *American Gladiators*.

Leng arrived with bad news. They had failed to score me a visa. They did, however, have some inside information: the waiting period would be one week. Stressing the positive, Leng pointed out that I wasn't missing much.

"The Vietnamese are not good people, always thinking about money. They have a smile on their face and badness in their heart. In Laos you are greeted by smiling girls and the Lao people have good hearts."

The ex-cop had another reason for keeping me in Laos. Leng was an ideas man. He reckoned that building a brewery was like owning a mint. How so? Laos had only one beer plant. Located in Vientiane, it often failed to meet the needs of a thirsty country. The more the capital drank, the less flowed to distant provinces. Savannakhet had been left dry more than once.

"Mr. Christopher, if you have a million dollars, we can build a brewery and supply the whole province."

I tried to explain that not every American had a million bucks at his fingertips. Leng sweetened the pot: "You can move to Laos and enjoy life. I will help you to marry a Lao girl." I said I would think about it.

The restaurant across the street from the hotel helped me decide. I considered myself a guerrilla eater up to the moment I read the menu. House specialties included "grilled moose bleeding," "minced barking deer," and "minced raw monitor lizard." The last choice, like the "minced scaly anteater," could also be served baked. I ordered vegetables, rice, and a plane ticket to Vientiane.

Frightening food wasn't the only thing driving me to the capital. I wanted to visit the Vietnamese Embassy. Watching the murky Mekong snaking below Lao Aviation's air-conditioned turboprop, I felt sure that clout, wiles, and greed would be easier to find at Hanoi's branch office in Vientiane.

My beeline to the embassy took me past magnificent and probably historic sights. Indeed, I later learned that a weathered slab of rock called the Black Stupa was said to house a seven-headed dragon. The same was said of the American Embassy. *Patuxai*, an ornate knockoff of the Arc de Triomphe, was a monument to fallen soldiers. But on my first pass through Laos's capital, sightseeing took a back seat to negotiating.

A serene, mid-career diplomat greeted me at Vietnam's compound. Like his counterpart in Savannakhet, the courtly Hanoi native served tea to a sweat-soaked American. We chatted about the past: the day the war ended was one of his life's happiest. We also talked about the present: Vietnam was so poor that he hadn't been allowed to bring his family to the overseas posting.

That sounded like my cue. I asked how long it would take to get a new tourist visa.

"One week."

"There is no faster way?"

"No. You must wait."

A quarter hour of nodding and winking didn't change the man's mind. He would send my visa application to Hanoi. He would not be bribed for faster service. The encounter left me wondering whether I had it all wrong. Was Vietnam's in fact the model of a scrupulous bureaucracy?

24

The Vietnamese were right. I would wait one week. I filled the frustrating delay by getting to know Laos's capital.

My main finding was that Vientiane was hot. Two knee-buckling bouts of dehydration taught me to avoid the sun after 9 A.M. Resisting the elements was like fighting the Tar Baby. Struggle all you like, but a human wasn't going to beat the 100-plus degree heat in the Lao PDR.*

Writing off broad daylight meant seeking indoor diversion. One option was the Morning Market, an all-day bazaar where "magic" mushrooms and opium could be bought in air-conditioned comfort. Another was the Lao Revolutionary Museum, which was located in a stylish mansion on a street called Samsenthai.

Photograph displays showed how violence had a way of finding Laos. The first blow came in 1893, when King Oun Kham gave France the keys to the kingdom. In a room devoted

---

* An acronym for People's Democratic Republic, PDR also abbreviated the motto of an overheated nation: Please don't rush.

to the betrayal, the culprits were depicted as pale, bearded scoundrels. A painting showed Frenchmen whipping locals in front of a burning village.

More disturbing were the photographs of the casualties of American bombing. The curators had juxtaposed snapshots of kids burned by napalm and monks shredded by explosives with images of Lyndon Johnson and Robert McNamara. The victims' main mistake was to live along North Vietnam's infiltration routes in eastern Laos. Bombs aimed at the NVA showed no mercy. Moreover, B-52 pilots returning to Thailand from sorties in North Vietnam often dumped unused bombs over the Laos's jungle.

Left alone, locals preferred not to fight. Indigenous Communists known as the Pathet Lao kept the safety catches on their weapons while overrunning Vientiane in 1975. The threat of violence was enough to convince government ministers and generals to flee to Thailand. Mementos of the revolution showed men idling with rifles, military police carrying paper, and dozens of soldiers talking sports. The U.S. Embassy closed for a day.

The Lao did seem a docile lot. Vietnamese poked and prodded strangers. An extroverted Lao might nod silently or whisper "*Sabaidii* [Hello]." Open a wallet in Vietnam and eyes popped, fingers twitched. Unable to communicate in Lao, I paid for things by fanning out my money and letting vendors take their due. Locals plucked banknotes as gingerly as grannies playing Go Fish.

Nonetheless, I itched to get back to Vietnam. Getting my name on Lao Aviation's list of Savannakhet-bound passengers took twenty minutes, about the time I usually spend listening to Muzak while holding for a United Airlines operator. The minutes passed quickly after a Canadian named J.R. introduced himself.

An engineer, J.R. and his wife had shopped Asia for a place to raise a family. Filthy and crowded, Thailand wouldn't do. Native charm and demand for technical skills drew them to Laos, where he was developing hydropower near the Vietnamese border.

"Do you spend most of your time there?"

"We can't work yet."

"Why not?"

"Bombs."

The average square kilometer of Laos, said J.R., received ten tons of bombs. About a tenth of the charges didn't detonate. In other words, the typical plot of Lao land had a ton of unexploded ordnance, some duds, some not, in part because Laos had refused American offers to clear the area. Dozens of development projects in Laos as well as Vietnam were held up while the sites were swept. Who did the dirty work?

"Not us," laughed J.R.

Spotting my interest in learning more about roving bomb-removal specialists, the engineer passed me the name of the outfit working at his site. He also crossed an X on my map of Vientiane to mark the spot where I would find a company whose uncreative name, Milsearch, smacked of a CIA cover.

A retired linebacker of a man named Ron welcomed me to his office with a heartfelt "G'day." The white-haired Australian listened in earnest to the story of my search for the Ho Chi Minh Trail. Without hesitation, he described the business of clearing "unexploded ordnance," UXO to insiders.

Ron explained that most of his colleagues were retired military personnel. They started out surveying and clearing former military land in Australia. Then Milsearch diversified. War-torn Southeast Asia was one obvious market. The Gulf War created another in Kuwait. "As long as people keep fighting, we'll be in business."

Business was brisk in Laos. Green and yellow flags denoting clearance jobs dotted a six-foot wall map. The biggest job lay 60 kilometers north of Xepon. To keep work going during the coming rainy season, when the jungle location would be inaccessible by road, Milsearch had built a camp for the forty full-time workers.

"Don't they get hurt?"

Ron said that accidents were rare. The Lao laborers worked in pairs, one carrying a metal detector, the other a shovel. When they found a bomb, a team located its edge and began to dig, gently. Experts had devised a disposal plan once the explosive had been unearthed and identified.

Nobody tried to move live bombs and mines. They blew them up. "Detect, expose, explode," was Ron's summary of his work.

Airplane bombs were the easiest to eliminate. Heavy, stable in the ground, and relatively insensitive to vibrations, the big boys were detonated by placing a smaller explosive on top. Built to explode on touch, these smaller explosives required more care. Ron shook his head while describing how the kids who picked up tennis-ball-size *bombi* were shredded by steel pellets.

Before returning to his desk, the gentle giant passed me his crib sheets. The stack of blue folders in my hand were military documents. Some were technical manuals used by U.S. Army bomb squads. One from the Department of Air Force had "SECRET" stamped on every page. I believed Ron when he said that all had been distributed through America's Freedom of Information Act. Nonetheless, holding wartime briefs made me tingle with a sense of danger, as if I had been handed the Pentagon Papers.

Drawings of mines, bombs, and bomblets filled the pages of one manual. Aimed at "Explosive Ordnance Reconnaissance Agents," the text had a list of rules worth remembering. Spend as little time as possible near live bombs. Don't touch unexploded bombs. Don't even touch the area near unexploded bombs. If you must touch a bomb, do it from behind a sandbag.

A document titled *Project CHECO* was an eyeopener. Prepared to help the air force fight "unconventional warfare," the folder was a guide to the Trail. A paragraph described how North Vietnam kept roads open, particularly in the area between Vietnam and Xepon, during the wet season. Another section described the Viet Cong practice of floating supplies down rivers. The flyboys even knew about the petrol pipeline over the Mu Gia Pass.

"Hard to imagine we* knew where all the stuff was and still couldn't stop them," said Ron.

A map in the air force booklet offered some explanation. Knowing the United States wouldn't bomb its own, Hanoi placed POW camps to the north and west of Xepon. However, war materiel never should have made it that far. The biggest mistake, in Ron's view, was not bombing ships arriving in Haiphong. "Supplies landed and disappeared. After that there was no chance to stop them."

I asked about Xepon. Could I spend a night there? Ron said that a blanket, a mosquito net, and a bucket of water for washing could be had at either the guesthouse in town or the forestry school outside. But he recommended against both. Seven Milsearch workers in the area had come down with malaria. In one case, a man came down with malaria *and* typhoid.

---

* Australian troops are often forgotten in America's vocal hand-wringing over the Vietnam War. They, in fact, may have been more adept at jungle warfare than GI Joes. A Viet Cong officer told me he was never afraid of Americans, who lived in well-lit encampments and tramped loudly when on patrol. Australians, on the other hand, gave Charlie the willies. They lived in the jungle, walked softly, and practiced many of the same stealth tactics as their quarry.

"It's pretty rough up there," said Ron.

Just how rough became clearer the following morning when the dark-skinned man standing in front of me pulled a black pistol from a holster beneath his blazer. I quickly calculated the damage a bullet could do if fired from a range of two feet. Meanwhile, the man behind me yanked a cousin of Wyatt Earp's six-shooter from his briefcase.

I told myself that this couldn't be happening in Laos, a country where Buddhist devotion had papered over man's tendency to gore his neighbor. And if this were really Laos, the shooting gallery wouldn't be in the airport.

"Your weapon?" asked a soldier manning a Formica desk.

"I don't have a weapon."

Double-checking, he pointed to a plastic sign to his right. Written in English and Lao, it said, "Please Show Your Gun."

"No weapon," I repeated.

The soldier's grunt didn't indicate whether this was shortsighted of me. He returned to collecting pistols from other passengers. After removing the bullets or ammunition clips from weapons, he gave the owner a receipt. Six men were disarmed before boarding the flight to Savannakhet. Why was everybody packing heat?

I wasn't planning to stick around long enough to find out. Back in Savannakhet, I guided a taxi driver along the shortest route to Vietnam's consulate. One week had passed since my first visit. I was ready to accept my new visa and the diplomat's thanks for my unusual patience. The diplomat flashed a smile of recognition when he saw me coming down his walk.

"So, my visa is ready?"

"I think maybe you will wait ten days."

I wanted to throttle him. Instead, I loosened my grip on the Nobel Patience Prize. "You said wait one week. I did. Now you want me to wait three more days? Or is it ten more? Why won't you let me go to Vietnam? I'll promise not to start another war."

The diplomat parried sarcasm with sarcasm. He reminded me that I was lucky to get any help: "If I wanted to go to your country I would have to wait. Right?" He suggested I visit "the places of beauty" near Savannakhet.

"I want to see the places of beauty in Vietnam."

"You can come here if you have free time."

"All my time is free."

"Then I think you will go to your hotel and drink beer."

On the way to do just that, I stopped by a temple called Sainyamungkun. Inside, a middle-aged Thai woman explained the local legends. The temple's top monk dispensed magic water, one sip of which ensured a long life and increased wealth. She also pointed out a small, brassy statue resting on a purple pillow.

"Have you lifted the Buddha?" she asked.

I hadn't. But by then I was willing to try anything.

25

"Christopher, do you remember what we talked about before?"

I was just midway through a skillet-hot morning. Local monks had already collected their alms and the Vietnamese Consulate had already rejected my daily visa plea. The Buddha hadn't cleared my head. Nor had Leng given up his own dreams.

"The brewery?" I said.

"Were you in California for the earthquake?"

I was, though I didn't see the connection.

"If you live in Laos there are no earthquakes."

The aspiring brewer fretted about the evident misery of his financial backer. He proposed a joyride. Would I like to see a famous place called the Ho Chi Minh Trail?

Leng outlined a trip that would take us east to Xepon and another town called Ban Dong. From there we could travel one of the Trail's main north-south axes. The way would be littered with fossilized jeeps and tanks. Time permitting, he could also show me the remains of American helicopters and jets.

For transport, the hotel's manager agreed to lend us his

car, for a day. Provided I loaned him a hundred bucks, forever. We settled on half that amount. I might have bargained harder had I known we were talking about a black Volga, a four-door box made by the folks who said cosmonaut instead of astronaut.

Signs of Russian craftsmanship were abundant when we boarded the vehicle at four-thirty the following A.M. Loose wires hung below the dashboard. A web of cracks crawled over the windshield. When the car moved, the speedometer swung like a pendulum. The petrol needle never budged from the far left.

"Volga is a river in Russia," said Leng, perhaps to sidetrack my suspicions that the car wasn't roadworthy. If so, he undermined the deception: "Do you have a flashlight? Once before the car broke in the dark and we needed a flashlight."

Worries gave way to admiration of Savannakhet's sunrise. The driver, a petite, serious man whose tanned skin was pulled tight over high cheekbones, pulled out of the hotel's gravel lot. The humid air turned lavender as the sun tried to burn through. A band of pink rimmed the horizon until a tangerine ball pushed through the obstruction and illuminated the tangle of green.

The driver fought to dodge potholes big enough to hide a cow. He swerved left to right, using both shoulders and at times the middle of the two-lane road. I tried to count my blessings. Befriended by Savannakhet's one English-speaker, I was headed for Lao sections of the Ho Chi Minh Trail.

How many Americans had seen the view out the Volga's window? Dry bushes and scruffy trees lined most of the road. Stilt houses appeared once in a while. Cows and buffalo rummaged through barren rice paddies which hadn't seen water for months.

Details of Leng's life surfaced bit by bit as the Volga jostled us east along Route 9. After the war, the former interpreter landed a job in the north of Laos. During one of his extended absences from Vientiane, Leng's wife fled to France. Devastated, he moved home to Savannakhet, where he found another wife and a new line of work.

Thousands of miles to the northeast, Japan's smelters were hungry for fodder. Short of heavy industry but long on scrap metal, Laos had a ready-made business boomlet. Once Vientiane began allowing shipments to Thailand, pieces of planes, tanks, and bombs became a leading export.

Leng was a junkman. He hired a truck and cruised Laos's panhandle-shaped south. A typical tour followed French-built Route 13, which meandered alongside the Mekong, the country's western frontier. If he hadn't filled his vehicle by the time he reached Cambodia, Leng turned left along Laos's southern edge.

Paris hadn't left behind a highway for scavenging the long border with Vietnam. But Hanoi had. For a scrap dealer, the Ho Chi Minh Trail was a road to riches. "Where there's war there's metal" became Leng's motto.

Natives of the jungle areas fed the growing appetite for metal. Locals scanned their vicinities for American and North Vietnamese leftovers. Those who didn't accidentally trigger unexploded ordnance piled the metal by the roads until Leng or a rival drove by and bought the lot at two hundred kip per kilo. Back in Savannakhet, the middleman resold the scrap to Thailand-bound dealers at four hundred kip, or about fifty cents at current rates.

A loaded truck held four tons. As the scrap harvests grew, Leng hired a second vehicle and a driver, and later a third, for ten-day convoys through the jungle. Where did they sleep? In the truck, said Leng. And with a gun. In a land as poor as Laos, a truckload of metal was as good as gold.

The business was doomed from the start. The supply of

the unnatural resource was limited. Within three years the jungle stopped generating loads big enough to cover costs. When all that remained were pieces too remote to reach, Leng gave up.

He spoke with regret as we passed a sheer, flat-topped mountain south of the road. "That was a base for the Royal Lao Army and American advisers. We found a lot of metal up there. Artillery, and also helicopters. But we couldn't get it down."

East of a town called Phalan, Route 9 doubled as a social club. The members belonged to hill tribes who made the Lao look pale and prosperous. Wielding scythes for slashing their burned land, men were reluctant to interrupt mid-road chats for a Russian car. Dogs were even slower to lift themselves from collision courses. Only the women swatting idle children moved fast to clear the way.

Where the road gently angled into the heat-hazed mountains a monument marked the western edge of the Trail. A concrete statue of two men stood tall in a plaza inhabited by goats and their droppings. One of the men was holding high an AK-47 machine gun, the other a Lao flag. The inscription read: "To remember the Lao and Vietnamese fighters who lost their lives."

Spread behind the tower was an eight-foot plaster mural of war scenes. Two men by a campfire shook hands and embraced a hammer and sickle. A soldier in a helmet and flak jacket whispered in a woman's ear. Two figures carried supplies on a pole bridged across their shoulders. Another looked set to fire a rocket-propelled grenade at a line of trucks. A plane in flames plunged groundward.

Farther along the dirt highway, craters announced that the center of the Trail was nearing. Mountains closed in on the road, which had been graded with Vietnamese aid money after 1975. The severe hills, said Leng, held caves first inhabited by ancient Khmers. During the war, torrential bombing had driven locals to refurbish them for stays of up to eight years.

Xepon itself was a letdown. The town of 5,000 was silent when we arrived late in the morning. The only movement was on a tiny puddle, where bugs skittered and plotted medical havoc for the coming rainy season. Leng pointed across the street to the guesthouse, a row of rooms on stilts that passed for the Xepon Plaza. I was glad not to be spending the night.

Leng led me through the market. There had been nothing here after the war, Leng explained. To rebuild, locals scrounged for sticks and stones not pulverized over the previous ten years. The pathetic result inspired the United Nations to finance the materials for the current grid, perfect rows of sturdy, tin-roofed stalls that resembled barracks.

Stunned stares followed me into an open vending area beneath a high roof. Nobody smiled. So I didn't. Leather-faced fogies froze and watched as if a spirit were passing. Seeing his first white face, a child screamed and ran behind his mother's grimy brown skirt. A quick exit looked prudent.

But Leng lingered. I found the upwardly mobile Lao among the hillbillies surrounding a table. A woman seated at the center of attention was riffling through a stack of lottery tickets. A hundred-kip chance could net as many as seven thousand, roughly ten dollars.

Leng bought a ticket and took me to the site of the old market. Formerly a bustling trading post—Xepon had once been the end of the line for Vietnamese trucks, which could now drive through to Savannakhet—a concrete floor and a rusted overhead lattice were all that remained of the structure. The only vendor was a toothless man in a white pith helmet. His lone item was the green casing of a two-foot missile, split in half and gutted like a fresh salmon. Painted *inside* were white-lettered warnings about the bomb's danger, as well as directions for disarming the thing.

Across the road I examined a photogenic bamboo building resting atop four-foot stilts. Leng said it was a barn. I moved to leave, but the stocky Lao held me by the arm and pulled me toward the structure's legs. The posts were oblong, not square. And metal rather than wood.

"Napalm bombs," said Leng.

The irony didn't need spelling out. Explosives that had blown or burned folks out of Xepon were now part of daily life. Nonetheless, Leng elaborated. "We used bombs to stop the growing during the war. Now they use them to store the harvest."

Just a few kilometers east, in Ban Dong, we stopped at the corner of Route 9 and Ho Chi Minh Trail. The driver popped the hood for a look at the Volga's steaming engine. Leng settled in the shade of a food shack, where the house specialties were rubber bovine and fish-head soup. I passed on the chow and examined the town's dozen or so homes.

Xepon's architect had a branch office in Ban Dong. Instead of a white picket fence, the owners of a flimsy bamboo house defined their yard with a row of green artillery shells. The porch of another shack was supported by bomb casings.

Down the road to Vietnam I found a homeowner with his own version of a lawn jockey. His patch was decorated with a rusting pile of war flotsam that included bits of bombs, helmets, radios, shovels, and mortar shells, some of which looked intact. How did all the infantry debris get into Laos, a country whose neutrality Washington once claimed to honor?

The Pentagon fibbed. Minus their uniforms, Green Berets regularly dropped into Laos during the Vietnam War. More rubble was left by Saigon's troops. Backed by American air support, South Vietnamese soldiers flooded across the border and down Route 9 in an attempt to cut Hanoi's supply lines. Known as Lam Son 719, the offensive was swiftly repelled by the NVA forces that saturated the area around Ban Dong, which lay just a few kilometers from the frontier.

With a grand gesture Leng piled us into the Volga. With equal suddenness he ordered the driver to halt about two hundred yards from our starting point. He marched over to a porch where men were playing poker and struck up a conversation. Five minutes later I followed.

"We must walk with the local people," Leng said.

I didn't argue, considering J.R., Ron, and a half-dozen books had mentioned the danger of unexploded bombs. To these I added five other well-documented dangers: common and king cobras; and green, Malayan, and Russell's pit vipers. Which one, I wondered, was the "two-step snake" feared by the MIA searchers? Until the region's serpents earned a new nickname, such as "harmless," I would be glad to have somebody walking ahead.

A local named Kham La agreed to lead us into the jungle, or whatever one called the post-defoliation greenery. Loyalty rather than bravery lured the lanky forty-year-old from his card game. As head of Ban Dong's cartel of scrap-metal collectors, he had been Leng's partner. With wind-crazed hair, gapped teeth, and weathered skin, Kham La looked to be just the sort of pirate I would expect to find trafficking in war debris.

Like other scavengers, Kham La had turned America's billion-dollar bombing program into a cash crop. But Ban Dong's top junk dog had paid his dues. "My suffering during the war became my living after the war," he said, with Leng translating.

The guide lit a cigarette and strolled down a path of crushed, dried grass. Leng shuffled in his wake. I brought up the rear, staying close enough to see where Kham La placed his flip-flops but far enough to be clear of a cluster bomb's shrapnel radius. After an accident-free quarter mile, I suspected the hazard had been exaggerated.

Two mortar shells showed that it hadn't. Lying side by side in the dried grass, the explosives looked too tidy to be deadly. Spotting my curiosity, Kham La warned me not to touch as he strode by. To be on the safe side of an accidental detonation, I tiptoed, held my breath, and tried to slow my heart rate.

Down an incline, and sunk in three feet of tall grass, a green army tank confirmed that I was in a nasty little corner of the world. Treads, armor, long cannon . . . the only difference between this and the tanks on the TV news was the front hood, which had been blown off during Lam Son 719. Frightened enough by Minsk breakdowns in Vietnam, I couldn't imagine the terror of a tank driver wrecked in Laos.

"Why didn't you sell this?" I asked Kham La.

"Somebody offered me one million kip. But I cannot take it. I would be prosecuted by the government."

"Selling scrap metal is illegal?"

"Selling this tank is illegal."

Leng explained that Vientiane had changed its policy as the scrap metal boom petered out. Concerned that the war would be forgotten, the government banned scrap traders from selling large vehicles. The remaining tanks and trucks were to stay put.

"The tank is now a hysterical monument," said Leng.

I asked Kham La where he had spent the war. The sultan of scrap pointed to a group of flat-topped mountains five miles to the south. American bombers had driven his family from the village to the shelter of caves. From there he watched the South Vietnamese soldiers pour down Route 9 and into an ambush. "The North Vietnamese stopped them," he said with boyish pride.

These days Kham La viewed the mountains with some embarrassment. The hills were still loaded with scrap metal. He knew the locations of five helicopters and a couple of planes. His attempts to move and sell them had failed. The mountains were too steep, the pieces too heavy.

Kham La led us through a gap in the thick, dry brush and down a narrow, beaten path. In a clearing shared by two houses he pointed out the turret of another tank, this one sunk deep in ground softened by season after season of heavy rain. A hole in a fence brought our trio and a stray dog to a patch of pineapples. There a shirtless man ignored the twelve-foot shaft of a cannon aimed at his head and hammered a wooden stake.

The hard nose of an artillery shell poked out six inches from the weapon's barrel. The property's tenant said he couldn't tell whether the explosive was alive or dead. He dared not investigate. Accepting the big gun as part of his life, the man simply cultivated the garden around the obstruction.

Leng scanned the pineapple patch as if something were missing. He turned a 360. Before long he was jabbering and gesturing to his former cohort. Slow shakes of Kham La's head met what appeared to be a series of questions from Leng.

"That is all for us to see."

"What about the helicopters and airplanes and other stuff?"

"The metal was here before. Now it is sold out."

26

Help was hard to come by at Savannakhet's bus terminal. Having walked more than a mile to catch the 5 A.M. to the border, I couldn't tell which of three rickety vehicles was going my way. Nothing indicated destinations. No conductors could be found. It took another passenger to save me from going to Pakse, the southern terminus of the bus on which I sat for twenty minutes.

The local to Vietnam was a refurbished flatbed. Seats were bolted to the area behind the cab. A roof was supported by two internal poles, which quivered under the weight of a five-foot stack of freight. When the "bus" began to roll, the movement shook the windowless side panels. Black exhaust spewed through a compartment holding more than seventy passengers packed seven per row.

The trip was an act of desperation. One more "You will wait" at the consulate pushed me over the edge. I packed my bag and headed for the Laos-Vietnam border. Maybe the border guards had the authority to let me pass their post. If not, perhaps they would make an exception for twenty bucks. I prayed they would, since the eight-hour ride was an experience not to repeat.

True, Euro-crunchy backpackers swore by public transport as the *only* place to meet "the people." Was that because global understanding was furthered by shared misery? It must be, since nobody on the bus discussed development theories or debt relief. My communications with fellow passengers were limited to "You Americans sure have hairy arms" and "You Lao sure pick your noses a lot."

The closest thing to a cross-cultural exchange came during a stop in Phalan. A swarm of children and young women descended to hawk munchies for the road. The vendors held up baggies of cold tea and lumps of sticky rice for inspection. One offered a barbecued rat on a stick. The guy to my right bought three wood skewers, each stacked with six roasted bugs. He offered to share. Keen to build bridges, I drew the line at chewing cockroaches.

The offer expired at one o'clock, when the bus reached the end of the line. Because the border was closed for lunch—every day, the soldiers shut the country for ninety minutes—I waited on the shady porch of the tree house turned border checkpoint.

A familiar face recognized mine. The potbellied, thumb-cuffing soldier smelled something fishy as I ambled, alone, toward the outpost. I sidestepped the thug and chatted with an equally chunky soldier wearing a white T-shirt and Ray Ban sunglasses.

We talked about how he might join his brother in Texas. Meanwhile, groups of women streamed under the guard's nose and toward Vietnam. On their shoulders were bamboo poles bearing giant loads of electric fans and cigarettes. I couldn't understand why the soldier didn't move to stop the obvious smugglers. Nor did I see the fun of his hobby, taking potshots at the passersby with pebbles and a slingshot.

Just as perplexing was the flabby soldier's decision to make a spot check. Bounding down the steps of his post, he grabbed two women carrying bulky shoulder bags. Shrieking, the pair let themselves be led onto the porch. They resisted only when brought to the door of the building. The guard grabbed each by an elbow and yanked. Arms wrapped around their purses, the women disappeared from view.

One made a break for daylight. The soldier caught her by the foot as she reached the threshold, sending the woman and several bricks of money spilling across the porch. Scrambling for her cash, the woman was dragged back inside by the ankle. A kick to her ribs elicited a cry of pain. The soldier improved his grip, jerked the woman to her feet, and slapped her square in the jaw. Judging by the sounds that followed, the beating continued behind closed doors.

"Lao girls number one," said the grinning soldier when he returned, Ray Bans in place, ten minutes later.

"Lao girls number one," I agreed, unwilling to play human rights watchdog with my exit to Vietnam on the line.

The blind eye worked. Technically, nobody could leave Laos without an entry visa to Vietnam. I explained that under a special arrangement I would be picking up my visa from the Vietnamese border guards. With the rogue male arguing my case, the captain of the Laos checkpoint made an exception. When the post reopened at two o'clock, the soldiers canceled my permit to stay in Laos and sent me into no-man's-land.

A cluster of Vietnamese officers gathered to watch me come down the pike. The team that assembled in the familiar interrogation room included the young, mustachioed official and the baby-faced customs officer. The crew struggled to understand why an American with no papers was at their checkpoint.

I reminded them of my previous visit. And asked whether

they had kept my old visa, which would prove that Hanoi didn't mind my presence on their soil. The yellow and white page was found within fifteen minutes. Would a canceled visa help me acquire a fresh one?

No. The immigration official said he had no authority to issue new visas. Not even for ten dollars. No. Not even for twenty dollars. Indignant, the policeman tensed his brow.

"No money," he shouted.

What was wrong with me? Why was I the only person unable to find a bribable official? More important, what was I to do now that I had no permission to enter either Laos or Vietnam?

"Why don't you return to Vietnam with this visa?"

"Wh-what?"

"If you want to enter Vietnam you may use this visa."

"When?"

"Now, if you like."

27

The staff of the brothel welcomed the return of a customer who, though no big spender, did pay his bills. One of the girls working at the mini-hotel wiped my face with a moist cloth. Her colleague lugged my pack upstairs and offered to do my laundry. She suggested a shower and, to my surprise, nothing else.

At dusk, Eddie invited me to his home, where he had stored my motorbike during my time in Laos. Not wearing his U.S. Army hand-me-downs, the stocky interpreter showed me his life. He introduced his dog and showed off the three-room house he had built in the sparse jungle near Highway One. A pile of building materials represented Eddie's savings. He bought bricks one by one until there were enough for a new wing.

I complimented the home as well as Eddie's four children. Displeased, the interpreter snapped back, "I have many more things before 1975. My family had fifteen million dong in the bank. VC took everything. Now I have no little money for my children to go to school."

"School isn't free?"

"Here, you pay for everything. You go to school, you must

pay teachers. You go to hospital, you must pay doctors, nurses. You don't pay, they don't help you. You dead in the morning."

Eddie's tirade stirred my memory banks. I recalled thoughts gathered during my last stay in Dong Ha. Residents of the former South Vietnam hadn't negated everything Northerners told me. They had, however, shot some holes in my vision of a unified people who had put the Vietnam War behind them.

Were cynicism and misery unique to Quang Tri Province? Or would I find more of the same in the rest of southern Vietnam? Curious, and disturbingly happy to be back in Vietnam, I departed after a day of rest in Dong Ha.

My destination was Aluoi. Below Quang Tri, on the western edge of Hue Province, the town and its vicinity had figured big on the Ho Chi Minh Trail. Once a base for American Green Berets trying to uproot nearby enemy supply lines, the town was overrun by the North in the mid-1960s. Hanoi then turned Aluoi into a relay station for southbound troops and provisions.

Opinions differed as to whether the place belonged on my tour. To a man, Northern veterans included Aluoi in their outlines of the Trail. Three colonels and a general had stabbed the dot on the map during our conversations. Sung, the lieutenant who operated in the region, told me that daily traffic on the road through Aluoi reached as many as ten thousand jeeps, trucks and tanks late in the war.

The MIA team had, of course, taken a different view. I recalled how my plans to visit Aluoi had pierced the pounding of The Doors in the Apocalypse Now. Four sailors lowered their beers and stared. "Me and Elvis shot JFK" would have attracted greater stupefied derision.

Greg's quivering tone when he said, "It's a bad, bad place," should have tipped me off. The sailor wasn't kidding. He meant it when he said that Aluoi, like Death Valley, wasn't the sort of place one dropped in for tea. But because Greg wouldn't say why, I figured he was exaggerating the danger. A simple dogleg west and then south of Dong Ha, Aluoi couldn't be so bad. If it was, I would move on quickly.

For the third time, I headed west on Route 9. On my way past two former American camps, three current Vietnamese bases, and 40 kilometers of stray animals and children, I kicked myself for being a nonsmoker. Or at least for forgetting one of my father's lessons: when in Vietnam, carry cigarettes.

Dad had always done so during his stint here. As a journalist, he wanted to get close to the war. As a parent, he didn't want to get too close. To stay in the comfort zone, he stopped at every South Vietnamese roadblock, shared a smoke, and discussed the stretch ahead. More than once local soldiers contradicted Saigon's assurances that a road was secure.

For once, the condition of the road wasn't the problem. Sung had assured me that the paved route south from the Dakrong Bridge led to Aluoi. Less certain was my ability to get onto the Trail.

Duy, the head of the province's tourism outfit, was disappointed when I spurned his offer to sell me a silver ring inscribed with "U.S. Army." His eyes reignited upon hearing of my plan to go west of the Dakrong Bridge. He said that the police wouldn't let me by without a permit and a government-approved guide. Total cost: twenty dollars.

"We don't want you to get lost," Duy said.

"But I know the road."

"The police don't allow foreigners to travel in that area."

"What area?"

"That is a border area."

"But I've been there twice. And across the border once."

"The police don't want foreigners to get hurt. There are many mines and explosives in the hills."

"Is Route 9 still mined?"

"It is dangerous."

Eddie explained what Duy hadn't. Foreigners *did* need a local guide to travel past the checkpoint. He had taken tourists from France, Japan, and other countries to Khe Sanh and war sights. But the interpreter hadn't accompanied Americans west of the Dakrong Bridge. Southern veterans were forbidden to travel Route 9 in the company of their former allies.

"What do they think we're going to do?"

Twenty years of paranoia-induced rules had taught Eddie how to shrug.

There was, however, a loophole. Foreigners with visas for Laos were excluded from the escort rule. The exception had got me by the checkpoint on my way to Savannakhet. If the guards didn't notice the cancellation of my Laos permit, it might work again. Still, my odds would have been better had I some Marlboros to distribute and smoke as I approached the striped pole lowered over the road.

The checkpoint Charlies recognized me. One of the uniformed men motioned for me to park beside a windowless concrete building. A young inspector led me inside the one-room facility, seated me in a wooden chair behind a wooden table and barked his demands: "Bazzbort! Beeza!" The booty in hand, he left to log the numbers of my documents.

An older officer, his gut bursting the buttons of a pale blue shirt with red epaulets, picked his teeth and watched the work of his junior. He poured two cups of tea and lifted one to his lips without taking his eyes from me. Moving to accept the hospitality, I noticed a black hair draped over the lip of my cup. Rather than jeopardize the journey, I drank.

"Americans make war here," said the tubby officer.

"Not me." I grabbed my passport and indicated my birth date.

The answer appeared to satisfy the man running the checkpoint. My Laos visa was also convincing. Unfazed by the pile of baggage I was carrying into the border area, the cops waved goodbye.

There was no missing the exit. At the north end of the Dakrong Bridge stood a vertical block of concrete thick enough to stop a truck. The giant yellow letters printed on the red background were clear. They would have been incomprehensible had Sung not translated for me: the southbound road from this point was a national monument, the Ho Chi Minh Trail.

The first milestone said Aluoi, 65 km. Paved with Cuban funds after the war, this section of the Trail wound along ridges cut into severe mountains. High above my head a slope of broad-leafed trees glimmered in the morning sun. Below, to my right, a river snaked between mountains tangled with an unthinkably dense layer of foliage. At road level tightly packed bushes and reeds twice my height meant that straight ahead, toward imposing shoulders of green mountain, was the only option.

Screeching cicadas and a buzzing Minsk were the only regular sounds. A Vietnamese army truck and a local bus were the sum of northbound traffic. Block out a past of horrific bombing, overlook a present of crushing poverty, and ignore the possibility of a mosquito injecting a cutting-edge strain of malaria . . . and mountains of Quang Tri defined tropical paradise.

As in northern Vietnam, the sight of a foreigner brought work to a halt and locals to their feet. Children cheered as if I were Patton entering Paris. Their parents limited themselves to wide grins and economic waves. After a deep breath everybody returned to wood gathering, ground hacking, or shade sitting.

The exception to the euphoria was a shoeless peasant. She

and six others surfaced when I stopped to admire the lush picture. While the others jockeyed to watch me scribble deep thoughts, the woman kept her distance and stared at the red-faced intruder.

She didn't flinch when I moved to admire the baby boy in her arms. The infant was pocked with sores and oozing green gobs from his nostrils. I wondered about the little guy's survival odds in mountains infested with microscopic ghouls. Probably a lot better if Mom cleaned and tried her hand at washing. The woman hadn't seen a bath in weeks. Her clothes may never have been laundered. Set to lecture her on hygiene, I was silenced by the rancid cloth swaddling the baby.

The child was wrapped in an American flag. Disparate thoughts and images collided, short-circuiting my brain. After a neurological breather, I began to sort them one by one. A dirt-poor Vietnamese. On the Ho Chi Minh Trail. A road pummeled by my countrymen. Was wrapping a kid in faded Stars and Stripes. Whoa.

"Where did you find that?"

The ragged woman pointed north, toward the mountains of the DMZ. Jingoism suggested I bring the flag home, where it belonged. Pragmatism told me to move on. Toting an American flag around Vietnam probably wasn't smart. And the woman certainly didn't have anything else in which to wrap her boy. When I left empty-handed, I worried that I had made the wrong choice.

I also worried about driving alone in the mountains on a Minsk. My maps indicated there was but one town, A Dong, between Route 9 and Aluoi. The milestones made me feel better. Should I break down, there might be help in A Ngo, A Le, or A Bung.

Or I might get help from the few people I spotted along the road. At a bridge strung high above the intersection of two rivers, two men were adding a six-foot bomb casing to three similar treasures. Would Southerners be angry at the folks who dropped the bombs? Or grateful for the living my government had provided?

This dubious theory was never put to the test. In A Dong, I floored the Minsk past a white concrete building with an official crest as well as the riverside town's thatch-roofed homes. Nor did I stop in A Le. At the edge of that town a short wooden bridge led to an incline steep enough to demand first gear. For fifteen minutes the motorbike chugged up and around the bends etched into the jungle. Resting at the top, I saw only tightly packed mountains smothered with an impenetrable green blanket.

Civilization reappeared when the mountains eased into rolling hills and then a valley. Stretched like a bony finger, the flat strip was bordered to the left by green monsters and to the right by a picket fence of rock faces. Just a pop fly from Laos, farmers plowed fields while water buffalo cooled themselves in muddy rain water gathered in bomb craters ten feet across. Aluoi, the biggest town for miles, couldn't be far.

I was ahead of schedule. Not yet eleven o'clock, there looked to be ample time to venture farther south to Ashau. Known to the North as a terminus where the Trail disgorged troops into South Vietnam, a mountain near the town was known to Americans by another name. "Hamburger Hill" was the site of a Viet Cong shooting spree that killed something like 240 GIs.

I wanted to see the jungle terrain. I wanted to see what kind of place Washington had deemed worth losing hundreds of teenage soldiers and risking the lives of hundreds more. To get there, I had to pass through the "bad, bad place."

28

Reaching Everest's peak must be a letdown. The months of planning, the physical and mental challenges, the expectations of epiphanies at the top, all come to what? Two realizations: remote summits are pretty dull spots; and there's nothing to eat.

At least those were my sentiments as I rolled into Aluoi, the place I considered the culmination of my search for the Ho Chi Minh Trail. A grove of trees formed a tunnel of shade over the road into the mountain town. I passed a guesthouse and a building flying a faded Vietnamese flag. On a strip of mechanics, soda sellers, and seamstresses, I found no cooks.

A second pass revealed two girls selling baguettes stacked like cordwood. Short of options, I steered down a dirt incline and toward their shaded table. A herd stampeded to watch me wrestle the Minsk into parking position. A man in a yellow T-shirt helped me steady the overburdened bike against a pole.

When I stepped back to admire our handiwork, the helper lunged for my spare gas. I shoved him away. He lunged again. A straight arm to the shoulder persuaded the helper to stand back. He began to scream and gesticulate. I began to wonder whether Aluoi was the sort of place an American might lose it all to a xenophobic mob.

The cause of the one-man commotion was a spout of pink fuel. Strapped atop my luggage rack, the petrol can had punctured. Gas had been leaking out for . . . I didn't want to know how long. The helper breathed down my neck as I squatted to unfasten the rubber cords securing the container. Hot and flustered, I shoved him back, perhaps too forcefully.

The next moment a heavy hand fell on my right shoulder. Irritability turned to anger; Vietnam had worn thin my tolerance for being pushed and shoved and grabbed and groped. My arm flew backward and slapped away the intrusive hand. The grip returned, firmer than before.

Fists clenching, I whirled to stare down the . . . policeman. The green hat and baggy doorman's uniform worn by Vietnam's finest were unmistakable. Holding the hand I had slapped, the cop stared at me, more in puzzlement than pain. What was the penalty for striking a Vietnamese officer? Imprisonment in a submerged, rat-infested cage seemed less than impossible.

Nghia 0182, the name and photo-badge number of the officer, didn't disagree. Enraged, the little man in plastic sandals tilted his face up toward mine, furrowed his eyebrows, and barked in Vietnamese. Missing the words, I understood slaps of his palm to mean "Let's see some papers. Pronto!" I was busted, though my crime was unclear.

I fumbled with my pockets and smiled: the tactic that had delivered me from previous brushes with the law as policemen concluded that I was too inept to be dangerous, too affable to arrest. But Nghia 0182 didn't go for that act. The longer I stalled, the harder the diminutive cop slapped his impatient palm.

"I. Vietnamese. No speak. Sorry."

Words that had served me well only angered the little fella. When he yanked on my shirt as if to drag me onto the road, I conceded round one and handed over a laminated photocopy of my passport. Nghia 0182 retreated to show the document to his partner, who was idling a red Honda scooter on the road. When the arresting officer returned, he pointed to me, my motorbike, and the road leading north. The constable was proposing I follow him.

I pleaded my case: "I'm a tourist passing through Aluoi en route to Hue, former seat of the Nguyen dynasty and a very popular spot with foreigners such as myself."

The cop's rotting grin gave way to an angry glare. He reiterated his interest in taking me to Aluoi's renowned North End, where I presumed we would find its famed police station and torture chamber. I gave up once it was clear that the policeman wouldn't. For the first time in weeks the Minsk started on the first pump of the starter. The red Honda led the way north.

Nghia 0182 was the first Vietnamese policeman I had seen armed with anything more potent than a billy club. Laughably small by American standards, his little pistol sparked visions of a quick shakedown and summary execution in a remote rice paddy. I toyed with the idea of making a run for it. That thought evaporated when the policemen turned onto the dirt drive leading to the building flying Vietnam's Star-no-Stripe flag.

Due process was dispensed from a row of padlocked doors. The partner, whose photo badge identified him as Binh 0592, led me to the last room on the left. But for the steel bars on the window, the room was more college dorm than jailhouse cell. There were two wardrobes, two desks, two chairs, and, in the rear corner, a bed beneath a mosquito net. My seat on a bench faced the only decoration, a girlie calendar.

Binh 0592 was older than his partner. The gray whiskers

flecking his dark stubble placed him close to fifty years old. His lined, bagged eyes looked hard at the photocopy of my passport, which he flipped over and back as if something were missing. With his hothead partner out of the room, I appealed to the veteran's sense of justice.

"I'm a tourist. Dong Ha, Aluoi, Hue."

Binh 0592 grunted but didn't lift his head. Nor did he flinch when I stood and walked out the door to prove to myself that I wasn't being held prisoner. Indeed, I felt more abducted than arrested. No hands had been cuffed, no rights read, no charges pressed. My sack was still on my shoulder, my motorbike keys in my pocket.

So was my wallet. Why hadn't the police simply demanded some cash and let me go? Had I misread the situation? Having failed at bribery, I wondered whether it was time to try again.

Binh 0592 didn't give me a chance. He ambled into another office. Eavesdropping, I heard voices jabbering in Vietnamese. "Dong Ha," "Hue," and "California" were the words that jumped out. I saw Nghia 0182 walk out to my motorcycle and copy down the license plate number. Then he asked for my visa. Having neglected to make a photocopy, I reluctantly handed over the real McCoy. Inside the office, somebody was dialing a telephone. Higher-ups were being informed

An hour later the partners reconvened in my holding cell.

"I'm going to Hue," I said.

"No, you're not," said their silently shaking heads.

As if to prove the point, Nghia 0182 pulled a chair over to the desk and pushed me into it from my standing position. Already seated, Binh 0592 spoke to me in Vietnamese. It took five minutes for him to grasp that I hadn't understood a word of his lecture. The older officer repeated his explanation, this time drawing a map as he spoke. He placed Lao Bao and Dong Ha at the end points of Route 9. The Dakrong Bridge was the midpoint. From there he drew a line to Aluoi. The last addition was the stretch of coastal Highway One running from Dong Ha down to Hue. I grinned at the success of the communication.

Binh 0592 frowned. He pointed to me and crossed a fat X over the route I had taken. It was then, ninety minutes into my detention, that I first considered the possibility that I had actually done something wrong. Maybe this was no mix-up. Maybe these were not greedy cops looking to supplement their meager incomes. Maybe I was in real trouble.

Having established my crime, the officer in charge moved on to the punishment. I made peace with the idea of spending —or doing—some time in Aluoi. With luck, my mosquito repellent would outlast my sentence.

It would. Binh 0592 ran his finger along his handmade map. The wrinkled digit started at Aluoi, moved north to the Dakrong Bridge, east to Dong Ha, and then south along Highway One to Hue.

"You want me to go back?"

Binh 0592 nodded.

I appealed the nonsensical decision. If my crime was traveling on a restricted road, why send me back the same way?

I reached for my phrase book, which was in the hands of Nghia 0182. The little cop resisted my tug, then ripped the book free with Doberman ferocity. He cast a glare that said "You want a pistol whipping, boy?" but gave up the prize when his partner ruled in my favor.

"Understand," I said, pointing to the word.

Binh 0592 smiled. Nghia 0182 fumed.

"But check this out," I continued.

Writing numbers on the segments of the map, I explained the obvious. It was 65 kilometers from Aluoi to the bridge and another 45 or so to Dong Ha. From there I was looking at another 100 or so to Hue. Let's call it an even 200 kilometers to my destination. Binh 0592 nodded. Nghia 0182 recaptured my phrase book, which meant I couldn't look up the word for "shortcut."

"Now say I go this way." I connected two dots, Aluoi and Hue, which were linked by the thinnest of red lines on one of my maps. "I get to the same place and only need to drive 60 kilometers." I underlined 60 twice.

Binh 0592 shook his head and crossed a big X over my route.

"Binh, cut me some slack here. So I had strayed into a border area, threatened national security, and destabilized the Hanoi regime. Hang me, shoot me, but don't make me back-track when there's a direct road to Hue."

My English babbling made Binh 0592 blink hard. He rose and walked to one of the wardrobes. Some rummaging yielded three forms and a green, pocket-size paperback bearing the red and yellow national emblem; it was a government document. Lest I underappreciate the weight of the moment, Nghia 0182 pointed to the words on the cover: *Phap Lenh*. Vietnamese for capital crimes?

The senior partner leafed through the booklet until he reached page 114. His lips moved as he read to himself. He turned the page so the print faced me and indicated Section 1C. There, in plain print, was the black-letter law.

Because the document wasn't a menu, the words meant nothing to me. I did understand the numbers—"twenty thousand dong" and "two hundred thousand dong"—buried in the text of Section 1C. My guess that these were fines was not wrong: Binh 0592 pointed to the larger figure and then to me. This was, after all the ado, about money.

The equivalent of twenty dollars was probably a bargain to

get out of Aluoi. Would I rather pay two? Naturally. My counteroffer was twenty thousand dong. The lowball bid infuriated Nghia 0182.

He slammed his palm on the table and shot me a glare that said, "No way we're going through all this trouble for a lousy twenty thousand dong." Grabbing the office pen from his partner, he wrote four hundred thousand dong on the edge of our map. He folded his arms and glanced at his holstered pistol.

"You win. Two hundred thousand dong."

Nghia 0182 flew into a spitting rage. Bonfires burned in his eyes as he screamed at the insolent prisoner. As I rose to right the balance of body language, the little man pushed down on my shoulder. Fanny on chair, eyes on pistol, I was too far from an American embassy not to be scared.

"One million dong," shouted Nghia 0182.

"Don't have that much."

"Four million dong!"

I kept quiet, in part to keep down the price of freedom and in part to catch my breath from the dizzying ascent from two to four hundred dollars, a large sum for me and more than a year's salary for a Vietnamese cop. The shouting and gesticulating didn't seem to distract Binh 0592 from the task of filling blanks on the forms.

"Four million dong," repeated Nghia 0182.

"I don't have that much."

"One million dong."

I still believed that twenty dollars went a long way in rural Vietnam.

"Four hundred thousand," said the officer.

To justify the amount, Nghia 0182 decided that I had violated Section 1D as well as Section 1C, two fines times two hundred thousand dong. There was no telling how many charges these guys could trump up at two hundred thousand dong a pop. As I couldn't appeal to a higher authority, the pair in green pajamas held all the power. But I had all the cash.

Nghia 0182 upped the ante. "Give us four hundred thousand dong or I'm taking your motorcycle," he said with a lucid combination of words and gestures.

I credited the bad cop with spotting my weakness. Did he know how scary Aluoi looked to a Westerner? How obvious was my fear of mosquitoes carrying Japanese encephalitis? Were two out of a series of three required injections enough to keep my brain from hemorrhaging from the infection?

Mentally caving in to the demand for forty dollars reduced the drama of the final half hour of my internment. Binh 0592 continued his scribbling on second and third forms. He asked occasional questions—age, rank, passport number—but was otherwise consumed by the task. Having no appetite for paperwork, Nghia 0182 lost interest in the proceedings. He left the room after placing my papers on the desk.

I snatched the documents with no protest from Binh 0592. Instead, he asked me to sign his completed forms, presumably some sort of confession that I hated Robert McNamara, William Westmoreland, and Jane Fonda. The officer took back the papers. Then he looked at my wallet on his desk.

I emptied the contents, small notes totaling one hundred thousand dong and a ten-dollar bill. Seeing no more, the officer accepted the payoff with a smile. Then he traced the shortcut from Aluoi to Hue with his finger and nodded. As far as he was concerned, that kind of dough bought the right to drive any place I pleased.

The arresting officers and four local urchins gathered to watch me leave. Their fond expressions were those of a proud family watching a son leave for college. All showed genuine concern when the Minsk didn't respond to the kick-starter. The delay gave Nghia 0182 time for second thoughts. Arms waving, jaw jabbering, he wanted me to stop.

I reached for the twenty-dollar note in my left pocket. I hated this little guy. Extortion didn't bother me. Mean spirits did. A vision of a reunion, one involving an Uzi and grenades, began to take shape. Nghia 0182 thrust a sheet of paper under my chin.

"What's this?" I asked.

"A receipt."

29

Captivity killed my appetite for Hamburger Hill.
My other plans were also scrapped. I dropped the idea of looking around the Ashau Valley. Nor would I consider spending the night in Aluoi; the cops weren't getting a second chance to jingle my change. I wanted safety and civilization in Hue.

A monument applauding the achievement of the Trail marked the start of the 60-kilometer, east-west stretch. Thunder rumbled as I directed the Minsk up a single lane of crumbling asphalt. Gathering clouds darkened the sky as the road turned to jagged stones. There being no shelter, the only course was to continue to twist up the tunnel cut into the mountain foliage.

At the peak, the angle of descent nearly tipped me over the handlebars. To the left, the mountain fell sharply toward a narrow stream. To the right, the slope was too severe to climb without ropes. Where one slope ended the next began, their proximity forming pointy Vs where the hills met. Everywhere I looked mountains shot up like rounded fists of green.

I thought of an American veteran I had met in Dong Ha. Bill and a van of vets had brought their wives for a tour of their personal war zones. Having fought along the Aluoi–Hue road, Bill had a suggestion. "Look around for old firebases. They're the hills that go unnaturally flat on top."

The former encampments weren't evident to me. The tree-covered peaks all looked pretty round. Those that were marginally flatter looked ludicrously isolated. The identification problem helped me deny that the Pentagon had thought it a good idea to station privates from Peoria in this evil terrain.

A near wipeout in a rocky puddle returned my focus to the road. An accident could be my end. How many hours, or days, would it take for another vehicle to come to the aid of a man with a broken leg? What insects would have chewed his hide by then? That's when a third threat presented itself.

A pitchfork of lightning rocketed down from a horizon growing grayer by the minute. I discounted hopes of finding cover. An hour had passed since the last sign of human life. Rather than travel home in an ashtray, I prepared to ditch the bike and hide under the next concrete bridge.

Fat raindrops and smooth pavement appeared simultaneously. A tiny valley opened between two mountains disappearing into a ferocious black cloud. Skidding to a halt under the eaves of a sturdy wooden shack, I watched jagged thunderbolts stab at the valley floor.

The darkest of the clouds had passed a half hour later. The clearing unveiled two rows of rounded peaks, one behind the next, to the east. Hue, I guessed, lay just beyond the second set.

A climb through a gap in the nearer mountains forced me to face my error. Peeking up behind the next wall of green was another row of hills. I gave up speculation after several rounds of expectation and disappointment.

"How far to Hue?" I asked six men gathered by the road.

"Thirty-seven kilometers," said a spokesman after consulting his colleagues. "You. American?"

"Yes."

"You want buy bomb?"

The spokesman drew my attention to a row of twenty bomb casings and mortar shells. I passed. Farther east, a gang of three armed with a metal detector was digging up similar debris in the rain-softened ground. Tempted to feel for myself the excitement of looking for scrap metal, I opted to keep my limbs.

Flat ground and motorcycle traffic suggested I was emerging from the belly of the green monster. A road sign—Hue 13 km—confirmed it. Minutes later the road forked. A coin toss, heads, directed me to the left.

I should have called tails. The road dead-ended at a river a half mile across. Late afternoon sun shone golden on the water. Long boats chugged silently in both directions. Children were swimming and women were washing. What the idyllic view didn't include was a crossing. I turned to double back.

A teenager ankle deep in water beckoned for me to drive down an incline to his spot. Named Hai, he said Hue was across the river, where he said he could take me. How? The young tout pointed to his "ferry," a giant canoe maybe thirty feet long and no wider than four across.

"You want to put a motorbike in that?"

"Of course, every Vietnamese people do," he said. Just then a woman in a flowing white *ao dai* presented her Honda scooter for Hai and another teenager to lift onto the makeshift barge. "We can put four motorbikes if we like. And many bicycles."

Roughly eleven hours on the road had numbed my ability to think for myself. Just as well, considering the trouble my contrarian bent had caused. While Hai loaded my motorbike onto his canoe, I envisioned the worst-case scenario. It didn't look too bad.

So what if the Minsk sank to the bottom of the Perfume River? In my hand were a plane ticket, a passport, and cab fare to Saigon. A hot meal in Hong Kong was just forty-eight hours away. Another sixteen and I could be in a California hot tub.

"How much for the crossing?"

"Ten thousand dong."

"How much for Vietnamese people?"

"Eight thousand. American must pay ten."

"How much to tip my bike into the drink?"

Unsure how to react, Hai lowered his head and shoved off with an oar twice his height. The load of two motorbikes, three bicycles, and seven passengers wobbled with each stroke of the oversized paddle. Straddling the boat's edge, the front tires of the motorbikes bobbed in and out of the water. The owner of the Honda looked unworried.

I mimicked her calm. Say the Minsk did reach the far bank. Its job would change. The prospect of breakdowns still scared me a bit. Another arrest more so. However, both fears paled compared to repeating the knee-buckling isolation I had felt when alone in the mountainous jungle. Avoiding a repeat overrode other priorities. The ride down the Ho Chi Minh Trail was over.

I was turning tourist. The job description included frequenting "places of beauty," gorging on indigenous delicacies, and, above all, sticking to Highway One. For once my timing was good: all three could be found in Hue.

The city of 200,000 was a tourist's paradise. It had history. Built in the seventeenth century, Hue's citadel became Vietnam's capital when, early in the nineteenth century, a French-backed prince named Nguyen Anh rolled back a rebellion and declared himself emperor. His successors, known as the Nguyen

Dynasty, ruled Vietnam's roost until 1945, when Bao Dai handed over the keys to Ho Chi Minh.

More than thirty years later, Hue leaped into the American vocabulary. On January 31, 1968, Hanoi launched simultaneous attacks on every major city and town in South Vietnam, which was celebrating *Tet*, or lunar new year. Repelled quickly in most places, the infamous Tet offensive lingered in Hue. The city wasn't liberated until the end of February. By then, roughly ten thousand bodies—a third of them civilians shot, beaten, or buried alive by the Viet Cong—had piled up.

The attack didn't wipe out Hue's splendor. The region was riddled with elaborate tombs and delicate pagodas. Sights came with exotic labels, such as Palace of Supreme Peace and Forbidden Purple City. The right kind of eye could spy the remnants of imperial pomp and evoke a vision of another era, a time when men were mandarins and women were concubines and eunuchs were neither.

The place had a sensual appeal as yet unspoiled by the charmless upgrades that were smothering Hanoi. Not yet reduced to a sewer, the Perfume River was a shimmering flow where sampans chugged. On either bank, broad, leafy avenues were still dominated by bicycles. Fathers held hands with their sons. Couples coupled.

Hue was the sort of place that sent Condé Nast travelers scrambling for a thesaurus. Purple became mauve. Green turned to emerald. An article in the glossy magazine told me that local girls didn't walk in Hue. Nor did they stroll. They fluttered like butterflies drawn to flower beds.

In Hue, past-present bridges were a dong a dozen. The city had retained its historic status as a center of learning. Visitors could stand outside Quoc Hoc Secondary School, Vietnam's answer to Eton, and speculate which of the teenagers might fill the shoes of previous graduates. That kid with the switchblade, was he the next General Giap? What about the skinny one with the peach-fuzzed chin? Another Ho Chi Minh?

Gripping a guidebook, I set off one early morning to devour the sights and drink the ambiance. A left turn out the door of my hotel on the river's right bank put me on Le Loi, an avenue named after the fifteenth-century general who cleared his homeland of Chinese invaders. Crossing to the left bank, I followed the river's edge to Thien Mu Pagoda.

The seven-layer tower resembled a giant wedding cake. Nice, I thought, but not as interesting as the vintage Austin sedan parked behind it. In 1963 the car had carried to Saigon a monk who torched himself to protest the anti-Buddhist tactics of President Diem, a rabid Catholic. The act elicited no sympathy from the President's sister-in-law, who said, "If the Buddhists wish to have another barbecue, I will be glad to supply the gasoline and the match."

A few months before my visit, an out-of-towner named Ho (no relation) had come to the pagoda, doused himself with petrol, and lit a match. He spent his last breaths chanting, "Buddha, Buddha." Already concerned about disgruntled monks, the government portrayed the suicide as the product of drug addiction, a marriage on the rocks, and possibly AIDS. Having established the motive as nonreligious, officials proceeded to arrest four of the monks in Hue.

Back in town, I entered the Citadel, a walled, moated fortress. Another set of towering walls, these protecting the Imperial City, lay dead ahead. With the summit of the leisure program in my cross hairs, my body and soul organized a walk-out.

They had two grievances. One was the heat, which had topped a hundred degrees. My head trouble was harder to explain. Having dropped the search for the Trail, I was on vacation. I was in the hub of Vietnamese history and culture, and I was bored rigid.

Cooled by a coconut's juice, I faced the facts. I was unable to relax and enjoy the sights. Buildings, no matter how history-steeped or architecturally endowed, didn't spin my wheels. True, liberal arts grads were *supposed* to appreciate ancient civilizations, foreign cultures, and public television. I just didn't. A bitter pill, there was no choice but to swallow it.

Another coconut helped. As did the friendly vendor, who invited me to join him in his shaded beach chairs. Quang was his name, though he introduced himself like this: "I know everything about the war. My father was a colonel fighting for the Americans."

I suggested his father had fought *for* South Vietnam, or at least *against* North Vietnam. Such distinctions meant nothing to the thirty-one-year-old merchant.

"My father was killed in 1970, but to some people he is still alive."

"What do you mean?"

"I applied to attend university after high school. I was qualified. But they checked my name and the government rejected me because my father was an officer in the army."

Barred from ordinary benefits, Quang knew his abilities were wasting. His brother had taken a different tack. Stripped of his job in 1975, he fled by boat to Malaysia. Three months later he emigrated to Toronto, where he saved enough to send for his mother and sister. The cash ran out before Quang's turn. If there was a bright side, it was that Hanoi's discrimination lasted just one generation. His sons' future wouldn't be linked to coconut sales.

"Can you tell me something about America?"

"Sure. What?"

"I can't understand Vietnamese boys in America. I read that some of them carry guns and don't go to school. Why would they do that?"

I had no explanation for the appeal of street gangs.

"They can go to school and the U.S. Government pays for it. If I am in the U.S. I study and study and study."

30

"Do not marry a Hanoi girl," warned Colonel Luc.

"Why not?"

"Because you are going to Hue."

"Which means . . . ?"

"Hue has the most beautiful girls in Vietnam. You must marry a Hue girl."

Luc was right. The one sight that never aged was the women of Hue. From the girls to the grannies, local ladies left mouths gaping and tongues lolling. After surveying the royal tombs, the fish market, and the bank, I decided their reputation was based on more than looks.

Hue's women had style. Their wardrobes were ruled by traditional *ao dai*. Sun hats decorated with flowers and white gloves which reached the biceps comprised the rest of the seductive uniform. Though not required, or needed, makeup and nail polish were common. Whatever the combination, the sum resembled . . . fluttering butterflies.

Maybe sightseer status wouldn't be so bad. To be sure, I settled in a shady lawn chair with views of the river and Le Loi. For three heat-hazed afternoons I sipped *nuoc mia*, fresh-pressed sugar cane juice with a dash of lime, and alternately watched the flows of river and human traffic.

The local government made it clear that looking was safer than touching. Glenn-the-vet had introduced me to Vietnam officialdom's fear of AIDS. Hanoi had looked at Thailand, where prostitution and promiscuity created a lethal epidemic, and declared AIDS to be a "social evil." Prudish Northerners fought a silent guerrilla war to prevent the disease.

Hue was in full battle gear. Spread throughout the city, multicolored billboards explained the danger in words and pictures. One poster showed a junkie shooting up. Another made clear that homosexual relationships were a no-no. A third targeted foreigners. Judging by the picture, a woman rubbing the back of a white male, the caption must have read, "Death wish? Do it with a Westerner."

Not that I should expect any physical contact with local women. A drinks vendor outside my guesthouse made that perfectly clear. Dressed in purple pajamas, the twenty-five-year-old stroked the fuzz on my forearm as I bought bottled water. When I returned the innocent gesture, she jumped back as if shocked by a live wire. Purple PJs pointed to an empty ring finger to say, "First, marry me. Then we'll talk."

So I went to a restaurant on the left bank of the Perfume River expecting no more than supper. Even that could be hard to get in Vietnam, a country with no translation for "The customer is always right." Not that I blamed them. The listless, clumsy crews of restaurants were victims of a system geared toward filling quotas, not providing service. For years, staff had had no incentive to "wrap it to go."

I fell in lust with the waitress who led me by the hand from the entrance to a stool at an upstairs table. En route I noticed the black heels supporting equine calves, which were mostly hidden by a flowered sundress. By holding back an explosion of black hair, a matching headband accentuated her lofted cheekbones. Rings on six fingers, hooped earrings and a gold watch finished the portrait. But for an accident of birthplace, she might be catwalking in Paris instead of hostessing in Hue.

Her brown eyes dancing, the waitress made a grand gesture of placing a menu before me. When taking my order, she made light of the language barrier with comically elaborate gestures. After fifteen minutes of watching her repeat the performance for other diners, I understood the source of her talent. The waitress was mute.

The Frenchwoman seated at my table, the Loner's & Loser's Table, knew as little as I about the speechless. A journalist, she was quick to note my fascination with the waitress. Embarrassed to have been caught, I expressed my admiration for the unusual attention she paid to customers.

"Especially the men," said *la journaliste*.

That perception proved correct. As I rose to pay, the waitress grinned and mimed matchmaking Patricia and me. I shook my head. Her next charade was also clear.

The waitress pointed to herself, then to me. She slowly breaststroked the air. She held up ten fingers. Her. Me. Swim. At ten o'clock. I nodded a little too eagerly. Then I went back to my guesthouse for a cold shower.

Not the self-pinching type, I dissected the night ahead. Moonbeams would guide a Minsk, a man, and a woman to a secluded clearing along the Perfume River. Or maybe all the way to the South China Sea. Keen to rinse off the sweat from a night's work, the waitress would drop the dress from her shoulders and wade into the water. The silhouette of her sculpted figure would persuade me to follow suit.

My date was waiting on the curb at ten. Her lipstick was

fresh, her eyes newly shadowed in blue. But the waitress couldn't get out of work. Could I wait? Definitely. Sitting with me at an empty table, she brought me a chilled beer, spooned chunks of mango into my mouth, and "told" her story with the help of a photo album.

She was the product of a mute father and a talking mother. Of her six sisters, five were also unable to speak. Looking around, I realized that the all-female staff had all along been communicating with a homegrown system of hand signals and facial expressions.

Her father was the villain. After enduring years of beatings, his wife upped and left, which the waitress explained by pretending to cut the middle-aged man out of a family photo. Marital discord became commercial competition when Mom opened a restaurant beside Pop's. Between good food and the gimmick of silent servers, business boomed. His daughters had all followed their mother, so the father instructed his restaurant's staff to boost sales by playing dumb.

A ruckus on the sidewalk punctuated the tale. A one-armed man and another with all of his limbs restrained a third man, a drunk. A dozen bystanders gathered to watch the rival restaurant owners grapple. The mother shrieked at her ex-husband, who was shaking a silent fist.

The range of our "conversation" was surprising. Her honed creativity meant the waitress could communicate better than the most vocal Vietnamese monoglot. She explained that her older sister's son could speak. I learned that she had lost a chance to go to France when her mother tore up a plane ticket sent by another admirer. Half in jest, we planned for her to accompany me to Danang, the next day's destination.

Perceiving my impatience, the waitress offered a plan. The restaurant closed at midnight. If I returned to my guesthouse she would cycle across the river for our moonlight swim. There was, however, one proviso. With a praying motion and the fingers of one hand she insisted that we be back by 5 A.M. A devout Buddhist, she had to be at the pagoda.

As I made my hopeful exit, the one-armed man asked for a lift. I hesitated, but decided my fear was groundless. With one limb securing his place on the back of a moving motorbike, the guy wouldn't have another one free to wield a knife. Between playing taxi to an amputee hitchhiker and awaiting a mute lover, my life had somehow turned into a Fellini flick.

At midnight a strobing streetlight was the only movement on the street outside the guesthouse. Antsy, I thought the next sign of life would be the gentle pedaling of a statuesque skinny-dipper. A bicycle did appear.

The rider was Purple PJs. Recognizing the fresh foreigner she had lectured on the evils of premarital sex, the soda seller stopped on my dim-lit street corner. She squatted beside me and demanded my name, age, and nationality. I answered quickly and told her to beat it.

Purple PJs stuck around. Speaking softly in Vietnamese, she rubbed the hair on my arms once again. She began to giggle. Further scrutiny brought her eyes to rest on my chest. Lifting my shirt, she manually explored a mass of chest hair unrivaled by local men. The sensation was not unpleasant. Nonetheless, I lifted the probing hands from my fuzzy pecs lest the waitress, now twenty minutes overdue, arrive and get the wrong impression.

"Let's go inside," said Purple PJs.

"You've gotta get outa here."

Suddenly, everything went black. Why couldn't I see? Had I been clubbed? Drugged? Had an overdose of libido short-circuited my senses? When my whiplashed brain caught up with events, I realized that Hue had been hit by a power failure.

Purple PJs thought faster than I. Moments after the darkness fell the woman sprang from her squat and straddled my outstretched legs. Hands gripped the back of my head and an inquisitive tongue sought a meeting with mine. Not quite a mugging, I was being mauled on the sidewalk by a woman who had warned she didn't shake hands on the first date.

I had to think. Where was the waitress? Would she brave the blackout or wait until the lights returned? Would that be a matter of minutes or hours? In the meantime, what should I do about this nymphomaniac on top of me?

Purple PJs wasn't subtle about *her* wishes. The sexual Magellan tugged my elbow toward the river and the cover of bushes. As devoted as ever to the waitress, I considered dropping my requirement—just this once—of developing intellectual and emotional bonds before proceeding to the other phases of a relationship. In other words, the bushes beckoned.

The MIA team had told about some Americans who had faced a choice similar to mine. Stationed not far from Hue in the late 1960s, the deadliest years of the war, the GIs were part of a unit ordered to set up a jungle ambush along a route frequented by the Viet Cong. The platoon was ready to spring the trap by nightfall.

A lithe Vietnamese woman distracted three of the soldiers. Still stunning when interviewed twenty-five years later, the seductress described luring the men from their positions. Buried deep in the jungle, her home was billed as the center of a three-ring carnal circus.

More like a carnage circus. The Marines followed the woman's unabashed lead and stripped naked. Whether the gang bang ever got under way wasn't clear to the speechless interviewers. What was made explicit was that the woman's uncle emerged from the bushes and placed a bullet in the skull of each soldier. The two Viet Cong then buried the bodies, for which they hoped to be paid a tidy sum by the Pentagon.

"Dumb fucks," said the sailor who told the tale.

Worried that the same might be said about me, I retired before the power returned or the waitress showed up.

31

South of Hue, the Truong Son Mountains jut out from Vietnam's long, curved spine. The section of Highway One that twists up and over the obstruction is called *Deo Hai Van*, or Pass of the Ocean Clouds.

Shopping for maps in Hanoi, I had found the capital's top dealer set up on a sidewalk near the central lake. He sold me two of his best. Because neither described road conditions, I outlined my projected course and awaited comments. The merchant had one. He stabbed his finger on the Hai Van Pass and said, "That road is very accidental."

Sure enough, the steep incline and hairpin turns put local steering skills to the test. Among those who failed was the handler of the DeSoto truck which veered into my lane during its downhill run. Uphill vehicles were nearly as dangerous: drivers tended to roll backward while shifting gears. Near the top, a line of vehicles was stacked bumper to bumper behind another hazard. A pile of cases, sacks, and bikes had slid off the roof of a bus and into a Rubik's tangle.

The passengers screamed at the bus boy. Other drivers

blasted horns at the passengers. I steered around the whole mess.

A gang of teenagers chased me down as I slowed at the peak for a breather. No biker groupies, they suspected an overheated foreigner might need cigarettes, a Coke, or both. Overwhelmed by hands pressing goodies against my face, I took refuge under a sugar-cane juicer's umbrella.

"You're American," said a man sharing the shade. Before I could confirm he continued. "You bought your motorcycle in Hanoi. You will take it to Saigon and try to sell it."

The man was dead right. But how?

Serene, aged around fifty, and wearing a baseball cap, Ban had been watching Americans since the age of fifteen. That was when a military officer in Danang, his hometown and my destination, offered a job to an eager lad living near the U.S. base. Ban started out shining shoes. Later he was promoted to selling sodas. Hard work and good English earned him respect, which he used to wangle carpentry work for his father.

The good life ended when the Viet Cong captured Danang in early 1975. He moved to a village where for fifteen years he had "nothing to do." Then *doi moi* created hope. He began making daily 10-kilometer trips to the 500-meter peak to intercept foreign traffic.

"More businessmen will be coming here now that U.S. embargo is lifted. They will need help from someone who can speak English and Vietnamese. I will meet the right one and ask for a job."

Ban fell silent so I could make him an offer. When none materialized, he handed me the card of a hotel that paid a commission for referrals. Mobbed again while leaving the rest stop, I was relieved to be clear of the hard sell.

The tactics at the Pass were subtle compared to standard

practice in downtown Danang. Ban's hotel demanded ten dollars per room, five dollars per load of laundry. Both prices halved when I noted the sign saying the room rate was fifty thousand dong, under five dollars. When the well-coifed receptionist tried to even the score by demanding that amount for parking, I checked into the Danang Hotel, a crumbling residence formerly inhabited by GIs.

Danang is the place where the first Marines splashed ashore. In time, tens of thousands of Americans called the coastal city "home." Many more knew it as an R and R spot just a short hop from the front. For current leisure options, I consulted my guidebook. There were museums dedicated to Ho Chi Minh and Cham sculpture. Another suggestion, China Beach, carried more appeal.

Across the Han River from the city, the stretch of sand had been Nirvana to war-weary soldiers, who were helicoptered in for a few hours of burgers, beers, and other fun. The Americans had been displaced. Along the southbound road I passed a unit of army rookies learning to march in formation near a field of petrol storage tanks. An air base, identifiable by immense half tubes of concrete that had once housed fighter jets, was a ghost town.

China Beach was nearly as deserted. Locals hawking "China Beach" baseball caps and other trinkets were the sole signs of life on the site of countless beach games. The China Beach Hotel looked dead. So I collected my motorbike from the China Beach Parking Lot where, in addition to a parking fee, I was shaken down for an extra buck for "watching motorbike."

(Only later did I discover that *this* China Beach was a fraud. The real McCoy, the place where American soldiers frolicked, lay several kilometers to the north. To attract guests and dollars, the government-owned hotel has co-opted the famous label for its less distinguished shoreline.)

The full-court pressure on my pocket picked up. Outside the former American Consulate, a square, colonial building reduced to a South Bronx tenement, a skeletal man tottered his bicycle to a stop at my feet. He didn't give me time to ask the whereabouts of his left arm. With his right one, he thrust a handmade business card at me. For a fee, he would rent me a bike, be my guide, or be my friend.

A block away, in a marketplace built of concrete, a woman grabbed my passing elbow. One by one she showed me bootlegged bottles of Johnnie Walker Scotch, Gordon's Gin, and Stolichnaya Vodka. Wandering aisles of T-shirts, golf caps, and cloth bolts, I watched listless vendors jerk to life upon sighting a foreign face. Their attention-getting chant—"You. You."—followed me everywhere.

The guidebook suggested a visit to the Marble Mountains, five stone hills just north of the phony China Beach. Some contained Buddhist and Confucian shrines. One had housed a Viet Cong field hospital during the war. All were recommended by locals as "places of beauty."

That, I soon learned, was Vietnamese for tourist trap. Three girls no older than thirteen gathered to help me park. The boldest asked my nationality. "America" drew rapid-fire responses.

"Totally awesome," said the bold one.

"No pain, no gain," cried her sister.

"Don't worry. Be happy," instructed a third urchin.

The trio designated themselves my guides. Traipsing in my wake as I clambered along stone steps and concrete paths that snaked through the tightly packed parabolas, they introduced the sights.

"Here you can see Buddhas, one sleeping, one sitting."

"Here you can see Shiva. Over one thousand years old."

"Here is the windy cave. Two years ago one Vietnamese girl fall thirty feet and die here."

Pilgrims flocked to the shrines during full moons and religious holidays. It was for them, as well as for the daily inflow of tourists, that a corps of beggars lay in wait. A ragged woman sought donations in an upturned rice hat. A man who had lost both eyes begged ten feet from another blind man. A one-legged man leaned on a crutch and held out a palm. How had they clambered into position?

At the end of the tour my guides produced handfuls of Buddhas, elephants, and wise men carved in marble, jade, and wood. Their sales pitch—"You buy one souvenir we very happy, very lucky"—was as resistible as their wares. But stiffing the girls, who had amused and informed me, seemed unfair.

I proffered a dollar. The bold one looked offended. I doubled the sum. Her sister shook her head and held out a wooden wise man for my reconsideration. Okay, I'd make it four. Urchin number three explained: "We no take money. You buy one souvenir we very happy, very lucky."

I wanted all the happiness and luck in the world for them. What I didn't want was a trinket. Or the burden of carrying it. Or the guilt from dumping a handcrafted piece. To save their face and my conscience, we compromised. I bought a Buddha, which immediately became my gift to the happy, lucky girls.

The all-female staff at the Danang Hotel had no such qualms about taking my cash. Their problem was devising new ways to persuade men to loosen their purse strings. It was the laundress who tipped me off.

She came to my third-floor room to collect my clothes. Dressed in a white smock, the cleaner paused in my doorway.

Her soft stare belied an interest in something dirtier than laundry.

"You like lady?" she asked.

"More than the alternative."

Confused, possibly hurt, but definitely rejected, the laundress sulked down the hallway linoleum. That didn't deter her colleagues. Shortly after turning in, I heard a light patter on my door. A message from the front desk? A chambermaid come to turn down my bed? On the threshold I found a heavy, fortyish woman in a black tank top and aqua running shorts.

"You like massage?"

"Uh . . . no thanks."

"You like boom-boom?"

Boom-boom? I could guess what she meant. But under the circumstances, I couldn't imagine its appeal.

Another knock followed fifteen minutes later. Now annoyed, I found a sparkling smile belonging to a girl barely old enough to buy her own six-pack. Hair moussed and lips sticked, she looked ready for a night on the town. Or a quiet one at home.

"You like massage?"

"No . . . thanks."

Unconvinced, she demonstrated on my bare chest. "Massage?"

"Not tonight," I said. "Very tired."

Like the rest of Danang, the masseuse hated the thought of a big fish getting away. She stepped back one pace to give me a better perspective on her product line. Hoping to lure a buyer with catchy advertising, she tilted her head slightly to the right, flashed her pearly smile, and lifted her dress clear of a panty-less crotch.

"Maybe later?"

"Maybe" was my way of saying "Good night."

32

Danang taught me tolerance for the persistent hectoring of peddlers. In fact, I came to respect the determination of the young trinketeers, bootleggers, and prostitutes who shadowed me. Growing up in a land of no opportunity hadn't dimmed their innate will to grab for the brass ring.

The desperate pall that followed Danang's older residents was harder to stomach. At least once an hour a lifeless beggar would stand before me, hands or rice hat held open for alms. My standard donation of two thousand dong, twenty cents, never brightened the faces of the paupers, who turned and shuffled off to nowhere.

Just as sad was the regular sight of men who twenty-plus years before had been stripped of their limbs and futures. I saw every permutation of amputee. No legs in wheelchair. No legs without wheelchair. Prosthetics. Crutches. One empty sleeve. Two empty sleeves. Nobody ever pointed an accusatory finger at me. Still, I felt a niggling responsibility.

The reason eluded me. Northerners, not Americans, had fired the weapons which destroyed these men. Then again, the flak might not have flown so fast and furious, or at all, had the

United States not intervened. What if Washington had stayed on the sidelines? Was a slow death from centrally planned poverty any better than a quick one from a bullet?

Unable to answer the Big Question—did America do the right thing in Vietnam?—I avoided the circumstances that begged it. Stuck in Danang until the Monday opening of the immigration office, I drove to the nearest beach.

There, from the shade of a bamboo shelter, an aging beachcomber called to me. He spoke without offering his name or asking mine.

"This beach used to be full of Americans, like you. *Beaucoup de* Americans. Too many. No Vietnamese. Except for girls, prostitutes."

The former South Vietnamese lieutenant explained that I had found the *real* China Beach. Technically, the name applied to the entire strip from so-called Monkey Mountain down to the Marble Mountains. But the GIs' fun and games were limited to the end nearer Monkey Mountain. "Here we are far from Danang and safe," he said. "In the city VC can find us."

Respect framed the beachcomber's monologue on the Viet Cong's wartime tactics. "VC was weak. He had only AK-47s. We had howitzers and missiles and boats and planes. But VC knew how to fight, especially in the jungle. They never stayed in one place. They would take careful aim, shoot one bullet or one mortar, and run. When the chopper came to look, VC was gone."

The veteran's disrespect for his own side was just as strong. He couldn't forgive or forget the greed of South Vietnam's top brass, whom he described as drunks who lived in big houses where they kept two, three, or six wives.

"Where did the money come from?"

"They took our supplies. How else could they pay for their luxuries? If the U.S. gave us ten rations, we only got five. If the

U.S. gave us one hundred liters of petrol, only fifty came to the men. The commanders sold the rest on the black market. They didn't have any interest in the army. When the North came to invade Danang, the commanders had all fled to Saigon."

The beachcomber considered himself lucky. As a low-ranking officer, his term in reeducation camp was short. Overcrowding led to his release after "only" sixteen months. But paroled prisoners still had to check in regularly at the local police station. Ongoing police surveillance of foreigners made sidewalk chats a risky business.

"Here on the beach they will not follow us. We are safe."

Being followed wasn't new to me. Before my arrival, a veteran journalist had warned me: "In Hanoi, anyone who speaks English well works for the government and will report your activities." Thus ignited, my paranoia invented dangers. How long had that green jeep been parked outside my guesthouse? Should I have avoided American veterans? Was I under suspicion for mingling with the MIA team?

The cloak-and-dagger games weren't just in my mind. Locals confirmed that, like other totalitarian regimes—and plenty of democracies—Vietnam had its snoops. One night I had dined with an American investor living in Hanoi. "Did you notice the three spies outside?" was his greeting. I watched another businessman grin upon learning of his removal from the "Watched List."

A Vietnamese official who invited me for coffee explained the surveillance like this: "The government wants Americans to come back. But they still don't trust you people. So they watch." The official said I ought not take it too personally. A roll call of invaders that included the Chinese, French, and Japanese had left Vietnam wary of outsiders. Nor should I worry. Spy budgets were being squeezed. And, like other government employees, the spooks played hooky to hustle for themselves. Finally, Hanoi was by far the country's most uptight city. Other places were more relaxed.

Except Danang. An American woman told me how the cops made the southern city an uncomfortable place to work. "The police follow me. They read my mail and tap the office phones. My home may even be bugged."

"How do you know?"

"Sometimes I see them. They don't always try to hide. But it's well known that the local police file a monthly report on the activities and visitors of every foreigner who lives in Danang. They take photos. They probably have pictures of the two of us together."

"They have pictures of me?"

Had the hidden cameras missed me, they got a second chance. After three extensions, a cancellation, and two entry stamps my visa was almost certainly invalid. If not, it was two days from expiration of the last extension. I had no choice but to drop in on the immigration police.

"Who is your sponsor?" asked a cordial man in uniform.

"I don't have one."

"You must have the sponsor."

A flashback to another police station told me the lawman was about to throw the book at me. Instead, he threw me out of the office. Individuals could not renew visas.

But Mien, the peppy manager of the East Asia Company, could. Unfazed by my visa's battered state, he promised a one-month extension for forty dollars. But first he needed my "itinerary." "Where are you going next?" he asked.

It was a question I had been ducking for days. The encounter in Aluoi had rattled my mental china. Alone in a remote town, I had got lucky. In Vietnam, overnight detention wasn't unheard of. Nor overweek. Stir in my memories of the daunting mountain road and a fickle Russian vehicle, and you had a recipe for my resolve to stick to Highway One.

But the coastal route had its own, more subtle, obstacles. Boredom was one. None of Vietnam's "places of beauty" held my interest for more than thirty minutes. Playing it safe, staying out of the mountains and off the Ho Chi Minh Trail, I was likely to fall asleep at the wheel. Moreover, the grating hard sell that plagued me in Danang was sure to continue along the increasingly beaten coastal path.

"Do I have to decide now?"

"I must give your itinerary to the immigration police," said Mien. After ten minutes of silent deliberation, I voted against boredom and handed Mien a list of my proposed stops in the Central Highlands. "This is impossible" was his delayed reaction.

"I'm not allowed to go to those places?"

"No, Vietnam is a free country. But you cannot travel on that road."

"Why not?"

"There are many rivers in the mountains. There used to be bridges. But they were bombed by the U.S. And the government has not yet rebuilt them. You cannot pass."

Mien recommended Highway One. "That is the best way."

"The best or the easiest?"

"In Vietnam the best way and the easiest way are the same."

In the end, it was Danang's police who determined my route. I edited my schedule into a Who's Who of coastal towns. Mien took it to the immigration police and told me to return that afternoon. I used the time to find a mechanic. A few hours in the hands of a toothless wizard named Hoang put the Minsk in racing form. To adjust to the improved handling and added power, I went for a joyride.

At least one Vietnamese woman wished I had opted otherwise. She was edging her Honda into a crowded roundabout. I was edging out of the circular traffic. Swerving to avoid a third motorbike which was perpendicular to mine, I clipped her rear wheel. The impact bounced the victim's child a foot in the air.

The baby landed back on the rear seat and gurgled. The woman skidded to a halt ten yards away. She scowled and shouted. Heads began to turn. With nobody hurt, I did what any unlicensed, uninsured driver would do. I fled.

Danang's finest outdid their reputation for thorough police work. Or so it seemed when the hotel's receptionist flagged me down as I passed her station. "You are in the newspaper," she said excitedly.

"What? Me?"

"Yes. You are the American who is driving a Minsk from Hanoi to Saigon. I read about you."

A former journalist, I had known better than to give interviews. Possible losses, either from verbal slips or shoddy reporting, almost always outweighed potential benefits. Indeed, "No" was my immediate reaction to a reporter's request during my second week in Hanoi. I didn't want the police thinking I was anything but a tourist.

Minh Tuan, a reporter for the *Great Solidarity Newspaper*, talked me into it. I protested that a tourist wasn't news. I stressed that I was a wannabe novelist, i.e., a nobody. He countered that readers would be interested in a young American's take on his country. I conceded this might be so and let him snap my picture. The long-haired reporter zinged his first question. "Do you eat rice?"

The interview that followed focused on my background.

Dull to me, the life and times of an American might actually interest a Vietnamese subscriber. A multiple of his monthly earnings, the hundred and twenty-five dollars per week I earned in my first newspaper job floored Tuan. He needed more time to recover when I told of thousand-dollar-per-month rents in New York. I only reserved candor when the questions bordered on the political.

What did I think about the changes? How did Vietnam compare to other places I had visited?

"British service is worse than Vietnamese."

When he moved to note my observation I reminded Tuan of my concern about being labeled a critic of the government. At least not until I was out of the country. Tuan said that he understood. A veteran journalist, he had learned that self-censorship was preferable to the whims of his newspaper's in-house monitor.

The discussion turned to my plan to see the Ho Chi Minh Trail by motorbike. He also asked whether I would like to invest in Vietnam. But, like any good reporter, Tuan saved his best question for last: "What do you think of Vietnamese girls?" My anodyne answer didn't make it into print.

The good news was that the article appeared on May 7, the anniversary of the Viet Minh's 1954 victory over French troops at Dien Bien Phu. The front page was spackled with photos of Ho Chi Minh planning, soldiers lugging weapons, and Frenchmen surrendering. The bad news was that Tuan referred to me as an American journalist writing a book about the new Vietnam.

Hanoi kept foreign journalists on a tight leash. Harmless slobs with dollars, tourists could roam alone. Most visiting reporters, on the other hand, were required to submit itineraries and travel with escorts. I would have some explaining to do if Danang's police linked me to the story.

33

Robert McNamara considered himself a hands-on decision maker. As Vietnam grew from a sliver to a slice of the geopolitical map, the Ford Motors whiz turned Secretary of Defense made several visits to Saigon to assess the situation. When he did, word spread.

Among those who heard was Nguyen Van Troi. An electrician by day, Troi moonlighted as a rabid patriot. Like many Southerners, he wanted the Americans out of his homeland. His occupation and avocation made him just the guy for a dirty job.

It's not clear whether Troi had help. What is clear is that he learned the route of McNamara's motorcade and planted a mine on the road. The bomb was discovered by Saigon's security forces. Naming no accomplices during his interrogation, the bomber was executed. "Long live Vietnam. Long live Ho Chi Minh" were his final words before a firing squad silenced the electrician.

Northernizing the cities of the South was one of Hanoi's first postwar projects. Saigon became Ho Chi Minh City. Rue Catinat, the downtown address of Fowler, the protagonist of

The Quiet American, was erased after 1954, when it became Tu Do, or "Victory." The Communists renamed it Dong Khoi, or "Uprising." Farther from the center, another avenue was renamed for the hero called Nguyen Van Troi.

The failed bomber's name was also splattered across his home province, Quang Nam. The main city, Danang, had a Nguyen Van Troi Street. The bridge across the Han River bore a similar label. Several kilometers to the south, in the hero's birthplace, few structures *weren't* dedicated to Nguyen Van Troi. Handing me a rejuvenated visa, Mien said I would find buildings, schools, and parks named for Dien Ban's favorite son.

To me, the town carried another label: crossroads. It lay at the intersection of Highway One and Route 14. The former was flat, paved, populated, and dull. Heading straight south, I could hit Saigon in a matter of days. The alternative led west, into the Truong Son Mountains, before turning south parallel to the borders of Laos and Cambodia. Nobody disputed that the road had doubled as the Ho Chi Minh Trail.

Its condition was debatable. Mien had sworn that Route 14 was impassable. I sought a second opinion from a Filipino with whom I played a set of tennis. His good will engendered by my double fault on match point, the international aid worker gladly suffered my queries. A regular on the mountain road, he promised it was passable. He recommended a Land Cruiser.

"How about a Minsk?"

"More difficult. But okay."

"In Hanoi they said I would be attacked by hill tribes."

The man giggled.

"Wild animals?"

The Filipino laughed aloud.

By Dien Ban, I was leaning toward believing the aid worker and heading west. An accident made up my mind. Just south of the intersection I saw a Honda crunched under the front wheel of a truck. The crowd of fifty rubberneckers surrounding the injured driver was growing fast.

Two policeman were already perusing the wreck. Between the difficulty of steering through the mob blocking Highway One, and the possibility that the cops might stop me, I saw an omen. I lowered the bill of my new headgear, an electric blue golf hat imprinted with "Danang Tourist," and veered right.

The Filipino said the road would get me to the Central Highlands town of Kontum in about six hours. That sounded bullish for a 300-kilometer journey. Whether I made it or not, the first stop was Giang. Just 60 clicks from Danang, the town had been a nucleus of the supply network. Other towns before Kontum—Phuoc Son, Dac Glei, and Dac To—read like a roll call of stops on the Trail.

The warmth of the early morning sun on the back of my neck reaffirmed the wisdom of my choice. So did the peaceful scenes along the winding, palm-lined pavement. The road teemed with school-bound children, the boys in white shirts, the girls in white *ao dai*. Women in rice hats spilled into the road from morning markets. Men lugged tools toward the stillness of rice paddies and vegetable patches.

The cratered shoulders of the road supported Mien's thumbnail sketch of the area's past. After American ground forces withdrew, the United States had bombed every road in sight. Some had only recently been repaired.

Bridges were next on the agenda. The asphalt ended and I found myself looking across two hundred yards of shallow river. Floating sections of aluminum linked the banks. On the far side, the dirt road bisecting the narrow valley inspired little more confidence.

"Where you going?" asked a vendor by the bridge.

"Kontum?"

"Too far. Many hills."

"Is that the road to Kontum?"

"Yes. I hope you lucky."

The road on the south bank looked worse from up close. Rocks the size of watermelons were so common that the road's unpacked dirt looked mined. Smaller, sharp stones threatened to puncture my tires. I drove the sides, where traffic had worn smoother paths.

A U-turn made sense. Traveling no less than 20 kilometers per hour, I would never make it to Kontum by sundown. I considered the other mountain towns. Would there be a roof to sleep under? A Holiday Inn wasn't necessary. A mosquito net was.

Before I could reverse course a pair of young men wheeled around the bend on Minsks of their own. One was honking and waving. The other was shouting. They wanted to ride with a foreigner. Before doing so, I sought their thoughts on the about-face under consideration.

Kontum? Too far, they said.

Giang? No sweat.

Phuoc Son? Two thumbs up.

Gas? Available everywhere.

The locals appeared to know the territory. That, plus their assurance that Phuoc Son was just one hundred kilometers, and four hours, away, convinced me to steam ahead. Guided by power cables strung atop fifty-foot steel towers, I followed the pair up a seam in the rugged green blanket covering the hills.

Roadside bottles of petrol and a pile of sliced melons beckoned in Giang. The sight of idle policemen told me to keep going. Over the next two and a half hours the no-stop policy took me past handfuls of loggers, up vertical rock piles, and onto the flat, dirt roads of Phuoc Son.

A mustached man rolled out of the hammock in his dusty food shack and ordered two girls to bring me rice and fish.

Speaking man to man, he said Kontum was 170 kilometers, about eight hours away at my current pace. Dac Glei, just 70 kilometers, looked a more likely place to overnight.

The day's third set of cops cut short the conversation. We watched the uniformed man scooter past my Minsk and circle back for a closer look. Our relief at his departure was short-lived. Within five minutes he and a partner returned to investigate. The officers looked at me and then at the owner.

"Where's he from?" asked one policeman.

"Russia," said my host.

The answer satisfied both law enforcers, who lingered to look over my backpack. Half finished eating, I paid my bill without arguing about being overcharged and forgot about my interest in a toilet. I wanted to leave town before the pair asked more questions.

The boy who pumped Phuoc Son's gas suggested I stick around. "*Mua*," he said, pointing to the darkening sky. The prediction of rain came to life within minutes. Steely clouds opened their taps as I crept up a rocky, southbound road gouged into a hillside so steep that the jungle nearly spilled onto my head.

Identifiable by bright green pants with a thin red stripe, an off-duty police officer waved for me to take shelter under the eaves of a lonely concrete building. When I did, we passed the time staring at each other and at the downpour. About twenty half-naked urchins stared at our attempts to discuss the weather. The officer's view? The rain would destroy the already horrible road to Dac Glei. I should stay the night.

The offer was generous. Looking around, I realized that I was on Vietnam's roof. Hours of climbing had brought me to a point where I was looking over, not up at, the caps of the Truong Son Mountains. Below the conspiracy of clouds rumbling over our spot was a sight line unfettered for miles of lesser peaks and valleys. When lightning began to strike, I felt safe. I was in the sky, not on the ground sought by the bolts.

"*Mua*," said the relaxed policeman. By that he clearly meant, "Don't even think about leaving." After one hour and a lot more *mua*, I left against his advice. More clouds were steamrolling our way. But one night in that remote outpost might be one too many: two friends in Hanoi had caught malaria in similar spots.

Driving alone in Charlie's heartland, I once again felt myself shrinking. Trees, bushes, and brambles formed a tunnel around the road. When the foliage cleared enough to offer a view, there were only seamless green valleys and rows of thicketed mountains. The jungle looked dense as a black hole. It wasn't hard to imagine an army of men and machines hiding beneath the canopy.

What I couldn't fathom was how Northern soldiers had survived a day, not to mention a decade, in the hyperactive wilderness. Physical strength wouldn't have been enough. To live in the bush, year after year, with bombs and bullets flying, Charlie had to have something more. What kept him going?

Depending on one's perspective, Hanoi was seeking to dominate or liberate South Vietnam. Soldiers were explicitly told that theirs was a one-way ticket until that goal was achieved. Ho Chi Minh was equally clear that the trip down the Trail was open-ended. "Your duty is to fight for five years or even ten or twenty years," he said.

Propaganda prepared soldiers for a long haul. The process of hardening men's minds began shortly after induction to the army. More than half of boot camp was devoted to lessons on the joys of Communism. The flip side, the misery of imperialism, was elucidated with photos of Southerners being beaten and tortured. To the passion to free fellow Vietnamese—after killing a few—each soldier could add personal rage about dead friends and family.

Motivated before hitting the Ho Chi Minh Trail, soldiers were given refresher courses along the way. Hanoi's willingness to devote scant resources to a corps of peripatetic political cadres underscored the importance of mental strength.

One Northerner put it like this: "Our arms and equipment were weaker than the enemy's. Thus we could only develop political and moral superiority and only then have the courage to attack the enemy, only then dare to fight the enemy resolutely."

Still, morale could slip. Political cadres couldn't shield their charges from the sight of northbound comrades. Soldiers saw men missing arms or legs, or victims of napalm attacks, and knew they might be looking at their futures. Desertions weren't uncommon. About a quarter million Northern fighters switched sides under the "open arms" program.

But the bulk of Hanoi's force hewed to the Party line, a sign of which was still visible near the Ham Rong Bridge on Thanh Hoa's outskirts. "Never give up" read the words chiseled into a hill. Individuals implanted motivators into their hides. A popular tattoo said, "Born in the North to die in the South."

Engulfed by Charlie's territory, I tried on his fatalism for size. After months of battling sun, rain, soot, and whatever else Vietnam threw in my path, I accepted the power of Mother Nature. Resistance was futile. All I could do was steer uphill and hope the jungle would let me pass.

It did, for a time. Steep rises led to impossible inclines. At the end of each bend was the beginning of another. Taking a break to scan the horizon for signs of civilization, I saw only more of the same.

Hundreds of sheer feet above the road, waterfalls fed

chasms that cut across the Trail. A concrete crossing bridged each stream. Plaques indicated that most had been built in mid-1993. Stopping to examine a marker, I met a different sort of obstacle.

A herd of water buffalo wallowed up to its collective neck in a pond of chocolate milk. When I stopped to take a picture, the largest of them stepped out of the mud bath and plodded toward me. I backed away from the incoming horns. The animal kept coming. With nowhere to run, I waited for the beast's next move.

The motorbike blocked its path. His chest just inches from the Minsk, the buffalo debated whether to tip the bike. The glare of his shiny brown eyes made clear that he, not I, was in charge. That clarified, he turned and lumbered back to the pond. Never had I been more desperate to see a human face.

A gang of construction workers in yellow hard hats provided my fix. Stopping at their tent city, I learned that Dac Glei was just 30 kilometers away. A Vietnamese man dressed in a blazer emerged from the group. Standing by a Minsk of his own, Vinh said, in shards of English, that he was headed my way. We set off together, each happier for company on the lonely road.

I counted the final milestones like an inmate counting the days of his sentence. Six kilometers from Dac Glei huts appeared. Along the road dark-skinned men and women carried scythes from the fields. Two teenage boys gave each other roadside haircuts. Children waved. I had made it.

Three kilometers from the finish line, that conclusion looked premature. Mien had been wrong about the lack of bridges along Route 14. The government had replaced nearly every bombed-out bridge with new concrete crossings. The missing link stopped the two Minsks dead on the edge of a river a hundred feet across. So close to Dac Glei, so far from Danang, the joke was a cruel one.

My partner wheeled left down a dirt path along the riverbank. On the opposite side, two hundred feet downstream, an uphill path taunted those stranded on the east side. I flopped onto the ground.

Vinh removed his shoes and motioned for me to do the same. I hesitated. He didn't. The rider plunged his Minsk into the river. With two feet of water lapping at his engine, I expected to see a midstream stall. Instead, the machine plowed ahead like the slowest of motorboats. Safe on the opposite side, the man put his shoes on and beckoned for me to follow.

There were two options: turn back to Danang or repeat the lesson in motorcycle durability. Steam rose when the heat of the engine met the chill of the mountain water. My tires slipped on the mossy rocks, causing the bike to tip toward the thigh-deep drink. I blocked the fall by planting a bare foot on a jagged rock. Upright again, the Minsk cut a neat wake through the water. The performance, mine and my bike's, surprised me.

Vinh was no less impressed. He lit a cigarette while I fussed over the bleeding sole of my foot. After a few thoughtful puffs he said, "You come with me in Dac Glei."

34

Vinh took care of me in Dac Glei. With the sun threatening to sink below the rim of the mountains we had just crossed, he led me to a set of concrete buildings on the northern edge of Dac Glei. One contained a pair of rooms complete with unmade beds and porous mosquito nets. The other was where I found a family of six gathered around the dinner table.

"Your family?" I asked.

"Friends," said Vinh.

The group gladly shared its dinner of fish, rice, and greens. My hostess, a fortyish woman with three feet of black hair, led the Q & A about my age, nationality, and marital status. Each of my one-word answers sparked five minutes of group discussion. As dinner wound down, the long-haired cook threw a curve ball: would I like to watch television with her? I didn't need to feign fatigue.

Awake at dawn, I got my first look at Dac Glei. Raw logs and wood planks were stacked beside the road. Opposite, empty trucks awaited their loads. Strung under the bellies of the vehicles were the hammocks of dozing, half-naked drivers.

Dac Glei fitted my preconception of a frontier settlement.

Set in a high-walled valley, the town had but one road. The dirt strip was flanked by a handful of buildings erected with freshly cut planks. A dust patina covered everything and everybody. Farm animals wandered at will.

The town hadn't always been so calm. A Southern veteran living near the town said the surrounding mountains were once riddled with enemy trails and encampments. The ground attacks ordered by Saigon spawned some of the war's fiercest fighting. When the guns stopped blazing, tigers roamed the combat zone and gnawed on the corpses.

Years later, my main worry was the weather. The previous day's deluge had stalled me. That night the skies let loose again. Were these freak storms or had the wet season begun? All I could get out of locals was "*mua* [rain]." Thunderstorm or monsoon, the midnight shower turned Route 14 into a slalom of puddles and ponds. My boots and pants were layered in mud almost from the start of my ride to Kontum.

Dark-skinned mountain men were lugging two-foot blades toward muddy fields when I passed at 7 A.M. Unprepared to dismiss seemingly ridiculous predictions of assault in hill tribe territory, I didn't stop to chat. The farmers showed no more interest in meeting me. Most likely focused on boosting their subsistence living, few Montagnards raised their heads to ponder disemboweling an American.

The women and children were more attentive. Alerted by the sound of my approaching motorbike, the mountain families raced to the road to inspect me. The sight of a pale face brought smiles to their dark ones. The grins disappeared as soon as the excitement passed. In my rearview mirror I watched the hillbillies return to dilapidated shacks.

There were some signs that the area was unsafe. Military bases dotted the landscape. Off-duty soldiers walked casually along the winding dirt road. But never alone, and never without the company of an AK-47. Because the men invariably waved, I concluded that the threat was no longer Westerners. Why, then, the buildup of defenses?

South of Dac Glei a single lane of dirt split from Route 14. Turning to investigate, I saw a path leading west across a narrow plain toward a row of mountains. My last encounter with Vietnamese touchiness about their borders had taught me to keep moving south. For those in need of instruction, bold letters spelled it out in English: "Frontier Area. No Trespassing." I wondered what bogeyman was, or had been, hiding in the hills.

Nor was I the only one curious about this corner of the country. America lost 58,000 soldiers during the war. The remains of 1,600 or so were still in Vietnam's land and waters.* A big chunk of the quarter million South Vietnamese soldiers killed were never found. Excruciating to the families of the deceased, both figures were tiny next to Hanoi's dead and missing.

About a million. That was the nearest guesstimate of the number of North Vietnamese soldiers killed during the war. Coming from a country that villainized Vietnam for its failure to find and return remains, I had felt my cheeks redden as beefy, nearsighted Colonel Sang tallied his side's missing. Again, the figure was rough. Hanoi's MIAs totaled more than 300,000.

The tally could have been far higher. One reason it wasn't was Northerners' maniacal efforts to carry off their dead comrades. American vets described surreal scenes after firefights. Checking areas blasted with machine gunfire and mortar just moments before, the ex-GIs often found blood and even flesh. But the bodies of dead enemies were gone. Those that were found were often bulldozed into unmarked graves.

---

* Many more Americans, 8,170, are still "missing" in the Korean War. The total for World War II stands at 78,750.

In a hamlet not far from Hanoi, a bent woman maintained a shrine in her home. Between the fresh flowers and ashes of incense stood framed photographs of five young men in uniform. Five sons, all killed during the war. "We were very lucky," said the lonesome mother. "All of the bodies were recovered."

The missing corpses prolonged Vietnam's anguish. The mostly Buddhist population believed the living were responsible for the souls of the dead. Offerings of mock money, cigarettes, or anything else that might come in handy on the other side were deposited at pagodas, shrines, and graves. With no remains to visit, one couldn't ensure happiness in the afterlife.

"It is important for the spirit to feel comfortable," explained a young man in Hanoi. "If the spirit is not comfortable, the family will be worried and unhappy."

The Hanoi-based language teacher, Mr. Hung, came to mind as I left the "No Trespassing" sign. One of Hung's brothers had been killed while withdrawing from an attack in Kontum Province. Buried on the spot, the Northern soldier's body never made it back to his family. The government didn't say why.

Like their American counterparts, the surviving brothers began digging for information after the war. Comrades remembered the coordinates of the fatal firefight. An officer drew a map of the terrain and the location of the impromptu grave. Still, Hung's family hadn't been able to bring home the bones.

Business had taken Hung's living brother to Kontum Province. The descriptions and map led him into the jungle, where he hoped to find the grave. Then he stopped and, reluctantly, turned back. Buried west of Vietnam's frontier, the dead brother was in a no-go zone in southeast Laos.

"We would like for the government to find our brother," said Hung. "But right now the U.S. has priority."

The morbid memory of Hung's sorrowful tone had diverted me from my sillier problem: another bout of rain had saturated my clothes and boots. The downpour had also turned the road's mud into mush. Spinning in search of traction, my tires sank six inches into the softened road.

It proved harder to get a grip on an incline bordered by streams of rainwater. The rear wheel spun triple time to move the motorbike forward through orange mud. I sensed the tire sliding left. I countered by steering the same way, but the slide continued. Though the ground was rushing toward my face, I felt detached from the midpoint of my first motorbike accident.

The out-of-body experience ended with my left side, head to toe, in six inches of mud. I checked my moving parts, which had been cushioned by the soft surface. Like me, the Minsk was dirty but not damaged. The engine started on the first try. The only casualty was my pride.

Conditions improved. The road broadened and showed hints of long-gone pavement south of an intersection where vendors hawked food, drinks, and batteries. The view also got better. The mountains were receding to the horizon. I assumed that the flat valley widening in front of me was the Central Highlands, an area controlled, for a spell, by American forces. The leftover runway just west of the road supported my suspicion.

A muscular woman in the next town, Dac To, reconfirmed that my compatriots had come and gone. Pushing her way through thirty truant schoolchildren who gathered to watch me eat bread, the woman skipped introductions.

"I think you American," she said.

"I think you're right."

"I think you not GI."

"Never was."

"I think if you here twenty years before you be GI."

On the mark again, Diane led me to the roadside stall

where she sold and sewed fabric for a living. A native of Quang Ngai, a town on the coast, she and five children had moved to the region when her husband found work in Kontum seven years before. And her English? Learned from American soldiers as well as her sister.

"My sister marry GI Joe," said Diane.

"Where is she now?"

"She dead. She met GI in Quang Ngai. Get married. Have baby. I got pictures. Then he gone, maybe dead, maybe home. We write so many letters. But hear nothing. My sister dead. Her heart broken."

35

Kontum spent most of the war staring down the barrel of the Trail. One of the outposts closest to the western frontier, the town was near the top of Hanoi's hit list. The mountains and jungle provided ample cover for badgering American and South Vietnamese defenders. The solution? The Pentagon flattened the terrain with B-52s.

Artifacts of the old days lined the road like rusting milestones. As Kontum neared, the piles of mangled jeeps, cannons, and bombshells along the highway grew higher. The debris looked harmless. Even an upright bomb, tall as a man but round as a barrel, looked more decorative than dangerous.

My snap assessment was wrong. The week before I reached the Central Highlands a public bus had left Dac To for points south. The passenger list included a dozen students from a teachers college. There was also an older woman who supplemented her income by collecting scrap metal. Piled among the jumble of luggage, bicycles, and rice bags atop the bus was the scavenger's market-bound stash of spent mortar and artillery shells.

Nobody knew that the load included a live bomb. Not the

woman. And certainly not the bus boys who, when the vehicle pulled into Kontum, unloaded the freight with Neanderthal delicacy.

Two feet long, the 105mm shell exploded on impact, ravaging buildings and flesh as far as fifty meters away. The entire town rushed toward the blast. What they found was a mess. Four people died on the spot. Six more perished in Kontum's hospital. Another twelve were maimed, among them a teenage girl who lost an arm.

The despondent amputee went home hours before I reached her bedside. Just as well. She might have linked me to the folks who had left the explosive behind. The stranger who begged me to accompany him to the hospital took another view. He said that the thrill of meeting an American would lift the girl's spirits. Learning that the bomb victim was gone, the stranger apologized.

We met in a hole-in-the-wall café beside Kontum's market. There I joined no less than twenty men who were killing the afternoon by sipping coffee and staring at a TV mounted on the wall. The owner had rented a video. In English, the movie needed no translation. The bad guys, a pair of bald and bearded professional wrestlers, sported tights with hammers and sickles. The clean-shaven, good guys wore stars and stripes.

The viewers gasped as the Russkies stomped heads and wrung necks. A tall but chunky man settled on the plastic stool beside mine. Dressed in an untucked T-shirt and a black baseball cap, he looked like a Little League coach. Wincing at a particularly rough body slam, he turned to say, "The Russians. Always so bad."

Which surprised me most? The stranger's English? His readiness to criticize Communism's birthplace? Or his belief that pro wrestling was for real?

"You were in Dac Glei," he said.

"How did you know?"

"Your motorcycle is very dirty."

More questions bubbled toward my tongue. How did this guy know about my Minsk? Was our meeting more than coincidence? Was he a cop? When I asked, the stranger lifted a hand to show me how far my guess was from the mark. Engraved on the rim of his fat ring was "U.S. Air Force."

Quan, like other veterans, was quick to tell his story. He grew up in Kontum and studied law in Saigon. High marks earned him a scholarship to a college in Tennessee. He also spent time in Texas, where the curriculum switched from contracts and torts to takeoffs and landings.

The lawyer became a flier. Quan reckoned he was an ace chopper pilot. Based in Pleiku, another big town in the Central Highlands, he logged two thousand hours flying GIs into trouble and plucking them from it.

The hazardous duty earned Quan twelve-hour days in the fields of a postwar prison camp. But neither the crime nor the punishment had dented the former lieutenant's fondness for Americans. Quan spoke with pride of bonds formed before and during the war, and with regret about contacts lost. When his capture was imminent, he burned his address book.

I couldn't imagine *not* wanting to befriend Quan. His expressive brown eyes were as soft as his manner was relaxed. He spoke quietly, but with the certainty of a man who knew right from wrong. When anecdotes ended with misery or death, the pilot punctuated them with a deep breath and his trademark phrase, "That's too bad for him."

Quan was the only Vietnamese I ever heard enunciate THE WORDS, the words that I, and probably any other American perplexed by the Vietnam War, had hoped to hear. In steady, shameless tones, Quan said, "I was glad when the

United States came here to help South Vietnam. Americans sacrificed their lives to protect my freedom. I am grateful to them."

There wasn't much else to say. Most of the café's other customers had exited when the wrestling movie ended in victory for the Americans. That left Quan and me sitting in silence among a handful of languid leftovers. The pilot apologized for the shortage of hospitality.

"You should have come here before 1975. I had a car, money. I would buy you dinner. Now . . . is now."

The pilot stiffened when I offered to buy us a meal. A fine idea, but there was a catch. A big one. He liked me and wanted to spend time with Americans. But such contacts invited trouble. Police control varied from province to province. Kontum's regime was one of Vietnam's strictest: seen chatting to an American veteran in 1993, Quan had been jailed and questioned. Heavily fined, he now trod more than lightly.

"The police are king. Because they can do what they want, I do what they say. If the police tell me that one plus one is three, I will agree. That is how I can survive."

There was, however, a way for Quan to be seen with me. One of the top cops had paid a visit in early 1994. He offered a deal. The province had recently lifted the ban on foreigners. The police granted Quan permission to work as a guide for travelers provided he dropped by the station with four dollars.

I covered the payoff. Still, Quan didn't fully relax when we made our first public appearance the following morning. We drove east on my Minsk, stopping at a broad, waist-deep river where children swam as their mothers washed clothing. Pointing past dry rice paddies to the green hills on the far side, Quan said that the flat top of a steep hill had been a Green Beret base. Lower hills and the surrounding jungle had been VC territory.

Nearby, a team of bulldozers was leveling the approach to a bridge in the making. Quan flattered the engineer, who took an interest in me. "A Russian?" he asked Quan.

"French," replied the pilot. When I asked about the fib he said, "You will have no problem with the police as long as you are with me."

I wasn't so sure. West of town, Quan directed me through a maze of narrow lanes that landed us at the home of his fishing buddy. His cheeks sunken, his skin shriveled, the man who met us at the door couldn't have been far shy of seventy. While his wife split a jackfruit—green, bumpy, and bloated like a pregnant football—he described his dream.

As the wartime chief of the district police station, he had been hated by Hanoi. Eight years of jailing Viet Cong earned him a similar sentence in a prison camp. Returning home to find that his considerable landholdings had been taken, the chief set his sights on America. After ten years of saving, he had enough money to emigrate.

The chief pulled a stack of papers from a sturdy cupboard. A half-dozen rubber bands bound six newly minted United States passports and a letter from the State Department. Having spent five million dong (about five hundred dollars, at the time), he wanted me to confirm the authenticity of the documents.

The passports looked like mine. But I didn't get it. Why would a man so old bother to leave Vietnam and start over?

The chief said he was moving for the sake of his family. Uncle Sam would provide six months of English lessons and a house with a long-term mortgage. From that base he hoped that his children, who were as old as twenty-five, could build better lives than Vietnam offered. As for himself . . . the old man showed me a bamboo fishing rod and several homemade hooks.

Quan was probably also eligible for the Orderly Departure Program. But he had other plans. In his own way, the pilot hadn't given up defending his hometown against the Northern invaders.

We walked from the market to a steepled church which was painted red. Quan explained that late in the nineteenth century a French priest had left the coastal city of Quy Nhon to "organize" the isolated mountain region. A two-month trek brought the cleric to Kontum, where, with local elephants and imported Bibles, he and a group of Vietnamese Catholics built a church and a following. Thousands of Montagnards still descended on the town for Easter and Christmas services.

The masses unnerved the government. Like other Communist regimes, Hanoi viewed religion as a threat. Somebody who followed God or Buddha might be less willing to listen to Ho Chi Minh. After the war, temples were shuttered, their monks sent to prison camps. The state hoped to stem subversion by banning the training of novices. Catholics were treated no better. Though churches, like temples, had been allowed to reopen, their future looked anything but bright.

Quan led me through a set of gates and up the shady drive of an elegant mansion. More than a hundred yards long, the two-story structure was a seminary. Of the dozens of doors, all but one was closed. A priest fiddling with rosary beads emerged to greet a familiar face. Ignoring me, he retreated and shut the door.

The seminary had been Quan's high school. The pilot took ponderous paces as we walked the outdoor corridor he had known since boyhood. Peering into a cobwebbed classroom, he described how the deserted building once shook from the footsteps of a thousand students. The grove of trees between the building and the fence had been playing fields. That changed in 1975. The new regime gave the budding priests a choice: go home or go to jail.

Attrition promised to claim the priests who were allowed

to remain. Without leaders, Catholicism would wither and die in Kontum. Quan was trying to fight back. Younger, at forty-five, than any of the seminary's eleven residents, he had resumed his religious education.

"If I do not become a priest, there will be no more priests in Kontum."

How did he reconcile years of pumping lead into Northerners with becoming a man of the cloth?

"I only killed my enemy," said the former pilot.

Quan's plan to become a priest didn't entirely surprise me. His sympathy for Kontum's poor was genuine. The warm reception he got in every village tipped him as a regular. Coming across a screaming spat between a mother and daughter, he led both women inside to settle the matter. He carried sweets for children. And it was the saintly man who took me on his daily visit to the victims of the accidental explosion.

His charitable bent extended to me. Late in the afternoon, I financed a round of iced drinks made from blendered fresh fruit. Quan took a delicate sip from his glass and said, "I saw you speaking with that Mr. Lai. You must be careful."

My stomach knotted. The reference was to a small man whose long gray hair was swept back from a tanned face. We met in an intersection near the market. Gridlocked behind a water buffalo, an ice cream cart, and two dozen bicycles, I shared a look of despair with the man beside me.

"Where are you going?" he asked in English.

"Nowhere."

"I'm stuck too. You are American?"

I nodded.

"I am leaving for America in five days. I worked for the consulate. The Communists thought I was CIA so they put me in prison for eight years. Now the ODP is sending me to Houston."

Several generations removed from immigrant stock, I was touched by Lai's excitement about leaving for America. More moving was his invitation to a departure party the following night. He would love for his grown children to meet their first American before touching down in Texas.

Quan ignored my question: how did he know I spoke to Lai? Instead, he warned me to skip the party. Lai's imminent departure meant the police were watching him closely. The proximity of freedom had made the consulate worker careless about contacts that once cost a rough grilling *and* a sizable bribe. An American seen in his company risked a nasty encounter.

"Why are you telling me this?"

"Because you are an American, I worry for you."

Quan's nosiness irked me. But not as much as his caution. I wanted to attend Lai's party. I didn't want to land in another Vietnamese jail. On the other hand, perhaps Quan was exaggerating the danger. A police state was *supposed* to breed paranoia.

The trait was easily acquired. Outside my guesthouse, I spotted an unusually neat set of clothes and a familiar face. But I couldn't place the guy seated on a Honda twenty yards from the door of Mini-Hotel 42. When I looked his way he raised a newspaper to cover his face. An inept detective? Kontum's Clouseau? Pleased with my fantasy, I continued the game.

A young man cut hair on the opposite sidewalk. I crossed to his "shop" and pointed to the man loitering atop the Honda. My Vietnamese had developed to the point where I could pronounce "*canh sat*," the word for police.

"*Canh sat*," he said with a nod.

Without thinking, I marched toward my minder. Again, he lifted the newspaper to hide his face. Lowering the disguise for another peek at his quarry, the officer found me bearing down on him. A man with no plan, I simply wanted to vent my outrage at being followed.

The spook didn't give me a chance. In the jiffy before I reached his spot, he folded the paper, started the engine of his scooter, and sped away.

36

Blood rushed to my face when Quan caught me ogling a village girl. His views on lust were clear. "Only 'taxi girls' sleep with men before marriage," said the future priest. "If my nieces do that, I will shoot them."

I could explain my staring. True, the young woman was striking, and not simply because she sat among three women with beef-jerky hides. Her lighter, smoother skin hugged a set of chiseled cheekbones. Long, fine hair spilled over athletic shoulders. Born to advertise something wholesome, like Corn Flakes, she looked vaguely familiar.

"She is the daughter of an American soldier," said Quan.

Lonesome GIs had left behind thousands of mongrel children, whose foreign features made them easy marks for discrimination. That's why the Orderly Departure Program had been bringing Amerasian kids to the States. But they missed one in Kontum. Should I embrace my semicompatriot?

Apparently not. Like the other Montagnards, the woman took notice of a stranger. But she neither rushed toward me nor shied away. Showing no second thoughts, the young mother resumed picking her son's scalp.

Quan continued our walk through the village, a cluster of houses on five-foot stilts. Children with soiled extremities played peekaboo. A leathery woman wrapped in a waist-to-ankle cloth chopped logs. Another sifted rice grains in a straw disk. A sinewy man in shorts emerged from the shade with a hand-held crossbow, which he demonstrated for the visitor.

Armed mountain men had a lot to do with Kontum's xenophobia. Vietnamese security got edgy around the 8 million inhabitants who didn't look or live like them. The main threat wasn't the country's biggest minority, ethnic Chinese, themselves the victims of centuries of popular antipathy and government-backed racism. The people who worried the gestapo were the mountain-dwelling "savages."

The United States Government had recruited heavily among the Central Highlands tribes. Some of those who signed up were employed as guides to the jungle and its trails. Others were armed and trained to fight the Northerners.

Not all of the guerrillas gave up in 1975. The resistance went by the name of FULRO, a French acronym for Unified Front for the Struggle of the Oppressed Races. Rumor had it that the holdouts supplemented their caches of America's leftover weapons with postwar help from the CIA. Nonetheless, most of FULRO's fighters were quickly killed or captured.

Quan said that a handful were holding out. "The Montagnards don't like the government. Some of them live in the forest," he said. Pointing west, toward a fringe of mountains near the Cambodian border, he added, "They have U.S. weapons and tanks."

"Tanks?" I protested. "Where do they get gas?"

The story gained credibility when Quan said the guerrillas were rife in the region around Dac Glei. Referring to them as "highwaymen," Quan said FULRO lurked along the mountainous sections of Route 14 and kidnapped Vietnamese soldiers.

Dragged into the jungle, the men were never seen again. The gun-toting soldiers and "No Trespassing" sign now made a lot more sense.

Discontent wasn't limited to armed bandits. The hill tribes were resisting Hanoi's attempts to "civilize" them. Forced collectivization of property? Mandatory lessons in Vietnam's language and culture? Yuck! Probably smart, replacing slash-and-burn agriculture with homestead farming was no more popular.

Most egregious was the ongoing effort to move tens of thousands of ethnic Vietnamese into the highlands. The busing program served two purposes. One was to ease overpopulation. With over 70 million people, Vietnam was heading for 168 million by 2025. Shifting people from the crowded, parched North to the open, fertile mountain plains made good demographic sense.

It was also good politics. The disintegration of the Soviet Union and Yugoslavia shocked Hanoi. Vietnam's leaders looked at areas dominated by Montagnards and saw the potential for similar civil strife. With machine guns and hand grenades available on black markets in the capital and Saigon, the cadres weren't taking any chances. Moving Vietnamese into the highlands would help to "pacify" those areas.

Not that all Montagnards were public enemies. Many of the sixty or so hill tribes had been Hanoi's allies during the war. The old man who led the expedition to reopen the Trail belonged to the Van Kieu tribe. Villagers on both sides of the Viet-Lao border fed southbound soldiers. Some became Viet Cong idols.

Nup was one such hero. I learned about the legendary Bahnar tribesman, who was known to all as Hero Nup, from Nguyen Ngoc. Just why the head of the Vietnam Writers Association agreed to meet me was unclear. Perhaps the French-speaking writer wanted to talk about the Ho Chi Minh Trail, which he walked first as a soldier and later as a journalist for the army newspaper. Or maybe he wanted to steer me clear of Route 14, a road he called "*accidentale.*"

There was also a third possibility. The tiny, graying man greeted me with a swift handshake on the ground floor of the Association's building. He led me past a table stacked high with bricks of banknotes—"The budget," he said—and up two flights of stairs to a reception room. The writer warmed only after the arrival of a tea tray. Then he spent the better part of an hour tracing the roots of his breakthrough novel, *The Village That Would Not Die.*

"The forces were unequal during peasant uprisings in the 1930s. The Montagnards had only bows and arrows. The French had guns and armor. They won every time. The local people said the French were not men. They were gods because they did not bleed.

"Nup was the first man in his village to question the legend. He wanted to find out if the French really were gods. Against the wishes of the village, he wanted to try to kill one. Nup said, 'If I kill one, it means the French are not invincible. Then we can fight them.'

"One day some French soldiers came to take the people's rice. They pillaged the village and raped the women. The people dared not move.

"But Nup would try. He pulled back an arrow, a poison one. He shot a soldier. Everybody was surprised to see the flow of red blood. They realized that the French were just men. That meant they could be beaten."

Ngoc added an epilogue. In part, he attributed the success of the novel to its timing. Written shortly after the expulsion of the French, the story appealed to Vietnam's affinity for David-beats-Goliath stories. Just as important, said the author, was his research. To capture the heroic spirit Ngoc had spent time with Nup and his neighbors.

"Hero Nup is a real person?"

"Of course, he is my friend."

"He's alive?"

"Of course. He is old, ninety-three. But he is alive."

The writer sketched directions to Hero Nup's hometown. Well west of the coastal town of Quy Nhon, one hit An Khe. Seven kilometers from there, Nup's village sat on a little hill. Only when I expressed enthusiasm for meeting the great man did Ngoc add that Hero Nup had moved to Pleiku.

"Do you think I can find him? Talk to him?"

"Hero Nup speaks French," said Nguyen Ngoc. "Ask anybody in Pleiku. They will know where he is."

That prediction proved too optimistic. The 50-kilometer drive down Route 14 was a breeze thanks to leftover American asphalt. Getting directions *within* Pleiku was next to impossible. I hailed a couple of teenagers near the town's market.

"Where is Nup?" I asked in my improving Vietnamese.

The pair gaped at me, then at each other, then back at me. I simplified: "Nup. Where?"

Big Foot syndrome struck. The teenagers couldn't accept that a foreign beast was attempting their language. Either that or I had mangled the two words. Assuming the worst, I found *o dau* (where), in my phrase book and showed it to the teenagers. Nothing doing. I left to find an Anglophone.

The Pleiku Hotel had two. Siu Cham, a Montagnard with a mustache, and Hai, his clean-shaven Vietnamese colleague, confirmed that Hero Nup lived in Pleiku. They also agreed that he wouldn't be hard to locate. Neither, however, could pinpoint just where one might find the famed archer.

My third shot hit the target, if not the bull's-eye. The good news was that the college graduate working the front desk of another hotel had seen Hero Nup the previous week. The bad news was that she had visited him in the hospital. Nup was not well.

The desk clerk showed me snapshots from her visit. A long, wispy, white beard was the only sign that Hero Nup was heading for a hundred. The rest of the little man's fine features suggested youth and exuberance. Though sick, he had donned a beige suit for his visitors. An immense smile looked at home on his lined face. The clerk bit her lip as I dwelled on the photo.

"If you want more information about Hero Nup you should go to the government office on Hai Ba Trung Street," she said.

Memories of recent run-ins with provincial governments brought a frown to my face. The clerk spotted my concern. "Don't worry," she said. "People in Pleiku are friendly."

Skeptical, I called off the search for Nup. I did, however, find another local legend. His name was Klong, as in Hero Klong. Beneath his likeness, a statue of a man with a rifle in one hand, a grenade in the other, was the inscription "Small but Valiant."

Like Nup's, Klong's story captured the cult of the underdog. His father killed by the French, the tiny Montagnard craved revenge. He killed his first enemy at age fourteen. His weapon? A slingshot. Grabbing the victim's gun, Klong dusted another enemy soldier with a single bullet.

Hero Klong wanted to keep killing, but he lacked access to guns and ammo. The Viet Cong spurned his request to enlist. They said the Montagnard was too short. So Klong armed himself by capturing weapons from Americans and their Southern puppets. Local lore had it that the little guerrilla was a one-man wrecking crew by the time the Northerners overcame their prejudice and welcomed the small, dark-skinned man.

37

"When in Rome do like the Romans do."

I double-checked that the place was Pleiku, that the speaker was Siu Cham, the manager of my hotel's tour office. Where on earth had the wiry Montagnard picked up his idiomatic English? And why did he think the cliché would get me to agree to a fat fee to visit the fringes of the Trail?

"You mean get burned?" I said.

Cham said the price was a bargain. He only asked thirty dollars from me. An American general and twenty vets had paid two thousand dollars for a tour of their former bases.

"I have my own vehicle."

"The price is fair. We pay twenty percent to the villages. They are very poor. This is the only way we can help them."

Back home, burgers and beers for two could cost just as much, before tip. I felt ashamed for trying to stiff Cham's people. The manager saved me from outright self-loathing: his brothers lived in North Carolina, not the nearby villages.

The soft-seller placed a call to his boss after I agreed to pay. Clearing the trip wasn't a cinch. Or so I judged from the angry barking on the other end of the line. Cham countered with his own arguments but was quickly silenced by more shouts. The bickering lasted a quarter hour. Then he hung up and translated.

"My boss says it's the rainy season. If you want to travel by motorbike you must take a raincoat."

Hai, the young graduate assigned to supervise me, ignored the advice. Spiffy in chinos, loafers, and a white dress shirt, he looked like a poster child for L. L. Bean. The local pilot boarded the Minsk and directed me east along Route 19.

Not since the onramp to San Francisco's airport had I seen pavement able to accommodate three cars abreast. Not that this was likely. In a region with little traffic, the highlanders turned the highway into an airing cupboard. Driving the route involved swerving around the rice and hay set out to dry in the sun and exhaust. Both were hastily swept up by attentive farmers when a flotilla of low-flying clouds loosened their load.

Hai looked more than miffed. He had spent years studying English and three bucks on a white collar. For that he expected a cushy office job, not a ride in the rain. I begged forgiveness and found a spot to wait out the shower. He forgave me when I made him a present of my orange windbreaker.

About 35 kilometers from Pleiku we turned left down the dirt road leading to "typical Bahnar village." There we were greeted by a brown man old enough to have learned his French from missionaries. After noting a preference for the next oc-cupiers—"The Americans were very big, very beautiful"—he led me into the "community house." Elevated on thick stilts, the wooden building's thatched roof was a fifteen-foot-high parab-ola. Inside, I found a fireplace, a guitar, and drums the size of beer kegs.

"The young men sleep here until they are seventeen. We tell them stories, play music, and dance. But no women may enter."

The codger explained other tribal traits as we walked down a leafy lane. Everything from a good harvest to the New Year was celebrated by sacrificing a water buffalo. At the cemetery, he described burial customs. Families buried and tended to their kin for about three years. The dead needed to eat, so the upkeep involved leaving fruit and rice. Smokers got cigarettes. At the end of mourning, the family partied, killing a buffalo.

A neatly dressed Vietnamese distracted my attempts to flesh out the details of Bahnar life. The green hat in his hand was police issue. Half listening to the old Montagnard, who wore only a homemade jockstrap, I wondered what the officer wanted.

"Let's go," my escort announced after a ten-minute chat with the officer. "Also, can we give this man a ride?"

"Where are we going?" I asked once our trio was under way and headed toward the main road.

"Now we will see the chief of the village."

"The chief doesn't live in the village?"

"He needs to be near the road to do things for the people."

"Hai, is the chief really a policeman?"

"Yes."

"Is he the chief of police?"

The sheepish guide submitted his excuses for our arrest in triplicate. "This is a mistake." Pause. "The chief didn't know you were coming." Pause. "I think he wants to serve us some tea."

True, true, and true, I learned once we were interned in a one-room police station decorated with two portraits of Uncle Ho and a dozen girlie pictures. The mistake was due to Hai's helmet and my windbreaker. We had been mistaken for two foreigners. A local busybody had reported the sighting to the cops, who weren't expecting company. And the top cop *did* serve us tea.

Hai's reign of error had a ways to go. The following morning we headed south from Pleiku and then west, across a brown and green plain, toward Cambodia. Passing through a place called Bau Can, Hai pointed out an overgrown helicopter base opposite a tea plantation. A left turn onto a road of red dirt took us into the gently rolling hills of the Chu Prong District. While Hai alerted the police to an American's presence, I kept my eye on a shirtless brown youth with a swastika on his forehead.

We stopped again in Plei Me. The plan was to look at the former American outpost and head farther west, onto Viet Cong turf. Sight lines were clear for miles in every direction. I couldn't see how Charlie had avoided detection and destruction.

"I came here with the U.S. veterans. They remembered their friends and they cried. Vietnamese veterans also come here. They also cry."

He told me how one American group received a particularly warm welcome from the locals. Odd, I thought. Not really, said Hai. That year two children had stepped on a leftover land mine while playing in a field. Both died. Another boy had lost a hand while digging for scrap metal. The villagers thought the vets would be able to pinpoint every mine in the area. They couldn't. So the bombs kept exploding. The month before my arrival another kid had stepped on a mine and died.

"Here is dangerous," was Hai's expert opinion as he led me toward a blockhouse that had been a command center. I believed him. Shallow holes left by successful scavengers pocked a path trodden through the tall dry grass. Pointing to a round, rusty ball nestled in weeds, the guide said, "Very dangerous."

A steel tube farther down the trail appeared to be no safer. A pair of intact mortar shells looked just as ready to blow up. I held my breath and assured myself that (a) Hai knew his way around, and (b) by walking ten yards behind him I would be spared the worst of any accidental blast.

"Let's get out of here," I said after a glance at the remnants of the blockhouse.

"You must take photos. The veterans took many."

"I'll look at theirs. I want to go."

Hai surveyed the dry dirt patch to our left. Then he scanned to the right, like a golfer looking for a stray drive. Stepping to the right, he said, "Over here, I think."

"What's over there?"

"No, over here," he said, switching to another vector.

"Hai, you know the way out of here, don't you?"

His tentative steps provided my answer. I stayed put.

"Hai, you *were* here before, weren't you? With the veterans?"

"That day was a very hot day," he said while taking more delicate steps. "I waited in the van."

To get home I would have to tiptoe through a field of American explosives. I tried to memorize Hai's paces. Doing so delivered me intact to the main road, where I intended to pummel the half-wit. I couldn't do it, not in front of a twelve-year-old in a baseball cap. The lad chattered and pointed to the field.

Hai paraphrased: "He says that is where his friend died from the mine."

38

I couldn't fault the Vietnamese for trying to surf the wave of incoming cash. But risking my limbs so somebody else could achieve a better life wasn't my idea of fun. Handing over my wallet was a preferable alternative. The men who greeted me in Buon Ma Thuot agreed.

Maybe 200 kilometers south of Pleiku, the mountain town's air was clogged with noise and dirt kicked up by the steady stream of Honda motorbikes. Nowhere was this more apparent than the central roundabout, where a Russian tank squatted atop a concrete pedestal. When I idled there and considered my next move, a pair of gaunt men, each forty-plus, set upon me.

"Do you have time to talk?"

"Sure."

"You are American."

"That's right."

"Can you give me five dollars?"

"What?"

"Five dollars. Can you give me five dollars?"

"Why?"

"You are American."

The receptionist at a rundown hotel took a similar view. Told the room rate was eight dollars per night, I asked the rate for Vietnamese. Without shame she said locals paid about five bucks. Her explanation? Foreigners could afford to pay more. Indifferent to my threat to leave, the clerk's reasoning triumphed.

The pressure on my purse made me snap at the next local who approached. My response to his question jolted the slender, soft-spoken man. Recovering, he introduced himself as Phuong, a medical student. Trying to be nicer, I asked about the green pouch slung over his shoulder. His medicine bag?

Phuong laughed. Stamped with "U.S." in big black letters, the bag had once carried a gas mask. "People here like American things. Especially since the end of the embargo."

The affinity extended to Americans themselves. Phuong asked whether I would spend the following evening with him and some buddies. I warmed to the idea of Saturday night carousing in Buon Ma Thuot, which I shortened to BMT.

We met at 7 P.M. Phuong had a favor to ask. Would I mind visiting his English class? It was due to begin in fifteen minutes. I drew an impatient breath, in part because I had been duped, and in part because such an appearance might attract the police. (I had been barred from speaking my native tongue for a class in Kontum by a government official.)

Phuong's teacher confirmed that his door was open. Dressed in a checked shirt that covered an affluent paunch, the former translator for the Southern army thanked me for coming. His English was good. But the instructor wanted students to hear the real thing. My role, then, was to talk about anything.

More than forty adults scrambled to their feet at the sight of a foreigner. Reseated, they went quiet. The boldest ran through the usual questions: name? age? married? Another asked me about my home. I said a few words about New York City, my birthplace, before describing San Francisco. Did I know Los Angeles? Not well, I said. California had an invisible north-south divide not unlike Vietnam's.

The crack relaxed the class. Questions began to flow. What was a Cadillac? An oversized gas guzzler favored by oversized beer guzzlers. Did I like Elvis? His music, definitely. His movies, less so. Terribly timid, a girl in the front row covered her mouth to ask whether it would be difficult for her to get to America.

I answered by chalking two sets of rungs on the blackboard. I pointed out that they were far from the bottom of Vietnam's socioeconomic ladder. Moreover, members of the class were clearly motivated to move up. "Go to America," I said, "and you're back to square one." I left open which was better. Heads nodded.

After class the instructor answered some of my questions. Lounging in a café beside the school, he described his war record and postwar trauma. Both proved he was ripe for the ODP. So why did he stay?

"I thought my life would be better here, in my home, with my family, than in a new country. I was right. I make three hundred dollars per month translating for a foreign company. Teaching English brings two hundred per month. In Vietnam, I am rich."

He was also smug. The instructor asked me to visit more classes. Or why not drop by his home to see how his possessions stacked up to my own pile? I accepted his address but said that lunch the following day looked unlikely. By then I planned to be far away.

Parallel to the Ho Chi Minh Trail, Route 14 south of Dac To had been controlled by Saigon for most of the war. Only in early 1975, when the North took Buon Ma Thuot, was Hanoi able to send men and machines along the main artery of the Central Highlands. Before then Charlie stuck to paths along the border and in Cambodia. One such path, said Northern veterans, could be traced by Route 14 out of BMT.

The drive *looked* simple on the map. Heading southwest, the road stopped just short of Cambodia, at a town called Dak Mil. Shortly thereafter, it forked. The left prong, Route 14, wandered toward Saigon. The right prong had no number. The thinnest of red lines, the route followed the border all the way to Loc Ninh, a place a former Trail trucker had said was the end of the line on his supply runs.

An affable employee of the province recommended an altogether different course. Nha Trang, he said, was a lovely beach resort and just five hours of asphalt away. Route 14's pavement, on the other hand, ran out 30 kilometers from Buon Ma Thuot. Most of the remaining 320 clicks to Saigon would be dirt and rocks.

"Can I make it with a Minsk?"

"The Vietnamese do it."

"What about the border area? Will the police let me pass?"

"Don't worry, this is a *friendly* province," he said. Then, with a grin, he added, "But are you afraid of the Khmer Rouge?"

I was. Like Laos, Cambodia had been treated by Northern strategists as a haven safe from Saigon's forces. That country's eastern edge was turned into a warren of supply trails, as well as a base for a big chunk of Hanoi's army. As with Laos, I investigated the possibility of following the Trail into Cambodia.

The first signs had been mixed. Fresh from a stint as chief of a news bureau in Phnom Penh, Sherie reported that visas were a snap. Buses and airplanes from Saigon to the Cambodian capital were frequent and fast. But the rest of eastern Cambodia was "pretty inaccessible." Were I to gain access, I would learn little.

"Remember that a lot of Cambodians have died since the war," Sherie said. "It will be hard to find people who will admit to being part of the Trail. Or anything else."

The State Department had thrown more cold water on the idea. The most recent U.S. Government travel advisory went like this:

> Sporadic military activity and widespread banditry continue to exist. In recent months an upsurge in banditry and incidents of military fighting have made tourist travel dangerous in some areas. Crime, including armed vehicle theft, is a serious problem in areas including the capital of Phnom Penh.

Cambodia's representative in Hanoi was equally frank. An official wearing tinted sunglasses handed me a visa application the moment I entered the embassy's immigration section. Seated in a cushy chair while filling in the form's blanks, I tried some small talk. I pointed to the portrait of a round-faced man and asked, "Is that Prince Sihanouk?"

"King Sihanouk," came an icy reply. "Western newspapers always call him Prince because they are too busy writing about how to make money in my country."

I changed the subject. Indicating Cambodia's north-east quadrant, an area once riddled with North Vietnamese byways, I asked about travel conditions.

"There are no roads, but many paths."

"Will a motorcycle be able to pass?"

"Maybe. Now most of the vehicles are ox carts." After reconsidering, he said, "Yes, the road is okay. But risky."

"Risky?"

"You may be killed."

"By the Khmer Rouge?"

"The jungle is very thick, very dangerous. It is not the place to go for fun."

The decision to withhold my application and the twenty-dollar filing fee looked smarter by the day. Most everybody agreed. In Vietnam and Laos, bad or overgrown roads would probably stop me from seeing the Trail. In Cambodia, armed, brutal thugs would almost certainly stop me from seeing home again.

It was Alia who put Cambodia out of my mind for good. Among the stories the Dutch woman spun during our day in the DMZ was one about her latest visit to Phnom Penh. A friend had warned her to take taxis after dark. She took the advice. That didn't keep a teenage boy from brandishing a pistol at the window as her cab left the curb.

A few nights later Alia found herself in a bar at 10 P.M. Just four blocks from her host's home, she decided to walk. A guy left with her. One block from the bar they heard a slow click behind them. Turning to find the source, Alia found a gun at her temple. Fear-buckled knees simplified the process of being forced face down to the ground and robbed. Alia knew she was lucky. Others in that situation had been shot in the skull.

The horror stories steered me clear of a country known for its "killing fields." Another well-documented obstacle kept me off the road that traced the Cambodian border.

The downpour in Dac Glei was no accident. Rain followed me down the Central Highlands. The cloudburst in Kontum had its pluses: my Minsk needed a rinse. In Pleiku, the first shower cost me my windbreaker. The second caught me admiring the statue of Hero Klong. Later, caught with several kilometers of open road between me and the town, I was too late to avoid a third set of black clouds and lightning bolting across the plains to drench me. The annual monsoon had come.

Not everybody saw the rainy season as a bad thing. Hanoi had concentrated its movement of men and supplies down the Ho Chi Trail on Truong Son Mountains' dry season. When was that? Most people agreed it began in October. Depending on the year, and whom you asked, and where you were, the dry spell ended in March, April, or May.

The effects of the monsoon were more certain. The rains turned jungle paths into streams. Roads became rivers. Because activity slowed or even stopped along the Trail, the supplies of the Viet Cong were limited. Once Mother Nature called time out, soldiers on both sides got a break from fighting until the skies cleared.

I grasped the implications of the rain delay during my stay in Buon Ma Thuot. The provincial official recommended I see some "places of beauty." One such gem, a lakeside palace built by Emperor Bao Dai, was just 50 kilometers to the south. A fine idea which turned sour when a sheet of steel gray enveloped a mountain halfway to Dac Lac Lake. I doubled back. And pudding-thick mud doubled the time of the return trip.

The following day I set off for another "place of beauty," Ban Don. Domesticated elephants were the draw of this hill tribe village, which was 55 clicks from BMT. The sun shone. But the damage had been done. I turned back after an hour and a half of plowing through chocolate mud and puddles. I described the trip to the official.

"The road will be closed for months," he said.

"How about the road along the border?"

"It will be no better."

Sunny, seaside Nha Trang, we agreed, was my only option.

39

"I've been on the road for two months, man. Burma. Cambodia. No hassles until I came to this fucking country."

The speaker was Johnny, an American in his late thirties. His tan and receding blond hair said St. Tropez playboy. The zippers on his designer jeans screamed *Saturday Night Fever.* But the wormlike man considered himself a social anthropologist, somebody with a feel for Asian culture. In fact, he was a war junkie, in Vietnam for his biggest fix to date.

"Hey man, have you been up north?"

"Just came from there."

"What was it like? Devastated? Was it just devastated? Did you see craters?"

"There are craters. But I wouldn't say . . ."

"Check *this* out, man. These are *real*. Not the fakes they sell to tourists." The American had spread four sets of dog tags on a table. To the pile he added a fistful of rusting bullets, some live and some spent. But his prize catch was a scrap of faded silver paper. "Look closely. You can see the word 'coffee.' This was a coffee packet! It's been out there twenty fucking years! A fucking coffee packet!"

Johnny was just beginning his Vietnam adventure. From Nha Trang, where we met in a shady bar near the beach, he was heading to the DMZ. Combat bases and craters were high on his wish list. So was inside dope, which is why he had hired Dung.

The Southern veteran was small but solid. His round face and mop of black hair belonged to a teenager. But his skin was creased and his eyelids drooped. Dung's permanent grimace was that of someone who had suffered plenty and seen even more.

"I found him in the street," bragged Johnny. "I pay him five bucks a day. He doesn't eat much, so maybe two dollars a day for food. And he can show me everything."

"For seven bucks a day."

"This guy worked with Special Forces, man. The Green fucking Berets. He is *tough*. Dung, show him that scar on your arm."

The sad Southerner touched his left biceps but didn't lift the sleeve. He rolled his eyes, as if to say, "It's a living."

Johnny wasn't the only American seeking cut-rate thrills in Vietnam. Wading in the gentle swells of the turquoise sea, I struck up a conversation with a guy named Clay. The chiseled workout buff said that he, a buddy, and twenty other close friends were celebrating the end of their MBA program by "doing" Asia.

Bangkok was already under their belts. So was Hue. That city's pride—beautiful women—had been their joy.

One night, multiple beers along the Perfume River led to a cyclo ride to Dong Ba Canal, a murky channel near the marketplace. The guys found what they wanted, a cluttered row of sampans moored to the muddy shore. There, young girls beckoned them onto boats that doubled as family homes. Ten bucks bought each MBA (was it Harvard or Wharton?) a romp on a straw mat in the cramped cabin.

Hadn't they seen the AIDS warning posters all over Hue? I asked. Weren't tomorrow's universe masters worried about nipping their careers in the bud?

"I double-bagged it," Clay assured me.

"Double-bagged?"

"Two condoms. I wasn't taking any chances."

Fresh off the overnight train from Hue, Clay and his buddy had yet to "sample the local fare." My own observations told me that the pair would be bloated by the time they skipped town.

Two young women in minuscule skirts had caught my eye the previous night. I was chatting with the cyclo drivers who idled along the beachfront boulevard. The ladies were struggling to cover up what their heels had hiked into the evening air. Once satisfied with their skirts, the pair freshened their makeup and disappeared into the dance hall in my hotel.

A matron in a green tank top was less concerned about appearances. Pulling up on a red Honda scooter, she didn't hesitate before saying, "You want massage?"

"Uh, I don't think so."

"You come with me I give you one-hour massage, every place."

"I'm . . . pretty tired."

A cyclo driver tried to help me overcome my evident shyness: "You go with her. Massage. Boom-boom. Number one."

Prostitutes weren't the only ones selling services in Nha Trang. During daylight hours the palmed beach was combed by women who gave less intrusive massages on the sand. I watched a French woman disappear beneath a pit crew performing a simultaneous manicure, pedicure, and hair removal. Children hawked "lucky" postcards, as well as sliced pineapples and mangoes. An old man sold dog-eared paperbacks left behind by GIs.

Westerners weren't the only customers. Said to be the site of a future Club Med, the pristine strip drew vacationers from all over Asia. A devoted Taiwanese tourist videotaped his young wife's entire half-hour paddle in ankle-deep water. Three bikini-clad girls from Hong Kong took turns posing for still photos. Seated at a table in the shade, a gang of Vietnamese Southerners surrounded an even bigger gang of empty beer bottles.

My own seaside activities were less intoxicating. A traveler who called herself L.J. was unimpressed by my exploits. She spurned what I considered an unbeatable offer, a drive to nearby Ba Ho Falls, where three waterfalls tumbled into three freshwater pools. Rejection bred depression. I wandered and mulled over my mistakes.

One was coming to Nha Trang. Had all those wrong turns and bum steers taught me nothing? Why, after 4,000-plus kilometers, was I still taking directions from a Vietnamese desk jockey? Not that my new course was without merit. The naval base at Cam Ranh Bah lay south of Nha Trang. I could also visit Dalat, a colonial hill station which had become the preferred honeymoon spot of Vietnamese. Still, at that moment I might have been rolling my wheels on the Trail instead of spinning them in sand.

Another detour bugged me a lot more. A Montagnard had invited me to his place during my time in the Central Highlands. Dark as Coca-Cola, he spoke soft but fluent English. I no longer needed to ask why.

His home was solid but simple. A portrait of Jesus was the only decoration in the two dirt-floored rooms which housed six people and two dogs. All mammals were dispatched so that we could "talk." The Montagnard offered me a stool and a cup of weak tea. He unlocked both a wooden cabinet and a box hidden inside. Seating himself on a stool opposite mine, he spoke just above a whisper.

"My friend has some bones. He wants to give them to the U.S."

I said nothing.

"In the jungle he found an American helicopter. There were the bones of two men. Also their pens, watches, and dog tags. He took them all home. But he had a problem."

I waited to hear my role in the probable hoax.

"He took one man's bones to the police. But he got no money." Sensing my dim view of Vietnamese seeking to profit from American angst, he added, "My friend feels very bad for the family of the dead man."

"I can't take bones on an airplane."

"No. My friend wants the family to come here. But if he tries to contact them he will be arrested. He wants you to contact them in America."

The mountain man showed me a slip of paper with a rubbing of the alleged MIA dog tag. The details looked real to me. But who was I to spot a phony?

On the other hand, what if this were the real deal? What if I was being offered a chance to help bring some peace of mind to an American family which had lost a son? I copied down the information—Edward C. Christian. 429967179. APOS. Church of Christ—and promised to do . . . something.

40

"You. You. Where you go?"

Touts shadowed my every move.

"You need cyclo? You rent motorbike? Very cheap."

The voracious chorus sang from dawn until well past dusk.

"You like postcard? Cigarette? Maybe you like girls?"

Short of staying indoors, there was no escaping the locals' crusade to turn my dollars into theirs. Still, I was glad to have reached Saigon.

Life could return to normal. Fear of stir-frying in the midday heat would no longer have me out of bed at 5 A.M. The blinding downpour that flooded my last, 200-kilometer drive might be my final unwanted shower. After a few weeks in Vietnam's biggest city, I would be home.

Regrets persisted. In addition to skipping the last leg of the Ho Chi Minh Trail, I gave short shrift to Dalat. On the other hand, I rolled into Saigon on May 18, the day before Ho Chi Minh's birthday. A city-wide bash would more than compensate for missing the mountain resort's waterfalls and paddle boats.

I dropped my bags and headed for Saigon's Times Square,

the corner of Le Loi and Nguyen Hue. Broad billboards filled my periscope. Propped atop low-rise buildings, the placards advertised Fuji film, San Miguel beer, and Daewoo refrigerators. There were no indications of a pending street party. The only sign of the birthday boy was a black statue set in a small park across from Aeroflot's offices. Inscribed beneath a bearded old man cradling a little girl were the words *Bac Ho*. This, I deduced, would be the epicenter of the gala.

It was, sort of. By seven-thirty the following morning fifteen times ten rows of folding chairs were facing the statue and the elegant town hall behind it. Though every seat was filled, the standing-room crowd was limited to a few cops in rumpled uniforms. A master of ceremonies said a few words. He signaled a herd of pixies in satin dresses to pitter-patter toward Uncle Ho. Cameras flashed. TV cameras rolled. The outpouring of affection was over by 8 A.M.

Had Communism ever taken root in South Vietnam's vanquished capital? Judging by the vendors swarming outside my hotel, the answer was no. Three women in pajamas and rice hats operated stands stocked with sodas, snacks, and cigarettes. Two others sold fresh sandwiches. A rank of at least five cyclos was always waiting. The entire cast sprang to life the moment a foreigner appeared.

Like the rest of Vietnam, Saigon was thinking "Every man for himself," not "Share the wealth." The difference was one of degrees. In Saigon, anything went, nothing was out of bounds.

A cyclo driver pulled alongside the moment I stepped out of my hotel. "You like restaurant? Later we go to lady bar. Maybe you need marijuana? You buy? You buy?"

Neither my refusals nor my silence deterred him. Nor did moving to the opposite side of the street. Pedaling against the flow of traffic, the Saigangster pushed harder: "I know girls very beautiful. Very long hair. Very young. Or you like boys?"

"Why you walk? Very bad. Very dangerous," said another driver, who picked up where the first left off. "I take you everyplace. You don't like, no money. No problem."

"No thanks."

"I introduce you my sister. She speak English and French. Number one."

Cyclo drivers weren't the only ones in overdrive. Most of the combat in the Vietnam War took place in the South. Because bullets, grenades, and mines could maim as well as kill, loss of limb was more common below the Ben Hai River than above, where bombs tended to kill quickly. Since Dong Ha, scarcely a day had passed without the unsettling sight of a man minus a body part. In Saigon, an amputee-free hour was rare.

In one quarter-mile strip, from the Rex Hotel to the Saigon River, I passed a one-legged man on crutches, a no-legged man in a wheelchair, and a guy missing both forearms and an eye. Around the bend a dolly supported the trunk of a man. Legless, he propelled himself with fists thrust into a pair of tattered sneakers. They all asked for cash. They all got some.

When sympathy turned to depression, I jumped aboard a cyclo. The move stunned the driver, a grinning twenty-year-old named Yung, who had never nabbed such an easy fare. He recovered and asked my destination. For the first time in months, I didn't have one.

"Never mind. I show you everything," he pledged

Relieved to have somebody else doing the thinking, and the driving, I relaxed like a sack of spuds. Was I hungry? Yung pedaled by La Bibliothèque, a law library turned French restaurant. Maybe a beer? Yung showed me Apocalypse Now, the bar whose Hanoi branch I knew too well. The driver seasoned the ride with commentaries on Saigon life.

"Don't go with girl on moto," he warned, pointing to a glamorous woman alone on a scooter. "Must pay twenty-five dollars for mini-hotel. More for boom-boom. And sometimes, girl not girl."

The tour continued past a cathedral and down an unlit street to the right. I didn't ask our target until we began passing shacks and piles of garbage. Yung promised that we were on track; he had something to show me. Ten minutes from the center, he pulled up to a one-room building. Five women, none over twenty-one, were loitering outside in their pajamas.

"This is lady bar," Yung announced with pride.

The quintet smelled blood. Or at least money. Two grabbed an arm apiece. Another yanked on my feet. The final pair motioned toward the door. Looking in their direction, I saw a room lighted by a red bulb. Inside, a dumpy Western man snuggled between a pair of attentive women.

"Let's get out of here."

"Lady bar. Very good. Very cheap."

"My place, now."

Yung reluctantly pedaled us away. But he didn't give up. Determined to show me a good time, the grinning driver decided I wasn't the "lady bar" type. Deeper in the maze of streets, we stopped in front of another dimly lit room. He vouched for the quality and price of the services inside. I threatened violence if we didn't leave immediately. Or sooner, was my thought when a peek inside revealed a man of fifty with his arm around a boy.

Cyclo drivers and prostitutes, many of whom had moved from rural poverty to urban misery, weren't the only ones proposing business. A middle-aged motorbiker intercepted me during my next sidewalk adventure. Handsome in a blue tennis shirt, he said he had been a captain in South Vietnam's navy. Still banned from working, he wondered whether I wanted to launch a joint venture.

"A company?" I asked.

"If you like."

"What kind of company?"

"Whatever you like."

Another Southern veteran had more specific ideas. We met in a sidewalk café. I was eating eggs. He was polishing off a bowl of breakfast noodles and his résumé. Like others, Ban introduced himself with a rundown of his war record. Not surprisingly, he had been another interpreter for the Americans.

Now Ban wanted to be a factotum for foreign businessmen. Translation for commercial transactions, business introductions, market research . . . you name it, the interpreter would do it. But he had a specialty in mind.

"You should go down to the Mekong Delta. Have a look at some real estate while you're there."

"Real estate?"

"If you buy land now and wait twenty years, you will make a lot of money."

"I'm not sure they want Americans buying the Mekong Delta."

"Before, you could not. Now, it is possible. I can help."

But most of the vets who approached me in Saigon told simpler stories. Out of work for years, the influx of foreign visitors and businessmen since *doi moi* provided a ray of hope. English-speakers rushed to government offices, which were short of linguists. All applications were received. All were rejected when records showed the applicant had fought on the losing side.

Propagandists were also mired in a twenty-year-old war. Having dotted Vietnam with Ho Chi Minh museums, Hanoi's spin doctors dedicated one more to demonizing Uncle Sam. The folks who stocked the Exhibition House of Aggression War Crimes mined a rich vein.

I knew the highlights of American atrocities. Billions of

tons of bombs and millions of gallons of chemicals were
dumped on Vietnam, North and South. Prisoners were tortured. Some "fell" from helicopters. And there was My Lai, the
hamlet where unarmed men, women, and children were slaugh-
tered by Lieutenant William Calley's 1st Platoon.

The photo exhibits fleshed out just how badly Sam had
treated Charlie. One blow-up showed a U.S. Army vehicle
dragging a corpse by a rope. Another displayed four GIs beaming beside a heap of human limbs. I couldn't judge who was
more pathetic, the half-starved prisoners tied at the neck by a
single rope, or the corn-fed giants leading them through the
reeds.

Most of the gruesome legacy spoke for itself. The face of a
man sprayed by a phosphorous bomb looked as if it had been
scrubbed with acid. A cluster bomb's pellets had turned a boy's
back into a minefield of oozing red holes.

When at a loss for words, the curators relied on the enemy.
The exhibit chronicled antiwar protests in America. One GI
had photographed a platoon posing, like a triumphant football
team, behind the disembodied heads of two Viet Cong. His
caption said, "The above picture shows exactly what the brass
want you to do in the Nam." A display of U.S. military medals
was punctuated by a quote from another solider, a Sergeant
William Brown: "To the people of a united Vietnam. I was
wrong. I am sorry."

One display was absent. Or maybe it was closed for renovation. I asked a guide to direct me to the exhibit of the North's
dirty deeds.

Had I missed the snapshots of Charlie castrating live GIs,
the footage of executions in the jungle? Where were the pix of
James Stockdale writhing without treatment for a broken back?
The Viet Cong often won hearts and minds by making a mur-
derous example of uncooperative peasants. Thousands of

Southerners were executed during the Tet takeover of Hue. Where was the register of these war crimes?

Walking through a wing devoted to showing the effects of defoliants, I learned that the Pentagon dropped 72 million liters of Agents Orange, White, and Blue over the jungle. It made sense that such chemicals mutate genes. But the link between them and the heart-wrenching photographs of kids without noses or arms couldn't be proven. Though it helps, you don't need a chemical war to create a birth defect.

Four girls on a school field trip pulled alongside while I was scrutinizing jars of malformed fetuses. I felt mildly uncomfortable as they chattered among themselves. Then I felt a sweat forming when one spoke to me in English. "What your name? Where you from?"

"Chris. America."

A consultation with her colleagues produced this response: "Chris, America number one."

One of us was missing the point. Was it the schoolgirls, who failed to grasp the museum's loud and clear message, that America ranked way below number one? Or was it me? Should I take a lesson from kids raised on the Big Lie and take more salt with my propaganda? The girls fled the stuffy room to sneak into a Huey helicopter parked outside. The question went unanswered.

On the surface, the American occupation was "all history" in Saigon. Eight boys playing soccer on the sidewalk paid no attention to the former U.S. Embassy, site of the rooftop scramble to safety in April 1975.

Three blocks down Le Duan Boulevard, traffic took no notice of the former Presidential Palace. Now Reunification Hall, the building only interested tourists, who could pay a dollar to sit in Ngo Dinh Diem's chair. When the President was overthrown in 1963, most Vietnamese hadn't been born.

The young population was too busy to dwell on the past. Teenagers patrolled the streets with armloads of newspapers. Lifted from incoming airplanes, publications such as the *International Herald Tribune* or *Le Monde* could be bought at a discount. Little boys offered to shine dirty shoes and sneakers. Little girls sold lottery tickets. A grown man offered to replace my mangled license plate. Forget the DMV. For three dollars an ironmonger stamped me a new one.

Industry filled the air. So did gunk. Saigon was choking on the exhaust of hundreds of thousands of motorbikes. Tiny chunks of soot and grit buffeted my eyes whenever I drove without sunglasses. That protection was useless at intersections, where idling engines spewed toxic clouds that burned my eyes and lungs.

Traffic posed a more immediate health hazard. Though mandatory, drivers' licenses were held by a fraction of those on Saigon's streets. At least that was the impression given by a corps of motorbikers streaming along Tran Hung Dao and other main avenues. Elbow to elbow, riders of all description jockeyed for openings on the straightaways. At roundabouts, the fighting went toe to toe.

Stoplights were rare. Because those that existed didn't always function, people devised their own rights of way. Slow vehicles let the speedsters pass. The cautious yielded to the daring. Still, too many drivers and too few rules had turned Saigon's streets into a massive bumper car ride. Only without the bumpers. Few of Vietnam's burgeoning industries outpaced the boom in business at the head trauma units of urban hospitals.

My injury-free run ended en route to Cholon, Saigon's Chinatown. The perpetrator wore the tails of a checked shirt loose over the beltline of loose slacks. His face was kind, avuncular. And the front wheel of his Honda was hard when it rammed my calf following my sudden stop to avoid another rider.

The perp shrugged and drove away. I could only do the same. Bruised but not broken, I considered buying a helmet. A better idea surfaced. Spooked by the vehicular mayhem, I considered selling my motorbike.

The decision was finalized a few days later. Slowing in deference to an evening drizzle, I slowed even more at the scene of an accident. Judging from the angles of the vehicles, the cause was a cyclo turning a slow U. Between darkness and a weak headlight, the motorbiker in the opposite lane probably hadn't seen the pedicab. His leg broken, the cyclo driver would live. The same couldn't be said for the motorbiker, whose bleeding head hadn't been moved from the spot where it met the curb.

"Zey are ruining zee country, *n'est-ce pas*?" said Elisabeth, a French commodities trader on vacation.

"I'm not so sure."

My response stunned the woman, who was back in Saigon for her second dose of "Viet chic." She described her admiration for the natural fabrics and dyes used by Montagnard craftsmen. Concerned for the future of native cultures as well as her studiously eclectic wardrobe, Elisabeth saw the writing on the wall. A boombox in Sapa, a Northern mountain town, had signaled the beginning of the end.

"Last year zey played cassettes with zeir own music. Zees year zey were playing Michael Jackson."

"Maybe they like Michael better."

"But zee local culture eez dying."

"I guess that's their choice."

41

The unusual calm of the Saigon side street made me hesitate in front of a home protected by a wall higher than my head. Visible through a gate and the thick foliage of an unkept yard, the small villa was probably deserted. It was certainly too peaceful to disturb. An old man rose from his squat and rang the bell for me.

The Vietnamese gentleman who emerged defied his billing. The friend who made the introduction had described Mr. An as a master spy, one of the Viet Cong's top agents. But the bony man coming down the walk looked nothing like the Party pedant I expected. Between plastic sandals and an untucked shirt, he looked too relaxed to be the gardener.

The man extended a hand weakened by illness. Once inside, An apologized for being home alone. He left me and prepared coffee for two.

Browsing the cool sitting room, I sought signs of my host's political leanings. I pegged him fast—a bookshelf held *The Essential Works of Chinese Communists* and *Khrushchev Remembers* —then scrapped my conclusion. Another shelf carried Winston

Churchill's writings, as well as Neil Sheehan's *A Bright Shining Lie*, a book about the Vietnam War.

"The Americans were always looking for infiltration," said Mr. An when, after settling into an armchair, he explained why he joined the Viet Cong. "What they didn't understand was that the people were already in place."

An was born and raised in the south. He attended a French school, where his favorite teacher was an America buff. In those days, Tarzan and Rin Tin Tin were beaming into Vietnamese homes. Young Mr. An fell in love with Shirley Temple. His mother agreed that American women were the world's most beautiful. She hoped her son would marry one.

His affinity for things American interfered with An's focus once he started work as a government censor. Unfulfilled by trimming dispatches filed by the likes of Graham Greene, he quit, claimed the pension funds set aside by Saigon, and left to study journalism in California. Back home, An was hired by *Time*.

"Journalism was exciting. You never knew what would happen. Where would the next demonstration be? When would the next bomb blow up? You had to be ready every moment."

About that time, An's second career took shape. "I lived in a place run by foreigners. Every day I felt small insults. There were also serious abuses. I knew it was my patriotic duty to fight them."

There was, however, a snag. Time in America, and more time among Americans in Vietnam, had burdened another loyalty. He likened the dilemma to choosing between a mother and a stepmother. "I loved my country, but I also loved America. No matter how I chose, I would lose."

He chose patriotism. Ordered by Viet Cong brass to become a spy, An learned the ropes on his own. In Danang to watch the first GIs splash ashore, he borrowed books from an American library. The best, he said, was called *A Short Course in Secret War*. Later he studied a French book, *Espionage in Six Lessons*. Adapted to local circumstances, these and other readings became the foundation of the Viet Cong's intelligence analysis unit.

As a professional, the spy came to admire the work of the CIA in Vietnam. The Phoenix Program was particularly adept at ferreting out his comrades. An could only pray they wouldn't catch him. Execution would be certain, torture likely. Fortunately for his side, An noted, the Pentagon had already steered America down an irreversible, wrongheaded course.

The story mesmerized me. Described in soft but factual tones, his actions made perfect sense. His knack for combining insight and feeling kindled my own candor. Showing no sign of offense, the retired spy answered my backlog of niggling, if indiscreet, questions.

"Did you think Vietnam would be better off under Communism?"

"In my business, I learned to judge people by their qualities, not their labels. That is the only way to make sense of the world. Ho Chi Minh . . . he was a very good man."

"Didn't you feel, well, bad about the deceit, about lying to your bosses?"

"Everybody in Saigon had to make a living. I made mine as a journalist. My spare time was a separate life. I never spied on the people I worked for."

"What about the people you killed?"

"Vietnamese believe that humans have a good side and a bad side. It is natural to do some bad things, and you try to make up for them by doing good things."

Others concurred with Mr. An's view, though in less explicit terms. Van's ministerial briefs had been propaganda and housing. Nonetheless, his position in President Thieu's cabinet put him in the middle of some nasty business. He didn't wait until the war's end to start righting the good-evil balance.

Frequent visits to pagodas were a start. He also gave money to support the families of his eight bodyguards. A better opportunity came when he was left in charge of a captured Viet Cong. "How could I kill her? What difference would one woman make to the war? I gave her some money and told her to run."

Acts of contrition weren't enough. "I saw so many things, so many people killed. I couldn't get them out of my head."

The nightmares brought Van back to Vietnam. But bad dreams only partly explained more than sixty trips to Hanoi since 1975. He liked to say there was big money to be made in Hanoi real estate. Maybe there was. But beneath the veil of greed lurked a supply-side patriot.

"If I can put up a few buildings I can create hundreds of jobs, help hundreds of families," said Van.

The cabinet minister turned developer wasn't the only exile returning to Vietnam. Around 135,000 Southerners fled as the North Vietnamese Army closed in on Saigon. Within five years over a half million more followed by land—refugees walked across Cambodia to Thailand—or by sea. In the Mekong Delta, entire villages would disappear overnight. Settled elsewhere, the *Viet kieu*, or overseas Vietnamese, were coming home. Most visited relatives, left some cash, and departed. Some stayed longer and opened businesses.

More than profits were behind the return of a *Viet kieu* named Hai. Born in Hanoi, his family moved to Saigon after the 1954 split of the country. Hai grew up to be a lawyer. Then he joined the navy. When his ship docked abroad, the navigation officer felt lonely and out of place. Offered the chance to leave in 1975, he stayed.

"I thought I could contribute to Vietnam. That mistake cost me two years of my life."

Now in his mid-forties, the thickset man rarely smiled. He always thought before locking onto a listener's gaze and speaking his few but well-selected words. When describing painful patches, such as the day he reported to a prison camp in the jungles near Cambodia, Hai closed his eyes.

"What happened in reeducation camps?"

"Hard labor."

"Do you still think about it?"

"For five years you cannot forget. After ten years I didn't want to think about it anymore. After twenty you can forget."

Once free, he tried and failed in three escape attempts. The fourth found the navigator, his wife, and child boarding a boat. Four days later the family reached Indonesia. Front there they emigrated to Australia.

The story might have ended there. The immigrant started as a laborer, learned computers, then went to law school for a second time. Hai reckoned he was only one of his Saigon classmates still practicing law. And the rest? "They're dead. Selling real estate in Australia. Driving cyclos in Saigon."

Like Van, Hai wanted to help his motherland. And like the consultant, the lawyer viewed foreign investment as vital to economic growth and job creation. To facilitate capital inflows, he translated Vietnam's commercial law, more than nine hundred pages of it, into English. Made possible by the sum of his experiences, it was a task Hai called his "destiny."

The lawyer had another reason for coming back. After

twelve years Hai still didn't feel at home in Australia. The instinctive reaction to his first sea journeys had been correct. There was only one time and place he had felt comfortable: his youth in Vietnam. The location shift was complete. Whether he could travel back to another era, or recreate his boyhood home, was an open question.

42

"How much you buy you Minsk?"

"Four hundred dollars."

"Ooohh! Too much. You pay too much."

The scene repeated itself at least a half dozen times in Saigon, usually at one of the red lights that worked. Because Minsks were less popular in the South, which was less comfortable with Russian machinery than the North, my black motorbike caught the attention of Honda riders who stopped alongside. A curious once-over and the question was popped: "How much you buy?"

Every inquirer shook his head and moaned that I had paid too much. Even when I lied, and lowered the purchase price to three hundred and fifty dollars, and later three hundred, they swore that I had overpaid. It was a matter of pride. No local would ever admit that a foreigner could strike a decent deal.

The bad reviews didn't affect my feelings. The only functioning dial on my odometer, the thousands place, had rolled over five times since Hanoi. Four hundred bucks plus gas money seemed a fair price for a ride down Vietnam. I could scrap the Minsk and still come out even.

That wasn't necessary. At a motorbike shop I announced my interest in selling. The manager sent the employee with the cleanest T-shirt to inspect the goods. After one lap around my Minsk, I overheard the recommended resale value, "*Bon tram do*," or four hundred dollars. The boss offered somewhat less, then jumped on my counteroffer of four hundred dollars. He also accepted my condition: I would hand over the keys in three days, after I had taken one last ride.

My men in Hanoi, as well as history books, were clear on Tay Ninh's wartime role. The province had two merits in the eyes of Northern strategists. Adjacent to the northwest rim of greater Saigon, the region offered ready access to the enemy's capital. Just across the border from Cambodia, it was relatively easy to supply. The logical place to headquarter the Viet Cong, Tay Ninh marked the end of the Ho Chi Minh Trail.

I expected a quick exit to the highway to Tay Ninh. At 7 A.M., rush hour would be flowing toward the city center. But workbound traffic co-opted most of the outbound lane. Navigating the resulting tangle took an hour. By then I was only as far as Tan Son Nhat Airport, which, thanks to American hangars and Vietnamese jets, still resembled a military base.

A broad, smooth stretch led across Saigon's flat suburbs. After about 40 kilometers, a blue-on-white road sign read: "Welcome to Cu Chi Tunnels."

The network of underground shafts was mythical. Some burrowed all the way to the Cambodian border. The length of those within the 420-square-kilometer district totaled more than 200 kilometers. The hidden entrances were countless.

The trap doors were the key to the Viet Cong's control of Cu Chi. Charlie's ability to hit, run, and vanish baffled troops in and around the capital of the South. The Americans had little more success locating and neutralizing the moles or their tunnels, some of which surfaced inside U.S. camps.

Ten thousand GIs couldn't find the tunnels. So the Pentagon bulldozed jungles and denuded paddies in hopes of stripping the enemy's cover. When underground trails were located, casualties among the human "tunnel rats" sent to investigate hit unacceptable highs. The region was declared a "free-fire zone." Anything that moved became a target. Carpet bombing, the last resort, was the only tactic that worked.

More than twenty years later, an American wasn't unwelcome in Cu Chi. Stopping at an intersection to examine my map, I was immediately jumped by five shirtless youths, all eager to direct me. Another man, older and fully dressed in slacks and a loose white shirt, hung back from the crowd. He circled warily, as if confirming an apparition, before nearing.

"You are American," he stated.

"I am."

"I am very happy to see you."

Of course, Tai had worked alongside the Americans. The Southerner started out selling watches, cameras, and other gadgets at the commissary that served the 25th Infantry Division. Following seven months of U.S.-sponsored English lessons, he accepted an offer to go to Virginia. There he trained as a helicopter mechanic. Unaccustomed to the cold, Tai needed all four of his coats and a pair of thick gloves to survive flying lessons.

America was otherwise flawless in Tai's eyes. Uncle Sam had provided all the things that had brought him joy. Tai met his wife at the commissary, where she worked as a cashier. U.S. child subsidies encouraged him to breed a litter of seven. Lately, his second language was lifting him from poverty.

After the war Tai was moved out of Saigon and onto a small farm in his hometown, Cu Chi. With no savings to attempt an escape, he had no choice but to work ten-hour days in his field. His best efforts couldn't fill his family's bellies. At night he cried—"Why doesn't the government, my government, want me to do something useful?"—and he prayed. The latter yielded results.

A South Korean sweater maker opened a factory nearby. After nixing four applicants for translator, the boss chose Tai. The sixty-dollar-per-month salary seemed a fortune after twenty years of paddies.

"Do you have free time to see my factory?"

I did. Down the road he led me through iron gates and onto the open floor of the sweater plant. The looms were idle on this Sunday. So was the crew-cut Korean boss, whom we found snoozing on a cot. Muscular despite his sixty years, the Seoul native seated me in front of his fan and behind a glass of water. He asked where I came from.

"California."

"Very good rice. Longer than Vietnamese rice."

I nodded to hide my ignorance, and offered my own pleasantry. Where had he learned his excellent English?

The manager fell silent. Then, in a lowered voice, he fessed up. He had fought alongside the Americans during the Korean War. Like the South Vietnamese, the South Korean had learned English from GIs. The connection, he admitted, was the basis for Tai's winning job application.

Tai begged me to visit his home. Before I could answer, the mechanic hopped on the rear of the Minsk. Several kilometers of dirt paths brought us to a roof over packed dirt. The two-room home was inhabited by a wife and the youngest of his children. The furniture was a table, four chairs, and a sleeping platform. On a bamboo wall hung a picture of the Last Supper.

There was also a locked wardrobe. From the cabinet Tai delicately withdrew a battered manila envelope stuffed with papers and a photo album. He showed me mementos, one by one. We admired certificates from mechanic training. I smiled at the young man grinning between Virginia natives, a pair of big-haired, bell-bottomed girls. Another photographer caught him beside a mammoth white convertible.

I noticed the absence of shots of Tai in uniform or with GIs. These, he said, had been burned. The police knew of his past. But photos and letters could compound one's guilt. Fearing a search, the mechanic also torched the book with the addresses of his GI buddies. He regretted the move.

"American friends used to come to my home for dinner. We talked, walked around. We enjoyed ourselves. Sometimes they stayed the night. That was the good time in my life."

Lately, things were looking up for a man who was once under police orders not to speak English. Signs pointed away from the dark past. A few months back, the precinct captain had visited Tai. He apologized for police harassment following the mechanic's recent chat with U.S. veterans. He promised it wouldn't happen again. There was one surer sign that the good times might return: an American face.

"I am very happy to see you," Tai said for the dozenth time.

The mechanic took me to the tunnels. A cemetery for Hanoi's martyrs and heroes reminded me that this, the "Iron Triangle," had been one of Vietnam's deadliest places. A lidless personnel carrier reinforced that message.

The scenery shifted when we reached the tunnel network's visitors center. Taxis and tour buses filled a dirt parking lot. A giant billboard described the Viet Cong wonderland: room of political commissioner, a makeshift hospital, a smoke-tight kitchen, and more. Four bucks bought a ticket to the sights, which were linked by a walkway through trees higher than town houses and around bomb craters deeper than swimming pools.

The concrete trail included several short crawls through tunnels which had been widened to accommodate wide-body tourists and swept of stray cobras. Near the final stop, an underground dining room, I heard several quick, sharp pops, which I imagined to be machine guns blazing at elusive enemies.

"What's that?" I asked Tai.

"Machine guns."

Minus the elaboration, I had guessed right about the sound. Opposite the entrance, the army had set up a firing range where tourists could live their military fantasies. For a buck a bullet, anybody could fire an American M-16 or a Russian AK-47.

I watched a Vietnamese soldier hand a weapon to a bloated man from Taiwan. Dressed in madras shorts and a golf hat saying "Don't Mess with This," the man took aim at animal-shaped targets maybe fifty yards away. The shooter squeezed off one round, then another. His four dapper buddies cheered and clapped.

The support fired the gunner's testosterone. He squeezed and held down the trigger. Pleased to have spewed eight bullets in a matter of seconds, he whirled, gun still leveled, to accept more plaudits. The soldier hit the deck. The buddies clapped some more. Then they took turns spraying lead into the targets and dollars into the army's coffers.

A Vietnamese man, too young for his dentistry's advanced rot, approached us. Like policemen I had come across, he asked his compatriot questions while tossing sidelong glances my way. Had Tai been too casual about fraternizing with an American? Should I have refused to let him endanger himself?

No and no. Tai introduced me to Don, "an old friend." But not that old. Because Tai grew up in the town of Cu Chi, because his father had served as an army captain on the side of the French, he had been destined to join the Southern army.

The friend came from the opposite side of the tracks. Don's family lived in a village 20 kilometers from the town. His father, a peasant, joined the Viet Cong when his son was ten. "If you grow up here, you are VC," he said.

The hometown boy invited us to the shack that doubled as a roadside café and his home. American calendar girls speckled the walls. In their midst was a draw sheet for the World Cup soccer tournament. A woman, Don's second wife, brought chilled tea and then bowls of noodles. After lunch he described his feelings about my country.

As a ten-year-old he took candy from soldiers. When he broke his leg, GIs took him to a hospital. His parents said that the new enemy was kinder than the old one. The French had a way of shooting first and asking questions later; Americans captured, interrogated, and often released locals. The Frogs were merciless rapists; the Yanks left village women alone.

The boy's impression worsened as he aged. American troops came calling more often, and in greater numbers. When choppers arrived in daylight, parents let the kids watch. At night, they joined their fathers and scrambled for the secret tunnels. During heavy fighting Don's mother hurried the children down a passage that emerged by the Saigon River.

The more he saw, the more Don feared the invaders. The South Vietnamese scared him too. As a teenager he was forbidden to go to town. Youths were drafted on sight by the South's army. Several of his village's Viet Cong fathers had sons in the opposing uniform.

Don knew that he was lucky. The war ended before he reached fighting age. Had the combat lasted, he knew which side he would have chosen. Did that matter any more?

The sun hung low in the sky and I needed at least an hour to reach Tay Ninh. Rising to leave, I offered to pay for our meal; judging by the surroundings, and his revelation that he too had seven children, Don couldn't afford to feed extra mouths. He refused my money. Tai's too.

43

Tay Ninh is no place to drop in for dinner, particularly after dark. Traveling small-town Vietnam had taught me to arrive before sundown. When I didn't, eateries were closed or closing. Guesthouses, hard enough to spot in broad daylight, became invisible. What I hadn't learned was how to get directions.

The trouble started in Go Dau. Situated at the bottom of Tay Ninh Province, maybe 40 kilometers from Tay Ninh town, Go Dau had one prominent feature, a forked road. At the town's center, one prong bent right. The other continued straight, across a bridge.

Already low in the sky, the sun was on my left. That meant the bend to the right went east. Checking the map, I figured it was the numberless road that curved up toward Route 14.

Steaming ahead, I saw a crew of soldiers in a guardhouse by the bridge. None looked up from their poker game as I passed. A road sign, a red slash through a camera, didn't apply to me: my Nikon was in Saigon. Besides, I had plenty of shots of water buffalo, though the checked cloths worn by women humping loads along the narrowing road were novel. My error became clear only when a stronger indication appeared.

Behind me, the driver of a car blasted its horn from close range. Only it wasn't a car. It was a jeep. And the driver was a soldier. And his comrades, three of them, had machine guns. They waved me to the road's shoulder. One jumped down from the back seat and shouted in Vietnamese.

"*Campuchia, nam kilomet.*"

"Cambodia, five kilometers," I mouthed.

"*Di, Go Dau.*"

The Vietnamese soldiers would have no trouble persuading me to go back to Go Dau. Had I needed further reasons not to visit Cambodia, recent press provided plenty. A newspaper article said that somebody had lobbed a grenade over the wall of an embassy in Phnom Penh. Another told of a traveler killed by mortar fire outside the capital. Two other tourists were being held hostage. The border guards didn't stick around after tipping me off. Khmer Rouge nastiness had a history of spilling into Tay Ninh Province.

Back on track, I brooded over the postponement of my plans. I had missed 6 P.M. prayers at the Holy See of the Cao Dai religion. Founded by a Vietnamese civil servant early in the twentieth century, the faith's two million devotees followed a hodgepodge of philosophies, Asian and Western, religious and secular. Buddha played a leading role. So did Victor Hugo.

It wasn't too late to see Black Lady Mountain. Visible to the north of Tay Ninh town, the lone feature on a plain of paddies loomed like a silent monster. Locals of all creeds saw the mountain as a shrine. So did I. The Viet Cong organized assaults in the fields around the mysterious peak. There wasn't enough light to visit. But the following day I would have no trouble finding the end of the Trail.

Discovering a bed wasn't so simple. My guidebook said hotels were east of "the triple-arch bridge." Darkness made it hard to spot a bridge or judge the east. I turned right at a broad but deserted roundabout. The undulating dirt road looked an unlikely home for the Ritz. Dehydrated, blinded by dust, I was ready to settle for the Bates Motel. Instead of Norman, I met a man in his twenties, a gardener at the Cao Dai compound.

The gardener wanted me to meet his mother. Unfortunately, it was impossible. She had taught English in Saigon during the war. For that she had been banished to the provinces. Her children were barred from education because of her link to the enemy's language, which she was now afraid to speak. What the gardener could do was guide me to an unmarked guesthouse.

Food was my problem. The shack beside my digs sold cookies and candy. The rest of the vicinity's shambolic structures were homes barely able to feed themselves. A pack of children followed a foreigner. None had a spare sandwich. More than a mile away, the main intersection had to have a restaurant.

A string of Christmas lights on a building near the central roundabout's southwest edge drew me like a moth to a flame. Inside, I found a room with a dozen or so empty tables. Six young ladies loitered around a counter.

Gleaning the establishment's core business took some time. The women tittered when I entered. More giggles met my request for a menu. A woman with a serpentine ponytail dabbed my face with a damp cloth. Another brought more hand towels wrapped around chunks of ice. A third did agree to bring chicken and rice, which I ate alone.

Most of the waitresses kept one eye on me. The exceptions were those shuttling in and out of the closed door of a side room. Judging by the one-way trips of beer cans and food trays, not to mention delighted shrieks and karaoke singing, a private party was well under way. One reveler took a break.

A blubbery man in a tennis shirt forgot his original mission when he spotted a foreigner. Struggling to avoid his teetering gaze by focusing on my guidebook—"Tay Ninh town (population 26,000), capital of Tay Ninh Province . . ."*—I failed. Resting his stomach on my table, the drunk leaned his face into mine.

"You drink beer," he said.

"In general, yes. But not tonight."

"You drink beer."

"No, thanks. Very tired."

"You drink beer."

The scene behind the closed door was now familiar. A gang of five men surrounded a rectangular table populated by dead cans of Vietnam's Budweiser, Bia 333. Glasses were kept full by five personal waitresses. To make the newcomer feel welcome, a sixth brew and a sixth waitress were ordered by a young factotum.

They were Saigon businessmen, he explained in English that might have rated a two on a sober night. The fat drunk (my words, not his) was the boss. Having closed a deal in Tay Ninh that afternoon, they were celebrating. And me? Who and what was I?

News that the man in their midst was American raised a round of cheers. Boss Hog lifted his glass, belched, "Amayreeka," and poured the beer down his gullet. He and the others stared at me. The factotum explained: "In Vietnam, it is custom to drink to the bottom with the boss."

Cultural sensitivity and fear of a beating made me chug.

* *Vietnam—A Travel Survival Kit* (Lonely Planet Publications, 1993), p. 221.

To be safe, on both counts, I chugged with another colleague whose toast went like this: "Kalifornya!" Two others seized the opportunity to impress the boss. Their salutes, each requiring a tandem chug with the American, were "Vietnam" and "Moscow."

I tried to stand. My personal waitress grabbed the forearm she had been stroking for half an hour and pulled me back into my seat. Nobody left without singing. Vietnam custom.

The factotum showed me how. Reading the words along the bottom of the karaoke screen, he belted out a local favorite. Can't read Vietnamese? He showed me a list of American tunes on the laser discs. My beery rendition of "New York, New York" won a standing O. There being no topper to a night in Tay Ninh, the businessmen staggered into a sedan and careened toward Saigon.

My trip to bed was far shorter, but no straighter. The absence of streetlights impaired my efforts to navigate the road's alpine bumps. A murky fog obscured anything beyond ten meters. When a halo of light illuminated the right side of the road, I wished it hadn't.

I couldn't make out the stationary vehicle beaming its headlights in my eyes. Yet there was no mistaking the men standing near the car. (Or was it a jeep?) Decked out in all too familiar doormen's summer wear—light blue shirt and baggy pants—a pair of police officers wanted to have a few words.

"Bazzbort" was the first word.

"Beeza" was the second.

I handed over laminated photocopies of the actual documents. If charged with drunk driving, I would have to plead guilty and throw myself on the mercy of the court of two.

I wanted to settle the matter quickly. An unlit roadside deep in former Viet Cong territory was no place to dither. Or to dicker. Aluoi had demonstrated the dangers of bargaining with

Vietnam's finest. But for his evenhanded partner, Nghia 0182 might still have me and my Minsk locked up near the Lao border.

Another worry broke through the fog and alcohol. A Vietnam-based lawyer had warned me that Southern police were far greedier than those in the North. Rougher, too. He illustrated the point with the misfortune of his mate Fred.

Fred had a way of staying out late when in Vietnam. The joy of *doi moi* kept him going into the wee hours. One midnight his car was flagged down at a military roadblock on the outskirts of Saigon. A soldier wasted no time clarifying the reason for the holdup. It was a holdup. An AK-47 touched to his breastbone, Fred handed over the contents of one pocket, ten dollars. Satisfied with the take, the soldiers waved the car on.

At best, the incident told me that Vietnam had some bugs to work out of its reforming system. That conclusion didn't make me feel any better about the prospect of an AK-47 pointed at my chest. I was tired of sparring with Charlie and I wanted to go home. Once the cops tired of the pretense of checking my papers and made their demand, I would pay fast and leave faster.

The policeman holding my documents began to speak. As ever, anything more than kindergarten Vietnamese was gibberish to me. So I cut the officer off with some words I did know.

"How much?"

"*Hai muoi do.*"

"Twenty dollars? You got it."

About the Author

Christopher Hunt is a native of New York City and a graduate of Dartmouth College and London School Economics. Working as a reporter for *South China Morning Post, The Asian Wall Street Journal,* and *The Economist,* he has covered business, finance and, in a pinch, politics. Between day jobs he has worked as a security guard and a stand-up comic.